MW00790954

Praise for *Indictment*

"*Indictment* offers a clear, compassionate, and practical vision for a much-needed transformation of the criminal justice system – a system consumed by the over-representation of Indigenous people and other marginalized Canadians. Through their powerful stories we find the key to doing justice better and breaking down the barriers that exist in our society. Building something new is never easy, but when we see this vision realized, it will be well worth it for all Canadians."

Puglaas, The Hon. Jody Wilson-Raybould, PC, OBC, KC, former Minister of Justice and Attorney General of Canada

"*Indictment* is nothing short of revolutionary. The implications of a truly trauma-informed perspective on justice require a reckoning. With sensitivity to the stories of survivors, Benjamin Perrin brings together the latest social science research and demonstrates the necessity for nothing short of a justice system overhaul. The writing style is beautiful, sensitive, and articulate. The case studies are authentic. Perrin's courageous book gives voice to a great many who have suffered at the hands of a cruel system of justice."

Robert T. Muller, Professor of Clinical Psychology, York University, Fellow at the International Society for the Study of Trauma and Dissociation, and author of *Trauma and the Struggle to Open Up*

"*Indictment* is original, timely, and easy to grasp. Perrin's conversations with people directly affected by Canada's criminal justice system, alongside his excellent research, offer compelling arguments for reform. He widens our focus and provides valuable guidance for transforming our understanding of this field."

John Borrows, Loveland Chair in Indigenous Law, University of Toronto

"If Benjamin Perrin were a physician, *Indictment* would diagnose multi-organ failure in his moribund patient – the justice system – caused by ignorance of the effects of trauma, systemic racism, and colonial violence. But he is a professor of criminal law, so instead he prosecutes his case with passion, evidence, and the testimony of compelling witnesses. His vision of a new transformative justice might also be the basis for a more just and compassionate social order. *Indictment* is a must-read."

Robert Maunder, Chair in Health and Behaviour at Sinai Health, Professor of Psychiatry, University of Toronto, and co-author of *Damaged: Childhood Trauma, Adult Illness, and the Need for a Health Care Revolution*

INDICTMENT

THE CRIMINAL JUSTICE SYSTEM ON TRIAL

BENJAMIN PERRIN

Aevo UTP
An imprint of University of Toronto Press
Toronto Buffalo London
utorontopress.com

© University of Toronto Press 2023

Library and Archives Canada Cataloguing in Publication

Title: Indictment : the criminal justice system on trial / Benjamin Perrin.
Names: Perrin, Benjamin, author.
Description: Includes bibliographical references and index.
Identifiers: Canadiana (print) 20230453333 | Canadiana (ebook) 20230455581 | ISBN 9781487506278 (hardcover) | ISBN 9781487533731 (PDF) | ISBN 9781487533748 (EPUB)
Subjects: LCSH: Discrimination in criminal justice administration – Canada. | LCSH: Crime and race – Canada. | LCSH: Marginality, Social – Canada.
Classification: LCC HV9960.C2 P47 2023 | DDC 364.10971 – dc23

ISBN 978-1-4875-0627-8 (cloth)   ISBN 978-1-4875-3374-8 (EPUB)
ISBN 978-1-4875-3373-1 (PDF)

Printed in Canada

Cover design: Kathleen Lynch
Cover image: Dhilan Seehra/EyeEm/Getty Images

All author royalties for *Indictment* are being donated directly to two charitable organizations profiled in the book: STR8 UP assists people in leaving gangs and criminal street lifestyles (https://www.str8-up.ca/), and Collaborative Justice Program: Restorative Justice Ottawa provides restorative justice services supporting survivors of crime and people charged with criminal offences (https://www.collaborativejustice.ca/).

We wish to acknowledge the land on which the University of Toronto Press operates. This land is the traditional territory of the Wendat, the Anishnaabeg, the Haudenosaunee, the Métis, and the Mississaugas of the Credit First Nation.

University of Toronto Press acknowledges the financial support of the Government of Canada, the Canada Council for the Arts, and the Ontario Arts Council, an agency of the Government of Ontario, for its publishing activities.

Canada Council   Conseil des Arts
for the Arts   du Canada

ONTARIO ARTS COUNCIL
CONSEIL DES ARTS DE L'ONTARIO
an Ontario government agency
un organisme du gouvernement de l'Ontario

Funded by the   Financé par le
Government   gouvernement
of Canada   du Canada

To everyone who shared their story with me

Content Note

This book includes potentially triggering content that may be difficult for some readers. Please refer to the Content Notes at the end of the book for chapter-by-chapter descriptions, and a list of Mental Health and Counselling Resources if you need support.

Disclaimer

This book is not intended to provide legal, medical, or therapeutic advice. If you need help with any of these things, please contact a professional for assistance.

indictment

ɪnˈdaɪtmənt • *noun*

1   a written statement accusing someone of a crime
2   a sign that a system, society, etc. is very bad or very wrong

Contents

PART TWO: A NEW VISION FOR CRIMINAL JUSTICE

CHAPTER ONE

"It Looked like Madness": Trauma

The rhythmic whirring of the swift blades of a police helicopter grew louder overhead, piercing the quiet solitude of the back-country wilderness of Kananaskis, Alberta. It ominously circled in the sky, like an unnatural bird of prey. Its quarry was my father-in-law, Greg.

The son of a Chinese-Canadian father and a Métis/Cree mother from the Young's Point Métis community near The Pas, Manitoba, Greg was dislocated from his mother around age three and sent away to boarding school at age five. He is a citizen of the Métis Nation of Alberta.

"Growing up pretty much almost like an orphan, I guess you could say, I didn't know myself at all," said Greg. "I had lost myself. I had no identity."

Greg was diagnosed with Fetal Alcohol Spectrum Disorder (FASD) and came to use substances, which was the reason he had embarked on a vision quest in the rugged wilderness of southern

Alberta. "I'm quite fine with people knowing that it was a crack cocaine addiction," he added.

"I remember, just about every time I was having a shower, I would cry to the Lord, saying, 'I just can't find a way to stop. Please help me.' There was nothing I could do," said Greg. "It was a horrible, horrible existence."

"My relationship with my wife had completely deteriorated. It was a very sad period in my life. I wasn't able to hold a job. I had huge money problems."

"I kind of figured I would end up on the street homeless, so I might as well learn to survive. I thought I would go to the mountains and try to survive out there and see how I did. Just before I left, I was watching PBS and I found out that going off into the mountains all alone is a thing called a vision quest that the Indians have been doing all the way back in time. I don't think it's used very often."

Greg set out with Cougar and Spirit, his two horses, who would be his only companions. He would live on the land, resupplying with basics when he could find a payphone. He left the chaos of his life to seek peace and healing. But it turned out he wasn't alone at all.

"When I first went out, realizing that it was indeed a vision quest, almost immediately I felt the Indian spirit saying, 'You come along, there hasn't been any Indian come out on a vision quest for quite a while and you're more than welcome.' And they, along with my dear Lord Jesus, was with me the whole time. The spirituality is amazing out in the mountains when you're completely immersed in the wonderful creation out there."

Greg wrote poetry and kept a notebook to record his experiences:

The sky was on fire with each and every star out, even the Milky Way stood out magically like an inviting trail to the universe, all before my eyes as I stared into deep space. The hooting of the owl treetop plays a melody as the stars dance to her tune. The river's eternal splash sings lullaby to my heart as the crisp cool evening air fills my breaths endlessly, and coziness sets in like the warmth of my covers. I try to fight off the sleep so as to savour that moment – but sleep had its own reward – a peace unknown before, and at last a dream about the trail, Spirit, Cougar, and I.

"You could feel that God had created this and what a wonderful amazing creation it was," said Greg. "The first thing I really noticed was the lack of distraction. Never before in my life, perhaps since I was a kid, could I hold a thought for hours on end. You get to know yourself, because you have to live with yourself. Whatever your actions are, you feel the consequence immediately. I had a lot of maturing and important decisions to make that my survival would rely on."

Greg found that he could survive and, at times, it was exhilarating. He forded glacier-fed rivers, followed wildlife trails, made shelters, built fires and rescued his horses when they wandered off. His confidence began to grow. Some of the trails he found were grown over from lack of use.

"In the end, through this process of being good in the mountains, I developed a very genuine and real sense of self-esteem. Self-esteem is one of the most important ingredients in a functioning and happy person. I began to appreciate each situation more and more as I progressed."

"Of course, there was bad interaction, too. I remember I came out near Lake Minnewanka, my horse had hurt himself, and I desperately needed to find a cell phone. I found a road that the cars were going by. I had tried to wave them down to try and use their phone. I suppose I did look quite dishevelled and all that. There must have been, well not quite, what seemed like a hundred cars go by."

There were also run-ins with park wardens. Greg had outstanding arrest warrants, so he tried to evade the wardens and RCMP as much as possible. Whenever they found him, he would give a false name. That worked for a while. But one day, the ruse came to an end. He had come across a campground and, with two horses, he stood out.

"I ran into some people that I knew," said Greg. "One lady that I met and her friend. We ended up getting into an argument and they left in the darkness and they were sure that I had followed them, which I never did. But they reported me to the RCMP and gave them my correct name and all that."

"The next morning, the helicopter flew over my campsite, and I knew what was happening. I was very close to escaping into the wilderness, where I probably wouldn't be apprehended. But, I had to stop – the horseshoe was coming off my horse. When that happens, you have to stop and you have to take it off."

"I was like Jesse James out in the mountains."

The manhunt ended with Greg being apprehended by police and arrested on multiple outstanding warrants. He was transported to the RCMP detachment and locked in a cell. Spirit and Cougar were also taken into custody by animal services.

Evenings under the canopy of the majestic stars. Mornings warming by the crackling fire, listening to bubbling streams. The warmth of his horse carrying him along as its enormous lungs breathed the crisp, clean mountain air, slowly in and out. The prayers. The poems. The peace. All of it was gone. The vision quest was over – or so he thought.

———

"Stop holding conferences. Stop with the symposiums. Give it up. You are wasting air. You haven't implemented the modest tinkering that you endlessly discuss. Your ideas are too little and too late," wrote Harold Johnson, a Harvard-educated lawyer and member of the Montreal Lake Cree Nation, in his book *Peace and Good Order: The Case for Indigenous Justice in Canada*. His tough talk didn't stop there.

"Instead of coming together for discussions amongst yourselves, spend the time, energy and money you presently waste by having those same conversations with Indigenous Peoples. If you insist on holding a symposium, make sure you hear from someone who has spent time in your jails. If your conference is in a city, bring in Indigenous people from the street, give them something to eat, let them warm up and then listen to what they have to say. You are never going to find solutions if you continue to have conversations about us without us."

I knew exactly what Harold (as he asked me to call him) was talking about. I'm a white male law professor and a settler. I have had challenges in my life but have also benefited enormously from that privilege. I've also been educated and indoctrinated into the Canadian legal system at some of the country's top law schools. I've spoken at judicial conferences at five-star hotels. I've attended beautifully catered Cabinet meetings on Parliament Hill. I've sat fireside at the Supreme Court of Canada listening to guest speakers. I've schmoozed at academic cocktail receptions. The food I ate at such events surpassed what is served at many weddings. These are elite places that exclude the people impacted by the criminal justice system whom Harold calls on us to welcome inside and hear from.

My first round of interviews for this book were with thirty-four "experts" – professionals working in, and around, the criminal justice system (I describe my methodology at the end of this book). I asked them: What are the major challenges facing the criminal justice system? And if they could design a new system, what would it look like?

I interviewed law professors; criminologists; Crown prosecutors and defence counsel; lawyers representing crime victims; a chief of police; a chief peacekeeper; an Elder; Indigenous leaders; Black and Indigenous scholars; staff from non-profit organizations that support survivors and people who have committed offences; public health officials; a forensic psychiatrist; gang outreach workers; restorative justice practitioners; legal aid lawyers; justice reform activists; prisoner and victims' rights advocates; disability, substance use, and mental health professionals; civil liberties proponents; a corrections officer; federal correctional investigators; and trauma experts.

They had many valuable insights but, ultimately, I knew something was missing. It was through this process that I met Harold. Already I was thinking I needed to interview people who had been directly affected by the system. After speaking with him, I couldn't ignore his call to action. They were the real experts.

———

Courtney, a thirty-nine-year-old Indigenous woman from Yukon, was the first person to respond to my research poster. It asked a simple question in big, bold text: "What was your experience like with the criminal justice system?" I quickly realized that I wasn't prepared to hear her answer. I awoke the next night with a nightmare about how she had attempted to take her own life in a maximum-security prison cell.

"I ended up becoming really suicidal and I cut my veins and I bled out and I almost died," Courtney had told me. "They had to give me a blood transfusion and take me to the hospital." When she returned to prison, instead of being treated with care and compassion, she was instead locked in a segregation cell alone for three months.

"That was pretty devastating on me because I was really trying to kill myself. I was so seriously suicidal at the time," said Courtney. "It's saddening to be so secluded when I go to seg. I believe I was treated extremely inhumanely when I was in seg. It was sad. I didn't feel I could make it."

In all, Courtney has spent twenty-five years of her life incarcerated – starting when she was twelve years old. At that age, she was already addicted to alcohol. She has lived most of her life behind bars in Yukon, Alberta, and British Columbia.

Within days, the emails and voicemails became a flood as more and more people contacted me to share their stories like Courtney. They wanted to talk – and for someone to listen.

"I know as a victim the system sucks," wrote one person. "I am very well aware of the injustices and I believe society should know about them, so glad to see a research study being done."

"I have never told my story publicly before and hope to shed light on how police brutality is covered up," said another. The calls and emails kept coming.

"Inquiring about your study but I'll tell you now if you're looking for me to say how the system is good, that won't happen. Our prison system is broken. If you are looking for the truth then I'm all for it."

"This gives me the chance to share my story, one I've barely told others and would love to get this off my chest and help others."

"Yes, we have laws and punishment for breaking those laws. However, we need to be sure that the men and women we send to prison come out better than when they went in. This doesn't happen often enough and the revolving door begins for far too many. So, if my words will help you in some small way, I will help."

They were survivors of assaults, death threats, sexual assaults, intimate partner violence, and human trafficking. People

incarcerated for murder, manslaughter, sexual offences, drug trafficking, robbery, assault causing bodily harm, firearms charges,
fraud, criminal harassment, and other crimes. Most of these individuals also told me about being victimized themselves, particularly as children and while imprisoned.

After accepting Harold Johnson's challenge and speaking with
three dozen individuals – many of whom were Indigenous – about
their lived experiences with the criminal justice system, I can cate-
gorically tell you he is right. I learned vastly more from them than
all the cocktail receptions, fireside talks, and conference panels
combined. In a single word, the common thread connecting all of
their stories was trauma.

———

"Trauma comes from a Greek word for wounding. So essentially,
trauma is a wound – it is a psychological wound," said Dr. Gabor
Maté, an internationally renowned trauma expert and author of
The Myth of Normal: Trauma, Illness & Healing in a Toxic Culture.
"Even if there is no conscious recall, the emotional memory is im-
printed in the brain, the nervous system and the body through
physiological mechanisms and these traumatic imprints then affect what a person believes, thinks, feels and acts throughout their
lifetime."

"Trauma is not the event that happens to you. Trauma is the
wound that the event incurred," explained Maté. "[It] leaves a long-
term impact that influences your behaviour without you knowing
it. It can be incurred by bad things happening, but also by children's developmental needs not being met, which is very common.
That's the essence of trauma."

At the most fundamental level, trauma arises from "experiences that overwhelm an individual's capacity to cope" and "feelings of powerlessness, disconnection, and loss of control."

There are six major types of what are often colloquially called "Big-T" trauma. First, single incident trauma arises from an unanticipated overwhelming episode, such as an accident, the sudden death of a loved one, a physical or sexual assault, a natural disaster, or witnessing violence.

Second, repetitive trauma involves ongoing emotional, physical, or sexual abuse; domestic violence; or war. It frequently involves being trapped, physically or emotionally.

Third, developmental trauma arises from early exposure as an infant, child, or young person to ongoing or repeated trauma, such as emotional, physical, or sexual abuse; abandonment; neglect; coercion; betrayal; or witnessing violence or death. Developmental trauma can lead to unique diagnoses, including C-PTSD (complex post-traumatic stress disorder) or developmental trauma disorder.

"The basic architecture of the brain is constructed through an ongoing process that begins before birth and continues into adulthood," according to Harvard University's Center on the Developing Child. "Early experiences affect the quality of that architecture by establishing either a sturdy or a fragile foundation for *all* of the learning, health and behavior that follow. In the first few years of life, more than 1 million new neural connections are formed every second."

Developmental trauma "can have especially negative consequences [on cognition and mental health], impacting the development of the brain and normal developmental progression." Because young victims of trauma are in survival mode, their brain development can become cognitively suspended or halted. Trauma in the first five years of life can result in diminished intellectual functioning, cognitive impairments, and communication issues that continue into adulthood. Later in this chapter I'll discuss the research on childhood trauma further and how it relates to the criminal justice system.

Fourth, intergenerational trauma is the result of the psychological, neurobiological, and emotional transmission of trauma to family members and people living with trauma survivors. Fifth, historical trauma is the transmission of massive collective trauma inflicted through the domination and subjugation of an entire group of people, such as genocide, colonialism, slavery, and war. This is a significant part of understanding how the criminal justice system affects and interacts with Indigenous people (as I will explore in chapters 4 and 5) and Black people (in chapter 6).

Finally, vicarious trauma is where someone may experience secondary trauma as a result of their exposure to the traumatic experiences of others, including people whom they are helping or interacting with in some capacity.

Not everyone experiences a potentially traumatic event the same way. There are a range of factors contributing to how someone is affected, including social, economic, and family supports; age and stage of development; previous experiences with trauma; resilience (ability to "bounce back"); cultural beliefs; gender; temperament; and the type, duration, and onset of trauma.

———

The girl in the photo had a big smile and pigtails. Jessica, an Indigenous woman, made a short video with photos of her childhood to tell her story. She had only shared it with a handful of people, so I felt honoured to see it. Jessica explained who each person was as photographs appeared on the screen. Her not-so-subtle language revealed the sexual abuse she experienced from an early age.

"These are my parents. That's me in the red pants and this is my story. My fourth birthday, I loved my dress. It was also the day my seventeen-year-old neighbour invited me in for an orange popsicle. I call him 'the popsicle guy.'"

"This is Mrs. H. She was my grandparents' neighbour. I could tell Mrs. H anything. Except what grandpa was doing. He said that was our secret."

"This is me at ten, the age when I told grandpa's secret. They said they would talk to grandpa. It stopped for a while. I am eleven now, and we moved to the new house."

In the decades that followed, Jessica would endure further physical, emotional, and sexual abuse and exploitation. Intimate partner violence. Sex trafficking. Her abuser would also abuse her children. She was diagnosed with anxiety, depression, anorexia, obsessive compulsive disorder, PTSD, and borderline personality disorder. She eventually tried to take her own life. But it wasn't the end of her story.

———

"The criminal justice system doesn't know anything about trauma," said Myrna McCallum, a Métis-Cree lawyer who has experience as both a criminal defence lawyer and Crown prosecutor. "And they really need to understand because trauma drives behaviour, particularly offending behaviour. And as long as you're just sentencing people, sending them to jail, upholding sentencing principles of denunciation and deterrence, you're really just putting a Band-Aid on a bullet wound."

Medical research has shown that trauma can cause lasting changes in brain structure and functioning. Notably, this includes the hippocampus (which supports "memory, learning, navigation and perception of space"), amygdala (which regulates emotion and memory and is "associated with the brain's reward system, stress, and the 'fight or flight' response when someone perceives a threat"), and medial prefrontal cortex ("regulation of complex cognitive, emotional, and behavioral functioning").

As a result, people who grew up without positive support, and especially those who experienced trauma, struggle with behavioural and emotional self-regulation. As Dr. Maté explained, the impulse regulation circuitry of the brain doesn't develop in these individuals – their behaviour is a reaction, rather than a conscious decision.

Medical research shows that people with unresolved trauma are often in a state of hyperarousal (fight/flight is persistently activated) and hypervigilance (overreacting), or listlessness and dissociation (being numb and disconnected in stressful situations).

During a perceived threat, the prefrontal cortex (the conscious thinking part of our brain) is inhibited and the amygdala kicks in (engaging our automatic fight-flight-freeze survival mechanism, which is done without conscious thought). "Fight" involves confronting the threat, "flight" consists of trying to escape the threat by leaving the situation, while "freeze" means shutting down to avoid the threat (think of a deer caught in the headlights of an oncoming vehicle and standing perfectly still). These fight-flight-freeze survival responses are amplified in people who have experienced trauma, including chronic childhood maltreatment. People who have unresolved trauma also respond to actual or perceived threats by "secreting large amounts of stress hormones long after the actual danger has passed."

This understanding brings a totally different perspective to criminal incidents, where the paradigm is that of a "rational actor" making decisions about their conduct and, therefore, fully culpable for them at all times. As Dr. Maté explained, for people with unresolved trauma, this long-standing assumption embedded in criminal law is "scientific nonsense. You look at their brain at that moment, that part is offline." We will see that this has massive implications for policing, courts, and corrections. It also has major consequences for how the behaviour of survivors is understood.

"Fawn," a fourth trauma response, is a submissive response that aims to please the source of the perceived conflict or threat in order to protect oneself. "Fawn" helps explain, at least in part, why a survivor of intimate partner violence may continue to engage in sexual activity with their abuser – it may be a survival mechanism aimed at mollifying the threat. Without understanding trauma, this behaviour could be misinterpreted as contradicting their disclosure about the nature and severity of the violence that they endured. Indeed, a courtroom that doesn't understand trauma risks disbelieving truthful but traumatized witnesses at every turn.

"Fawn" also helps explain why some Indigenous people plead guilty even while they're innocent, according to McCallum. Accepting allegations and punishment avoids further conflict. It's a trauma response to self-protect because disagreeing with authority figures (i.e., an abusive parent or guardian) in their childhood would lead to more harm. You don't fight, you acquiesce.

———

"I don't like to use the term survivor. But I'm an overcomer. Because I no longer live in the trauma of those experiences," said

Jessica, whom we met earlier in this chapter as she shared photos of her childhood and the abuse she endured throughout her life. "It is like a memory of someone else's life."

But it wasn't the criminal justice system, child welfare system, or health care system that helped her get to this stage of recovery and healing.

"I would reach out to police, I would go to shelters, seeking help. And it was just pointless," said Jessica. "Medical institutions also labelled me with all kinds of mental illnesses – but never, ever once screened me for domestic violence. So, there's a failure in systems in general."

"And I had no escape because police wouldn't help me."

"Like when I look back at it, I think, wow, do you know how many times there was possibilities they could have intervened? I can't even count how many times, hundreds probably."

All of these systems were blind to her trauma, making it worse. Eventually, Jessica could no longer cope with the violence.

"I took my kids out for ice cream and told them how much I loved them. I dropped them off at a babysitter's. I went home and hung myself on the basement rafters."

Jessica's abusive partner heard the noise coming from the basement. He came down and, without a word, cut her down. "He told me that he cut me down because he didn't want to be blamed for my death."

Jessica didn't stop there. Next, she tried swallowing pills. The police arrived a few minutes later and took her to the hospital. But, unlike the literally hundreds of unhelpful and negative interactions with police she'd had before, this time was different.

While Jessica was in the emergency room, she asked to go to the bathroom. She still had pills with her and was intent on following through with her plan to take her own life.

"I sat on the floor in the bathroom and started chewing the pills I had in my hand, one at a time. The officer asked the nurse to open the door because I was taking too long."

"He picked me up off the floor and in the kindest voice said, 'Oh, sweetheart, no, don't do this.' And he took the pills from my hand."

It was in that single moment of kindness and compassion, after decades of indifference and abuse, that Jessica's life began to change. She escaped from her abuser, went into therapy, and attended a naming ceremony where she was given a traditional Indigenous name. With time, her lengthy list of mental health diagnoses (over ten in total) evaporated, except for PTSD. In her case, they were all related to the trauma she had been enduring.

Today, her life is unrecognizable from before.

"I took a leap of faith and married my second husband," said Jessica. "Had three more little girls, graduated college, learned how to parent without fear. Took the time to enjoy each moment. Bought a house in a forest, and I just graduated from my Bachelor of Social Work."

"I work at accepting who I am every day. I am beautiful and deserving of love."

———

Despite seemingly insurmountable trauma, Jessica was able to start her healing journey after that moment of kindness in the emergency room. Unfortunately, most people with lived experience whom I interviewed hadn't yet had that kind of life-changing transformation.

The Adverse Childhood Experiences (ACEs) survey is a simple but powerful tool to help understand the ripple effects of trauma in the lives of people like Jessica. It identifies potentially traumatic events experienced under eighteen years of age: physical, emotional, and sexual abuse; emotional neglect; poverty; parental separation; living with a family member with mental illness or substance use issues; family violence; and having a family member imprisoned – these are the "original" ten ACEs. Other supplementary ACEs have since been recognized based on the research, such as experiencing racism, being bullied, the death of a parent, feeling unsafe in the community, living in foster care, poverty, serious accidents or illness, parents who often argued, and not having close friends.

How prevalent are ACEs? Researchers estimate that about 60 per cent of people have experienced at least one of the original ten ACEs. About 15 per cent of people have experienced at least four of them – a level that significantly increases the risk of negative life outcomes. The more ACEs that someone has, the greater the risk – but not inevitability – that their life will be detrimentally impacted.

ACEs increase the risk of prolonged health problems, substance use, mental health issues, education and employment challenges, poverty, and being involved in the criminal justice system.

"Given the cascade of negatives that ACEs trigger, they can fairly be called the unacknowledged 'cause of causes,'" wrote Dr. Robert Maunder and Dr. Jonathan Hunter, professors at the University of Toronto's Department of Psychiatry, in *Damaged: Childhood Trauma, Adult Illness, and the Need for a Health Care Revolution*. A massive body of scholarly research demonstrates that an accumulation of childhood trauma is associated with "radically different life-course trajectories."

ACEs are not randomly distributed throughout the population. Those at greatest risk include "First Nations, Inuit, and Métis children; LGBTQ+ youth; homeless, street-involved youth and youth who misuse drugs; children with low socioeconomic status; children who have experienced previous violent victimization; and immigrant and racialized youth of first-generation and ethnic minorities." It is no accident that these very same marginalized groups are disproportionately impacted by the criminal justice system.

Residential school survivors are estimated to have experienced, on average, six of the original ten ACEs, placing them within the upper echelons of developmental trauma. In terms of intergenerational trauma, a peer-reviewed study noted that "[o]ne of the most enduring predictors of parenting behavior in published studies is how parents were parented themselves," and that "[m]aternal and paternal residential school attendance were each associated with increased ACE score among adults raised by survivors." In other words, the children of residential school survivors themselves also reported increased adverse childhood experiences.

"You've got people who are traumatized in the community, who self-medicate with alcohol and other substances, who, in a state of intoxication, commit atrocities and traumatize themselves some more," said Harold Johnson. "And then we bring them into the justice system and we run them through a preliminary hearing and a trial that are traumatizing, and then we send them to prison where we know they're going to be severely traumatized. Then we release them and ask them if they've learnt their lesson. And this is the system that we're in. But the longer I was in it, the more it looked like madness."

———

There's a saying that "hurt people hurt people," meaning that people with unresolved trauma may, in turn, harm others – physically, emotionally, psychologically, or sexually. This is what's called the "victim/offender" overlap.

"As a prosecutor and as defence counsel, I quite often saw that a person in court as a victim who's giving testimony would later be in court as the accused," said Johnson. His observations are corroborated by scholarly research.

"[T]he victimization rates for incarcerated populations are much higher than in the general population," wrote Professor Sandra Bucerius, director of the Centre for Criminological Research at the University of Alberta. "[O]ur research findings clearly show that almost everyone incarcerated in Alberta, regardless of gender, were victims *before* becoming offenders."

"95% of incarcerated Indigenous women and 86% of Indigenous men in Alberta experienced violent victimization in their lives (in contrast to 90% of [incarcerated] white women and 79% of white men), with the majority of these victimizations happening during the childhood and teenager years."

"People look at, you know, it's 'good guys' and 'bad guys' – it's 'us and them.' And if you're bad you go to jail," said Kimberly Mann, executive director of the Collaborative Justice Program in Ottawa. "Really there's no 'us and them,' there's only 'us,' right? ... We have all hurt somebody at some point, whether or not there was criminal charges attached to it, but we've all hurt people."

"Some people will re-enact what was done to them, and they do it all the time," said Myrna McCallum, who is also host of *The Trauma-Informed Lawyer* podcast. "All the more reason why we need to get educated about trauma."

While the overwhelming majority of incarcerated people were victimized as children, most children who are victimized do not go on to abuse others. However, their trauma can profoundly affect them in other ways, including making them more vulnerable to further victimization throughout their lives.

ACEs are "a key risk factor for offending and victimization" alike. ACEs increase the risk of an individual becoming a victim of crime or a perpetrator of crime – or both, as we saw earlier with the victim/offender overlap. Research has shown that "children and adolescents exposed to [ACEs] are at increased risk for experiencing violence across their life span with accumulating risk for poorer health and social outcomes." For example, survivors of child sexual abuse are at greater risk of subsequent sexual assault and intimate partner violence. Individuals who have experienced five or more of the ten original ACEs are eight times more likely to be sexually victimized as adults, compared with people who hadn't suffered these childhood traumas.

Criminologists have also long observed correlations between exposure to ACEs and criminal behaviour. Children who are exposed to violence are more likely to commit violence themselves later: "childhood maltreatment ... increases the risk of later criminality by approximately 50%." Not surprisingly, higher ACEs also increase the risk of incarceration. "ACEs not only increase the chances of involvement in the juvenile justice system, but increase the risk of re-offense."

ACEs increase the likelihood of challenges with school or work, substance use, family challenges, and developing antisocial personality patterns. These very things are also known to be criminogenic (factors that increase the chances of offending). Additionally, substance use is criminalized in many ways, contributing to stigma and marginalization, exposure to use of force by police and imprisonment – further potentially traumatizing incidents. ACEs also increase the risk of mental health issues, which contribute to a greater risk of a wide range of negative criminal justice outcomes, including dying during or immediately after contact with police as well as self-harm and suicide if incarcerated.

The criminal justice system itself also causes ACEs. It does so directly, such as when a child's parent or guardian is incarcerated (having a family member go to jail is one of the ten original ACEs), and by racist conduct by police and other criminal justice actors that is experienced by racialized children and youth. The criminal justice system also indirectly causes ACEs, including by failing to prevent physical, sexual, and emotional abuse of children; failing to protect children from witnessing family violence; children and youth not feeling safe in their neighbourhood; parental separation due to incarceration; and material deprivation due to loss of income from either incarcerated parents or due to criminal victimization.

———

To some, trauma may feel like a life sentence. Something irredeemable. But, as Jessica's life shows, trauma does not need to be the end of someone's story. Wounds can heal, even if a scar remains as a reminder of the pain. Indeed, a "central belief of trauma-informed practice is that people can recover, and the approach is grounded in hope and the honouring of each individual's resiliency." Even the brain impacts of trauma can be healed – "neuroplasticity" is the remarkable ability of our brains to grow and reorganize, even later in life.

Recovering from trauma can even lead to "post-traumatic growth," which refers to the "positive psychological growth some people report once they have had the opportunity to heal from their negative experience(s)." It leads to "the development of resiliency and adaptivity for future events." In other words, trauma can be transformed. As the saying goes "trauma that isn't transformed gets transferred" onto others, repeating the tragic cycle.

"Healing childhood trauma involves a balance: attending to the wounds of the past while living in the present," wrote Dr. Arielle Schwartz, a licensed clinical psychologist who specializes in treating complex trauma. People in recovery from trauma talk about "doing the work" – the ongoing and difficult work of identifying, understanding, and working towards healing. I believe that there is hope for individuals and families, and I also want to believe that there is hope for marginalized communities, Indigenous Nations, and society to heal from trauma.

———

#MeToo. Black Lives Matter. Defund the Police. Decriminalize Drugs. No More Stolen Sisters. These aren't just slogans, protests, and movements. Discontent about the criminal justice system is not only a growing social and political force – it's backed up by statistics, reports, inquiries, commissions, and scholarly research that is shaking its very foundations.

Issues like how sexual assault and intimate partner violence survivors are treated by the system, Missing and Murdered Indigenous Women and Girls, mass incarceration of Indigenous and Black people, police misconduct and brutality, anti-Black racism, the toxic contaminated drug poisoning crisis, police-involved deaths of people in mental health crisis, and many other issues related to the criminal justice system are typically treated in isolation. But this hides their interrelationships, cumulative impacts, and underlying causes.

Our criminal justice system is facing an existential crisis. In part 1 of this book, you will hear from witnesses directly impacted by the system and read the evidence for yourself as we put the criminal justice system on trial. This crisis of confidence is so serious that a Justice Canada public consultation asked: "If you could create a new criminal justice system from scratch, what would it look like?" Part 2 of this book aims to provide one answer to this provocative question, setting out a compelling new transformative justice vision for Canada.

An understanding of trauma will be our guide because trauma is deeply interwoven with all of these issues. Literally every encounter people have with the criminal justice system, whatever their role or involvement, needs to be informed by a compassionate understanding of trauma. The stakes are high. As we will see, when a trauma-informed approach is lacking by victim services, police, lawyers, judges, courthouse staff, corrections officers, parole officers, community corrections, and other justice system practitioners, we witness greater harm, worse outcomes, and even the tragic loss of life.

PART ONE

The Criminal Justice System on Trial

CHAPTER TWO

"Set Up to Fail": Criminalizing People Who Use Substances

"I grew up in a very conservative Christian home. I am a lesbian, so that was difficult. That was a struggle for me growing up," said Kaila. "And then at age thirteen, my father committed suicide."

While Kaila and her family were profoundly affected by the loss of her dad, they didn't talk about it. Everyone turned to different ways of coping. Her mother began drinking and gambling. Her brother's pain turned into anger.

"After that I very quickly turned to substance use," said Kaila. She began using alcohol, followed by cannabis, cocaine, and meth. "I didn't stop and it escalated. So, it went from the drinking to really whatever I can get my hands on. I was very impressionable. I was very naïve and I really didn't care. My philosophy was 'I'll just kill myself like my dad did,' like, I really did not give a shit about anything."

Despite her escalating drug use, Kaila was still haunted by the trauma of her father's death. Her friend had a suggestion: "Why don't you cut yourself?" She began to self-harm. That too quickly escalated.

"I started cutting myself, cutting my wrists and cutting my legs to the point where you couldn't hide it anymore. It was consistent stitches, consistent hospitalizations, mental health and they'd never hold me. I was a smooth talker, I can talk my way out of anything. I would just say, 'Everything's fine, it's a one-time thing' – even though the record showed I'd been there thirty, forty times."

While it may seem counter-intuitive, self-harming can release neurochemicals that temporarily provide relief from emotional numbness or pain and can elevate mood. The harmful behaviour can become addictive. Hospital staff would tend to Kaila's cuts even while earlier stitches were still in. No one ever offered her help for her unseen wounds at the hospital. They just sewed her up and sent her out.

"It was trauma, 100 per cent," said Kaila looking back on those years. "I didn't know who I could turn to. At such a young age I turned to my friends who had the worst ideas that were unhelpful. If you don't have any other resources, then you're just going to go with whatever other people tell you to do, your peers. You're so impressionable, right?"

———

There are many different ways people cope with trauma and stress. Adaptive coping strategies are constructive approaches that directly address the issue, including problem solving, identifying and expressing emotions, emotional regulation, and positive thinking.

On the other hand, maladaptive coping strategies may provide some relief or escape – at least in the short-term. But the underlying sources of distress remain unresolved. Excessive eating, alcohol, drugs, work, exercise, shopping, pornography, sex, dating, television/video streaming, checking the news, social media, gaming, gambling, volunteering, caregiving, hobbies, sports, leisure, religious activities, obsessing over finances, and over-functioning – quite literally anything can become an avoidance strategy, even things that superficially appear to be "good."

Maladaptive ways of coping, in turn, lead to "high levels of psychological distress, such as symptoms of anxiety and depression" and can cause other problems or difficulties in a person's life – including being victimized and becoming involved in the criminal justice system. People living with unresolved trauma are at greater risk of abusing substances as a maladaptive coping mechanism. People who experienced five of the ten original Adverse Childhood Experiences (ACEs, as discussed in chapter 1) are at seven to ten times greater risk of developing a substance addiction than someone who had an ACE score of 0.

It's important to approach this issue with compassion – towards ourselves and others. These coping mechanisms served a purpose for a time because they helped a person to survive being overwhelmed by trauma. But in time, these solutions become the problem as their origins go unaddressed.

———

"We know that alcohol alleviates all of the symptoms of PTSD," said Harold Johnson, who also wrote *Firewater: How Alcohol Is Killing My People (and Yours)*. "These people who are drinking, self-medicating their trauma ... when they self-medicate that PTSD with alcohol and then the spinoffs from that – the feedback loops – more people get victimized, beaten, sexually assaulted and trauma is the result."

Johnson witnessed this first-hand as a lawyer in Northern Saskatchewan where approximately 95 per cent of all criminal incidents in the region involved alcohol in some way.

Indigenous peoples have long resisted alcohol in their communities because of the devastation, violence, and disorder it causes. During the negotiations of Treaty No. 6 in 1876, Indigenous representatives asked for "the exclusion of fire water in the whole [of] Saskatchewan." The final text of Treaty No. 6 included language that "no intoxicating liquor shall be allowed to be introduced or sold" on reserves and that laws to "preserve Her [Majesty's] Indian subjects inhabiting the reserves or living elsewhere within Her North-west Territories from the evil influence of the use of intoxicating liquors, shall be strictly enforced."

However, Johnson points out that rather than respect this treaty obligation to keep alcohol out, the Canadian state instead punished Indigenous people (via the *Indian Act*) for drinking alcohol. Thus, settler colonialism introduced not only extensive historical traumas against Indigenous people, but also introduced alcohol to self-medicate those traumas – despite knowing of its deleterious effects on individuals and communities – and then introduced the "solution": criminalizing and imprisoning Indigenous people to address those ill effects.

Trauma. Alcohol. More trauma. Incarceration. More trauma. Repeat. Rather than accept responsibility for this vicious cycle, the system has instead increasingly foisted blame and punishment on Indigenous people.

Likewise, the criminal prohibition on opioids in Canada has racist roots, dating back well over a hundred years. In *Overdose:*

Heartbreak and Hope in Canada's Opioid Crisis, I documented how the history of the criminalization of opioids is rooted in overtly racist motivations – namely, harassing the Chinese-Canadian population in the late nineteenth and early twentieth centuries by, among other measures, criminalizing opium.

"My general sense of the criminal justice system is that it's misplaced," said Michael Bryant, executive director and general counsel at the Canadian Civil Liberties Association. "We have severe public health issues with respect to mental illness and addiction, and we ought to have a health care response to those, to this serious public health problem."

Today, we know that substance use disorders are medical and social issues. A number of factors contribute to people developing substance use disorders, including "early drug use, peer influence, trauma, genetics, psycho-social [their surrounding environment], and mental health concurrent disorders." However, the system continues to punish people who use substances based on the fundamentally flawed conception that they do so by "choice" and that punishing them will deter them from using.

Criminal offences are supposedly about punishing people for their morally blameworthy conduct, but this logic rests uneasily with the reality that substance use disorders render the idea of "choice" illusory. Substance use disorders are clinical diagnoses. The American Psychiatric Association, in its authoritative *Diagnostic and Statistical Manual of Mental Disorders* (DSM-5, published in 2013), describes a substance use disorder as a *compulsive* and prolonged pattern of problematic use.

The weight of criminalizing people who use drugs falls disproportionately on racialized and marginalized people, including Indigenous people, and those experiencing poverty, homelessness, and mental health issues. To be clear, criminalizing people who use drugs goes beyond simply criminalizing the use and possession of certain substances. It encompasses all the myriad ways that the system treats substance use as a criminal law issue – rather than a public health issue – and the flawed tools it correspondingly relies on to do so. There's a saying, "if all you have is a hammer, everything looks like a nail." That sums up how the criminal justice system treats people who use substances.

Dr. Sandy Simpson, chair in forensic psychiatry at the University of Toronto's Centre for Addiction and Mental Health, explained that the increasing toxicity and potency of illicit drugs combined with "an increasing policing of disruptive behaviour and poverty … sucks up into the criminal justice system a lot of people on the fringes of society."

I interviewed a senior criminal defence lawyer and asked what would happen if I were charged with drug possession and called him for help. He didn't want to go on record with his name.

"We gotta make sure we win. You probably won't go to jail, but you won't be able to go the States, so people want to fight that. For a day-long trial, there would have to be *Charter* issues to exclude the evidence. Without that, you will be found guilty. I would charge something to someone who can pay, I'd charge $20,000 to $25,000."

In other words, I would have a chance at beating the charges with a high-priced criminal defence lawyer. Even if not, they could help me get a more lenient sentence by presenting me in the best possible light as someone who is a remorseful, rehabilitating, responsibility-accepting, productive-member-of-society, who-made-a-mistake-and-needs-a-second-chance kind-of-person. People without the money to get top-notch legal representation don't have a way out of this legal labyrinth.

"I didn't know about lawyers or anything. So, I went in and essentially just pled guilty every time and took whatever came at me," said Kaila, whom we met at the start of this chapter.

"When you look at incarcerated women in the province of BC, the number of those women with fairly low-level drug crimes is very, very high," said Dr. Shannon McDonald, acting chief medical officer at the BC First Nations Health Authority. "It's easy to devalue and dehumanize people when you look at them only with shame and blame. ... There's no reflection on the system for having failed you."

Our criminal laws continue to threaten and punish people who are addicted to substances when they possess and use those substances. Nowhere is this more pronounced than in the ongoing toxic contaminated illicit drug crisis.

———

The "opioid crisis" is an ongoing national public health emergency that has only grown worse. Between January 2016 and September 2022, over 35,000 people in Canada died from unregulated drug overdoses.

In BC, unregulated drug deaths are the leading cause of unnatural death – more than homicides, suicides, and car accidents combined. Fatal overdoses disproportionately impact men, people between thirty and fifty-nine years of age, Indigenous people, people with concurrent mental health conditions, people who have been incarcerated, and people who are experiencing poverty or homelessness. Indigenous women also have a substantially higher risk of fatal overdose than non-Indigenous women.

A poisoned illicit drug supply is fuelling the crisis, with approximately 80 per cent of deaths involving fentanyl – a powerful synthetic opioid. It isn't naturally occurring like heroin, but made in laboratories or even at home with basic college chemistry knowledge and skills. Fentanyl is thirty to fifty times more potent than heroin and fifty to one hundred times more potent than morphine. We are also seeing even more powerful "analogues," such as carfentanyl, showing up in illicit street drugs – and autopsy reports. Carfentanyl is one hundred times more potent than fentanyl and ten thousand times more potent than morphine.

Opioids aren't "party drugs." Rather they are powerful pain relievers and anaesthetics, used widely in medical settings. It is now understood that many people who use substances are self-medicating unresolved trauma.

"If you look at the opiate circuitry of the brain, opiates are essential brain chemicals," said Dr. Gabor Maté. "We have our own opiates. They're called endorphins – endogenous morphine-like substances. They are essential for love, for connection, for attachment, for pain relief and for experiences of pleasure. Now, those kids that are traumatized, those circuits don't develop, now they need to get their endorphins, dopamine from the outside, now they turn to [illicit] opium. Now they're criminals, you know, heroin or other forms of opiates."

"A lot of these kids were doing drugs – doing meth, doing heroin – at eleven, twelve, thirteen years old," said Fritzi Horstman, founder and executive director of Compassion Prison Project. During my interviews, I heard the same thing time and again. One person even first started using substances (alcohol) at just five years of age to cope with their trauma.

"Heroin is a drug that makes you think the world is OK," said Jimmy, a fifty-six-year-old man who spent thirty years in prison for murdering his friend when he was eighteen. "I describe it as a warm terry cloth robe you just took out of the dryer. And as long as you keep feeling it, it stays nice and warm and the world is fine. We're good, right? So, it was an easy coping mechanism because I didn't know how to cope. And there wasn't any real mechanism set up to try and help me cope."

———

I've had fentanyl. It was administered in a medical setting as a sedative for a procedure. I felt peaceful and serene – not a care in the world – as I fell in and out of consciousness, without a nasty hangover. Chances are, if you or your pet have been sedated or needed strong pain relief medication, it may well have been fentanyl or some other opioid. The reason why it is safe in medical settings is two-fold. First, the contents and potency of the drugs are known and carefully titrated. Second, if you are sedated, your heart rate and respiration are carefully monitored by an anaesthesiologist so that if you are getting too much of the drug, action can be taken to prevent a fatal overdose.

When people use illicit drugs and these safeguards are not present, the results can be deadly. First, street drugs of all varieties have been haphazardly contaminated with fentanyl, absent any "quality control" of their potency. Drug squad investigators told me that kitchen blenders have been used to mix fentanyl with "buffers" like caffeine. Fentanyl's potency is such that the difference between a nonfatal dose and a fatal dose may be as little as the equivalent of grains of sand. So, on any given day you have no idea what you're getting from street drugs. Second, if someone using unregulated drugs experiences an overdose, they are at a much greater risk of dying if they are using alone. Without intervention, the breathing of a person who is over- dosing slows and may eventually stop. Naloxone is a temporary antidote to an opioid overdose that can revive someone who has overdosed, but depending on potency and the presence of other drugs, it may not be effective. They may also need assistance breathing.

"Criminal justice deals with the opioid epidemic by harassing and incarcerating drug-dependent people," said Professor Joshua Sealy-Harrington at Toronto Metropolitan University's Lincoln Alexander School of Law. Drug prohibition is not only costly and counterproductive but, as I documented in *Overdose*, it is fuelling the opioid crisis. Criminalizing drugs encourages people to use them faster to avoid police detection, making an overdose more likely. The stigma of criminalization and fear of being caught in- centivizes people to use alone, where they're significantly more likely to die in the event of an overdose.

A large and growing chorus of people are recommending the decriminalization of people who use drugs. In addition to public health experts and academic researchers, the Canadian Associa- tion of Chiefs of Police has even called for the decriminalization of simple possession. So too have groups of people who use drugs, and surviving family members of those who have died, like Moms Stop the Harm.

———

As early as fourteen years of age, Kaila (whom we met at the outset of this chapter) was already known to police in Moose Jaw, Saska- toon, and Regina for her prolific drinking and drug use.

"They would just brush me off, they really didn't take the time. I didn't end up in custody. I was never charged," said Kaila. "They would essentially just cuff me, take me away from whatever was going on and just plop me down on another street."

Kaila is white. Her experience also highlights how police discretion plays a big role in who is arrested and charged with substance-related offences. Based on my interviews, I can tell you that Indigenous youth in Saskatchewan weren't so fortunate. At any rate, the police didn't help Kaila. Their interventions simply displaced her. A lot of policing is about moving "undesirable people" out of view and away from middle class parts of town, wealthier neighbourhoods, or high visibility areas.

When Kaila turned eighteen, she was charged with impaired driving for the first time. It was just the first in a series of charges that would expand to include uttering threats and assault with a weapon.

"There was no guidance. There was no court worker. There was no anybody that said, 'Hey, what's going on here, do you need some help?' There was nobody like that."

"That just continued for years and years, the same pattern. Again, I'd go out, back to my old ways: drinking, partying, driving, fighting, whatever it was. End up back in custody. The police let me go the next day, off you go, nowhere to go. Well, who do I call? One of my friends. And we're back at it again. And it just went over and over and over again until finally in 2014 – I got into custody."

It was then that Kaila was incarcerated in provincial jail.

"Lots of times, when you're in court and you have a substance use disorder or there's substance use involved in your defence, the judge will say, 'I want you to go to treatment from custody' or 'I want you to do treatment' or something along those lines," said Kaila.

But there was a waitlist of up to six months for substance-use treatment programs. She couldn't even get in without a medical exam, which she couldn't get while in jail: "they think that people are just going to use it for bail or an early release." In more ways than one, the system was setting Kaila up for failure, then blaming her for it.

Two hours is the optimal time window to get someone into a rapid-access treatment program when they express an interest in getting help with an opioid addiction, according to medical experts. A six-month waitlist might as well be a lifetime for anyone struggling with addiction. Not only were options for substance use treatment and recovery unavailable to Kaila in jail, she also didn't get any support for addressing her underlying trauma that was driving it.

"They don't have any trauma therapists in there," said Kaila. "They're going to call jail 'rehabilitation'? I have not seen it when I was there, nor have I seen it now working in the field. [It's] solely punishment, and it's setting people up for failure. And then, when they come out, the same thing happens, and it's going to continue to happen because we're not addressing the root issues."

When Kaila got out of jail, she was sent to a halfway house. She was good at masking and put on a brave face. I asked Kaila what could have been done differently by the criminal justice system.

"I think right from the very beginning, even if there was somebody in the courtroom or even the first officer, any of the times I spent in cells, if any one of those people had taken the time to say, 'What's going on? Why do you keep coming back here? Why do we keep arresting you? Is there someone that we can call? Is there someone that we can connect you to?' – would have made a whole difference. But that never happened. And I must have been arrested over fifty times."

Rather than help Kaila address her substance use and the traumatic origins of it, the system punished her – in an escalating manner when lesser sanctions "didn't work." When probation didn't work, a short-term jail term. When that didn't work, a longer-term jail term. In and out, in and out. The system was doing what it is designed to do – trying to deter Kaila through unpleasant sanctions – rather than seeking to understand the reasons for her behaviour and providing opportunities for healing the deep wounds she was carrying.

"They just saw me as this drunk that caused havoc around the town or around the city. And, so, here's a punishment, here's another punishment, here's another punishment. And again, I always thought well, whatever, life gets too hard, I'm going to kill myself, OK give me a punishment. Nobody actually was like, 'what is really going on here?' or 'can I point you in a direction?' I would have done it. I was so desperate at times I would have tried anything."

———

Compassion, not condemnation, should be how we approach dealing with people who use substances. We need to get beneath the obvious symptoms and go deeper to the "cause of causes" – their physical, mental, emotional, social, and spiritual brokenness and wounds. Instead, the criminal justice system is deliberately ignorant of how it is causing extreme harm to people who use. The impacts begin with street-level policing.

"Canadians with a mental or substance use disorder are nine times more likely to come into contact with police for problems with their emotions, mental health or substance use, and four times more likely to be arrested than Canadians without a mental or substance use disorder," according to Statistics Canada.

"The presence of a mental or substance use disorder was associated with increased odds of coming into contact with police, even after controlling for related demographic and socioeconomic factors. Furthermore, those who perceived a need for help with their emotions, mental health or substance use also had greater odds of contact with police, regardless of whether those needs had been met."

A disturbing policing practice is to arrest people who are intoxicated and lock them up in police detention cells to "sober up" – the so-called "drunk tank." But someone who is severely intoxicated is at risk of suffering negative health outcomes, including death. They need medical monitoring and, potentially, intervention to survive. Again, the system is dealing with a medical issue using criminal justice tools – instead of nurses and hospitals, police officers and cells. "Drunk tanks" are often not properly monitored. A CBC investigation found that at least sixty people have died in police custody between 2010 and 2021 after being arrested while intoxicated.

Kaila's story of people with substance use disorders experiencing the criminal justice system as an endless revolving door is all too common. I heard from many other people who use substances that they were repeatedly given conditions by courts and parole boards that they abstain from using the substances they were addicted to.

"We are asking a person with alcoholism to refrain from drinking alcohol when it's a disease that they don't necessarily control," said Brandon Rolle, managing lawyer of Nova Scotia Legal Aid. "We're fundamentally failing that person, and we're setting them up to stay involved in the justice system."

People may come to a crisis point in their lives, like Kaila, and get into treatment and begin a recovery journey, but they should not be forced or coerced to do so. For that reason, I heard criticism of so-called "drug courts" from both practitioners and people with lived experience. These specialized courts use criminal charges as a basis for putting people with substance use disorders on strict conditions and mandatory treatment. They typically mandate abstinence from illegal street drugs for someone who has an addiction, without providing an alternative safer supply. They claim to address the "root cause" of the crime – substance use – which we have seen is often itself a symptom of unresolved trauma. This is all the more problematic given that voluntary evidence-based treatment and recovery options remain inadequate in much of the country.

"Drug court is a good example that's on the backend, and that's very, very expensive," said Dale McFee, chief of police at the Edmonton Police Service. He suggested that rather than spending so much money on drug courts *after* someone has already harmed others and become involved in the criminal justice system, we should instead provide greater access to treatment and recovery *before* things get to that stage. In short, address problematic substance use as a public health issue. "Do it quicker, faster, cheaper, with better results for people."

Threatening someone with imprisonment for using a substance that they are addicted to is counterproductive, cruel, and increases their risk of death (because their tolerance rapidly decreases during incarceration due to the forced abstinence from substances, or, at least, their reduced availability). Yet so-called "abstinence conditions" – that the individual not use substances – are routinely applied by police, judges, prosecutors, and parole boards across the country. Often on-site urine tests are required to enforce compliance. This is one of the most pervasive and insidious ways the system criminalizes people with substance use disorders. Again and again and again, people subject to such conditions rightly described it as being "set up to fail." This is particularly egregious given that Indigenous people are more likely to return to custody for things like violating conditions, rather than committing new criminal offences, and given the direct link between intergenerational trauma and substance use.

"My experiences of people I work with, like, all struggle with addictions and if they've been in jail for a period of time, they're still using in jail. And so, when they get out, that's why they're breaching, it's because of their addiction," said Stan Tu'Inukuafe, co-founder of STR8 UP, a Saskatchewan-based non-profit organization that helps people exit gangs and criminal lifestyles.

"We had this individual where he relapsed. And we're encouraging him to tell his parole officer, OK, to be honest," said Tu'Inukuafe. "We asked him to tell his parole officer he should go to treatment. But his parole officer said that he can't send him to treatment, because on his condition it says, 'you can't use drugs,' so if you go to treatment, it's like assumed you broke your condition, right."

"So, instead of being proactive, people are like, 'OK, thank you for being honest, but you can't go to treatment and we've got to send you back to jail.'"

Jerry Soltani, resident Elder at the Fetal Alcohol Syndrome Society of Yukon (FASSY), shared a similar story with me of the system not recognizing the need for treatment to support people with substance use disorders.

Elder Soltani visited a thirty-five-year-old man twice per week while he was incarcerated. He was a victim of severe abuse, homeless, exploited by others, living with Fetal Alcohol Spectrum

Disorder, and addicted to drugs and alcohol. Yet, during his five-month incarceration, he managed to get sober. Elder Soltani said he was making "big plans" for his new life. Despite his progress, the system paid no attention to what would happen next, despite professing an interest in rehabilitation.

"Bingo. They let him out of jail, no housing, no place for him to go, with all these conditions again, but there is nothing provided for him to help him with these conditions," said Elder Soltani. "So now his only alternative, basically, is to breach and go back to jail, because he doesn't have a place to live, and guess what, it's going to start raining this afternoon and tonight so it's going to be pretty cold out at his campsite."

"It's setting them up for failure. There is just no possibility of a win for any of them, as far as I can see."

I heard from multiple interviewees in different parts of the country that people experiencing poverty and homelessness would sometimes intentionally breach their conditions just so that they would have a dry place to sleep and three meals per day.

———

"I'm either going to join a gang, I'm going to kill myself, I go back to jail, or I'm going to get sober." Kaila knew those were her only options when her last criminal charge was resolved in 2014.

Kaila started looking for a counsellor and found the Circle Project in Regina – an agency focused on helping Indigenous people get healing in the community. Although she isn't Indigenous, Kaila said she felt a connection to Indigenous culture and was welcomed by the non-profit. She vividly remembers the moment she first walked into the Circle Project building.

"I was so hesitant about what I was walking into, and this lady just came up to me. She must have been about sixty years old. She just sat beside me and said, 'Do you want a coffee?' Sure. And she just started praying," said Kaila. "And I always had that piece of religion in me, right, growing up in that conservative Christian home, and that's what I needed. I instantly connected with her and just kind of went from there."

The staff member helped Kaila get into a treatment program in Saskatoon and find a doctor who prescribed her medication for her anxiety and depression. The cup of coffee and prayer from a stranger was a turning point in Kaila's life. It was the start of her recovery journey.

"So, from that moment on, I did stay sober and the first year was terrible. I had no idea who I was. It was just basically a fight to stay sober. Every day it was like, 'Hey, I need to make it through today, that's what I got to do.' After the first year, things got better."

"The second year was still hard, but I started to discover who I was again. Man, I really like hiking, I like biking, I started trying new things, I got a new job. Things were going relatively well. Still had struggles, but it was a lot of self-discovery. And then, by the third year I was like, 'you know what, I want to go to school, I want to be an addictions counsellor. I think that I know some of the things that are missing and I want to help fill those gaps.'"

Kaila followed through and became a certified addictions counsellor. She moved, got a job, married her wife, has two kids, bought a house, and got her driver's licence back.

"It's just crazy," said Kaila. "I never thought I'd be at a desk, I never thought I'd get my licence back or a car, never thought I'd own a home – these things that were impossible, right?" said Kaila. "It's just mind blowing."

Today, Kaila is an addictions counsellor at STR8 UP. Her clients are predominantly Indigenous people between fifteen and thirty years of age with gang affiliations, who are considered a high risk to reoffend. Kaila is one of just a handful of counsellors who treat individuals in provincial custody – something she wished she had had access to. And she doesn't have a lengthy waitlist, usually seeing new clients within the week.

"It costs a whole lot less for someone to see a counsellor than for them to sit in jail, so give them that trauma therapy or whatever it is. So, if the government's concern is finances, then maybe they should weigh the options of helping someone as opposed to punishing them."

———

Not only are people with substance use disorders more likely to be in contact with police and to be arrested, they're also disproportionately imprisoned.

"Upon admission to federal custody, almost 70% of federal offenders are assessed as having some level of substance abuse problem requiring intervention," according to a report by the Correctional Service of Canada. In some provinces, like Saskatchewan, up to 93 per cent of people in provincial custody have a substance use disorder. In comparison, among the general population of Canada, 3.4 per cent have a substance use disorder, 5.5 per cent have a mental disorder (other than a substance abuse disorder), and 1.0 per cent have both.

Analysts at the Correctional Service of Canada noted that half of federally incarcerated people believe that their substance use directly or indirectly contributed to their offence. Among those severely affected by substance use disorders, 97 per cent said that they were using substances the day they committed their offence. In addition to driving under the influence, the other offences with the highest rates of being connected to a person's substance use were assault (69 per cent), theft (66 per cent), murder (58 per cent), break and enter (56 per cent), robbery (56 per cent), and sexual assault (45 per cent).

What this shows is, for a vast proportion of people, we do not have a "crime problem" – we have a substance use problem, which is often a trauma problem – the "cause of causes" that we explored in chapter 1. So how does incarceration impact substance use?

"We've got a drug trade that is through the frickin' roof. It is unbelievable the amount of drugs that you can get inside of the prison," said James Bloomfield, a federal correctional officer with the Correctional Service of Canada, and Prairies regional president for the Union of Canadian Correctional Officers. "We know we have drugs in every single area of the prison."

Virtually every person that I spoke with who had been incarcerated in provincial and federal custody spoke about the widespread availability of alcohol and drugs inside. Invariably, they also spoke about the intimidation, racketeering, and bloodshed that is part and parcel of the illicit prison drug trade.

"The amount of blood and teeth that I saw on the range [cellblock], fighting, just unbelievable. Makeshift weapons of all sorts. Yeah. Just unbelievable. And this is – it's a daily occurrence," said Martin, a fifty-seven-year-old who has spent time in provincial custody in Ontario. I was told by a prison guard and countless formerly incarcerated people that drugs are frequently smuggled inside body cavities.

"Internally is where inmates hide drugs. It's not something that I can go and get, and it's not something I'm interested in going to get," said Bloomfield. "No, we don't do that stuff anymore. We are so scrutinized as a correctional group, as correctional officers that it's career suicide to pull some bullshit like that, essentially. So, it's all protecting your own ass at the end of the day."

Several people who had been incarcerated told me what they saw happen when someone new was admitted into custody – after corrections officers were out of sight. Other incarcerated people would immediately approach the new arrival.

"Guys show up on the range, right? And the first thing they say is 'What's your charge? Do you have any drugs?'" said Martin. "And I saw them take one guy into a bathroom stall and literally forced him to sit on the toilet until he defecated out whatever he was carrying. They stood there watching it and said, 'We're going to kill you unless you give us what you have.' Because they're looking for the drugs, obviously, that's what they're doing."

"If you had anything, they [the other people who were incarcerated] would just beat you when you came in, for someone to shit on the floor and take all their stuff," said Nate, a thirty-six-year-old who was imprisoned in a provincial facility in Quebec. He is in recovery from drug and alcohol addiction and was living in a tent when I spoke to him. He asked if he could receive the modest honorarium for our interview right away so he could get a $30 hostel to get out of the cold for the night. He told me he couldn't go to local homeless shelters because they were too triggering for him – both for his PTSD that he developed while incarcerated and because being surrounded by people who were actively using substances made it difficult to maintain his sobriety.

I was also told by people who had been incarcerated about drugs allegedly being brought behind bars via corrupt corrections officers and even drones, which land in the outdoor areas of correctional facilities. I was quoted $3,000 as the going delivery rate for anything a drone could carry inside a Quebec corrections facility. I was even given a recipe for how moonshine is made in prison and how it is hidden in plain sight. It's a never-ending game of cat and mouse. It all points to the desperation of profoundly traumatized people with long-term substance use disorders being locked in cages where their existing trauma, substance use, and mental health conditions are exacerbated, and they are exposed to fresh traumas. The prison environment is not conducive to recovery. This inadequacy is seen in the lengths to which people have gone to access these substances while incarcerated.

"One of the most horrendous things you would see is there's a number of people who are heroin addicts who get methadone instead," said Martin, who spent time at a provincial maximum and medium-security provincial jail in Ontario. Methadone is one of the medications used to suppress opioid use. But it can also be abused. "So, they provide them with a methadone drink, and you have to go down once a day. It's very tightly controlled. They drink their methadone. There are guys that would come back to the range after their methadone, vomit through a sock to filter out the vomit and save the methadone and then sell it."

"You do get a buzz from the methadone but it's not like shooting heroin," he said. "But things like that, you think, you're going to drink somebody else's puke to get high? That's how desperate some people are on the inside for drugs. One guy told me, 'From the moment the cells crack till I go to bed, I am high. I'm never not high. And that's how I cope.'"

You quite literally could not intentionally design a worse place than jail for someone with an addiction to substances. The rampant violence inside, the reuse and sharing of syringes which increase the transmission of communicable diseases such as HIV/AIDs, Hepatitis B, and Hepatitis C. For some, the outcome of being incarcerated with a substance use disorder can be fatal.

———

"I can remember one day in the prison hearing that there had been sixteen overdoses in one day at the facility. I myself witnessed half a dozen overdoses. Literally tried to save one gentleman," said Martin. With no guards around, it was up to Martin to try and help this fellow incarcerated person who was suddenly unconscious and not breathing. "Was on top of him grinding my fist into his sternum, trying to get him to come around, to no avail." Despite Martin's best efforts, the man died.

"Opioid-related deaths are increasing among incarcerated people," according to a report by a group of researchers at Dalhousie University. "Post-release, their prospects are even worse: in the two weeks after release, a prisoner's risk of overdose mortality is more than 50 times higher than in the general population."

Two-thirds of all unregulated drug deaths in British Columbia were people who had been imprisoned or were under community supervision by the province at some point in their lives, according to the BC Coroners Service. Alarmingly, almost one in five people (18 per cent) who died in BC of a fatal overdose had been released from provincial custody within the previous thirty days. In Alberta, 50 per cent of fatal overdoses since 2017 were people who had spent time in a provincial correctional facility within the previous two years.

Indeed, multiple peer-reviewed studies have found that people who are incarcerated are at substantially greater risk of dying from an overdose, especially in the weeks immediately following release. Why? A key factor is that, while drugs are widely available behind bars, supply is more limited. Tolerance to substances correspondingly decreases so that, once someone is released and uses drugs again (opioid-use disorder is considered to be a chronic, relapsing condition after all), they are at much greater risk of dying from an overdose.

"People die because they think, 'Oh I'm going to do what I was doing again.' And the tolerance isn't there," said Duncan, a twenty-eight-year-old who is in recovery from a fentanyl addiction and has experienced homelessness and incarceration. He's also a childhood sexual abuse survivor. "I remember looking at a piece of fentanyl I was going to do. I'm like, this is stupid. It's a crumb. Like I used to smash chunks, like ten, fifteen times the size of this. Like, and I OD'd [overdosed]."

"There's no option for you to sign up when you're getting sentenced or something like, 'Can I go to a halfway house to get help when I get out of here, at least? Or do I just have to go back to the streets?' Because there's no option for that," Duncan added.

Even if someone with a substance use disorder has a place to go upon release from custody, their conditions typically include a requirement not to use substances – or end up back imprisoned. This encourages them to hide their consumption and use alone, especially at places like halfway houses or treatment centres, dramatically increasing the risk of a fatal overdose as we have seen.

Looking at all of this evidence leads to a stark conclusion: for many people with substance use disorders, imprisonment is equivalent to a death sentence.

CHAPTER THREE

"From Protectors to Villains": Mental Health, Poverty, and Homelessness

"I need help for my husband! I think he's going to kill himself," Audrey told the 911 operator.

Will, her husband, was struggling with a range of mental health issues, including anxiety, depression, and addiction to alcohol, opioids, cocaine, and prescription drugs that began in his youth.

"I had a good childhood up until about seven, and my dad came into the situation," said Will, who is thirty-six years old and has spent over a decade behind bars. When Will was seven years of age, his dad was released from prison. It was the first time Will met him. His dad quickly became violent. "Beat my mom up every day. He almost killed her. The last time I seen her she was in a coma, broken jaw. He burned her face on a frying pan. That stuff, you know, had a bit of an effect on me when I was a kid, but it is what it is. But never learned coping mechanisms." The childhood trauma that Will endured set him up for a whole cascade of harms. His story is tragically not an isolated case.

When his mom "couldn't handle" him and his three sisters, she placed Will in the custody of children's aid. "But the system group homes are even broke, right? Everything's broken. The whole system is a very broken system. There is no quick fix. I'm still attached to the criminal system right now. I'm on probation. The system's just – it's fucked up. I've actually called the treatment centre that I was on the list for and I missed a call – so I fell off their list. I've called them three times in the last month and left messages." The day his wife called 911, Will was suicidal.

"I took a bunch of lorazepam [Ativan] to try to get rid of my anxiety. I ended up stabbing myself in the head, stabbed myself in the arm. My wife said that I was so gone that she was scared," explained Will. "I was suicidal."

"She called 911, said that she wanted to get help. She didn't say I threatened her, nothing. She said, 'I'm afraid he's going to kill himself.' That was the 911 call."

The police were dispatched to respond. They took Will to the hospital for treatment. But after he was stitched up and the hospital released him, the police kept him waiting.

"They had me in the back of the cop car and they said, 'I don't know what we're doing, hold on.' And they charged me with mischief and possession of a weapon for stabbing myself with a steak knife from my house, and stabbing my own house, a wall."

Will spent forty days in jail in relation to the incident. No help after his suicide attempt, just more hurt after he had already hurt himself. He was released the month his youngest son was born. Will was just coming up on ninety days sober when I spoke with him – about the longest he's gone before relapsing in the community.

"My sole focus right now is my mental health and my sobriety. I'm trying to focus on these things because I've never taken the time to focus on them. I have a newborn son, he's four months old, and I've let my kids down."

"The one thing I know is, I'm not stupid, I'm not a bad person. I have an amazingly big heart. I just don't know how to do – my anxiety, my depression, my mental health, I don't know how to cope. I don't know how – I've never learned anything. You know, I've never learned anything my whole life because it's always been – you end up in jail."

———

"The link between childhood adversity and adult mental health issues is scientifically documented to be as strong as the link between cigarette smoking and lung cancer," said Dr. Gabor Maté.

Trauma can affect people in myriad ways. It impacts emotional well-being. It can cause emotional distress, including feeling numb, disconnected, confused, shocked, angry, anxious, terrified, helpless, powerless, irritable, depressed, and ashamed. It can involve nightmares, intrusive thoughts, and flashbacks ("reexperiencing a previous traumatic experience as if it were actually happening in that moment"). Often, this will be caused by a "trigger," which is any "reminder of the traumatic event: a noise, smell, temperature, other physical sensation, or visual scene."

Trauma increases the risk of mental health conditions, as we saw with Will at the outset of this chapter. This includes post-traumatic stress disorder (trauma is a broader concept than PTSD), depression, dissociation and dissociative disorders, panic disorder, generalized anxiety disorder, and somatoform disorder. These conditions are linked to trauma's impact on the neurochemistry and structure of the brain as we examined in chapter 1.

Trauma can impact cognitive processes, including memory, attention, and thinking. Trauma affects the brain in a way that "leads to narrative incoherence" or "uncontained communication that has no walls or structure ... Events are out of sequence, gradations of severity are lost because everything is really bad." This has massive implications for the criminal justice system, which relies heavily on witness testimony to determine what happened. It calls into question the ability of judges and juries to correctly discern the truth due to the risk of disbelieving truthful traumatized witnesses.

Trauma can also manifest itself in the body, as alluded to in the title of Dr. Bessel van der Kolk's acclaimed book *The Body Keeps the Score*. This can include chronic pain, gynaecological difficulties, gastrointestinal problems, asthma, heart palpitations, headaches, musculoskeletal difficulties, insomnia, increased susceptibility to autoimmune disorders, and exacerbation of existing health issues.

Trauma erodes social well-being. It can make it difficult to trust others and benefit from relationships, including among family members, friends, the community, and even people offering resources or support. We also know that childhood trauma interferes with parenting later in life, leading to ongoing intergenerational impacts.

Finally, trauma impacts spiritual well-being. In some instances, people experiencing trauma report "increased appreciation of life, greater perceived closeness to God, increased sense of purpose in life, and enhanced spiritual well-being." Conversely, others experience "loss of faith, diminished participation in religious or spiritual activities, changes in belief, feelings of being abandoned or punished by God, and loss of meaning and purpose for living."

———

"When the healthcare system fails to treat mental illness, the criminal justice system punishes the symptoms," said a John Howard Society report.

People with psychotic illnesses are "bouncing between police, jails, emergency departments, patched up acutely, back on the streets, never getting well, never getting adequately followed up," said forensic psychiatrist Dr. Sandy Simpson. "So, they never get the sort of service that will be supportive, and they've never got the social infrastructure necessary to support them, and the criminal justice system sucks them up."

"Forty per cent of people in their first episode of psychosis could have been charged with a violent criminal offence. It is a common – not a rare – but a common complication of acute psychosis," said Dr. Simpson. What determines their long-term prospects, future risk to others, and the long-term financial costs to society is how we respond. "People who have a psychotic illness who are treated have the same or lower rates of violence than the general population. So, it's treatable if care is available and acceptable and delivered in the right way to people in need."

Yet, what is the first question you get asked when you call 911? "Do you need police, fire, or ambulance?" The police are frequently the default when someone is in a mental health crisis, especially if it is a rural or remote community, after hours, or on weekends. The outcome can be deadly.

Over two-thirds (68 per cent) of the 555 people identified in a CBC investigative report who were killed during encounters with police between 2000 and 2020 had mental health and/or substance use issues. The number of fatalities has continued to grow on a per capita basis. A subsequent investigation by the *Globe and Mail* found that police officers who kill or injure someone are rarely charged or disciplined – the vast majority refuse to cooperate with independent oversight bodies. In BC, a mere 2 per cent of almost 200 officers investigated by the Independent Investigations Office in the last five years fully cooperated. This represents both a failure of police accountability and our societal response to complex, often inter-related challenges.

"What, fundamentally, I see going on in this area is that there has been a widespread failure of social policy to provide appropriate care for people with serious mental illness," said Dr. Simpson. "So, lack of adequate income support, lack of adequate housing, creating huge structural barriers for people."

Mental health calls are a major component of policing today and the way police respond also intersects with race. In Toronto, 20,000 calls to police were related to mental illness in one year. In Edmonton, Chief of Police Dale McFee estimated that 30 per cent of calls to the dispatch centre involved serious mental health concerns.

Paradoxically, while mental health calls to police are less likely to be about serious offences, people with mental health concerns were more likely to be arrested for minor offences than someone who didn't have a mental disorder. Cases abound of people experiencing a mental health crisis dying during police "wellness checks" – visits prompted, ironically, by someone calling in and expressing a concern that the person was in distress and might need help.

In some cases, it was that person themselves who called 911 for support, but police arrived, and it ended fatally. The risk of a fatal encounter appears to be heightened when the person is racialized and/or also using substances. Here are just a few examples of publicly reported incidents from May and June 2020.

Chantel Moore, a twenty-six-year-old Nuu-chah-nulth woman of the Tla-o-qui-aht First Nation in British Columbia, was fatally shot by police in New Brunswick on June 4, 2020, during a middle-of-the-night "wellness check." An ex-boyfriend had called police worried about her safety. She was asleep when police woke her up with a flashlight. She emerged with a knife and was shot by police twice in the chest, once in the abdomen, and once in her left leg. She died as a result. During a subsequent investigation clearing his name, the officer told investigators that "he regretted not giving himself an exit from the confrontation." In May 2022, a coroner's inquest jury found that Moore's death was a homicide and recommended an independent review of police use-of-force policies. Indigenous leaders called for an Indigenous-led inquiry into systemic racism.

Regis Korchinski-Paquet, a twenty-nine-year-old Indigenous-Ukrainian-Black Canadian woman died after falling from her twenty-fourth-floor balcony just minutes after Toronto police arrived at her apartment on May 27, 2020. Her family told reporters that she was experiencing a mental health crisis. Her mother said she called police to de-escalate the situation and take her daughter to the Centre for Addiction and Mental Health. The province's Special Investigations Unit (SIU) cleared the officers of wrongdoing.

Ejaz Ahmed Choudry, a sixty-two-year-old Muslim man from Pakistan with schizophrenia, was shot and killed by police in Mississauga, Ontario, on June 20, 2020. A family member had called a non-emergency line for help while Choudry was experiencing a mental health crisis. According to the family, Choudry had diabetes, heart issues, and was frail from recent lung surgery. Prior to arriving at the scene, police had been told he could "barely walk or breathe." Police shot him twice in the chest, killing him. The police officer who fired the fatal shots refused to give a statement or hand over their notes to the SIU. Nevertheless, in April 2021, the SIU cleared the officers of wrongdoing despite finding that the "wellness check" consisted of police kicking in Choudry's balcony door and shouting at him in English – which he didn't understand – to drop a kitchen knife. The officer in charge said he was concerned Choudry was at risk of "self-harm." Yet it was police who shot him.

"The law is clear that police officers are not required to measure the force they used with exactitude or to a nicety," said the SIU in clearing police.

"Ejaz committed no crime. He did not deserve any of this," said a statement by the family.

I asked Dr. Sandy Simpson, who has over thirty years of experience as a mental health professional, why people in mental health distress are disproportionately killed during police encounters. He explained that to secure compliance, police predominantly "use dominance to control." To illustrate the impact of this approach, he described first how it tends to work with a person lacking any serious mental health conditions.

"If you're an antisocial guy in the middle of a bus stop with someone else, and there are three large guys with tasers and body armour coming up to tell you to calm down, you kind of weigh up the risks and you back off."

In other words, the display of dominance by the police is intended to subdue without recourse to force. Forceful and authoritative language, weapons carried or displayed, physical presence and stature, large numbers of officers present, even the intimidating style of their uniforms and vehicles all send a message: we are in charge, we are more powerful, you have no choice but to submit to us. Resistance is futile. The best-case scenario is compliance with their verbal commands so no escalation to physical force is required. At least that's the idea.

What Dr. Simpson described sounded so primal – like something I'd seen on nature documentaries with lions roaring at one another over territory or silverback gorillas pounding their chests, both species baring their teeth. If the rival doesn't back down, force is used to subdue and, potentially, kill them. However, the assumptions behind using displays of dominance play out very differently for someone who is experiencing a mental health crisis.

"Heavy police, militarized police-type responses to deal with people who can't read dominance dynamics doesn't work," said Dr. Simpson. "That doesn't work with people who can't process the social cues of dominance. Or if you're acutely paranoid, a dominant display is a cue that heightens your arousal."

In other words, displays of dominance – the primal threat of overwhelming force or death – by police or corrections officers may *escalate* rather than de-escalate situations for people in mental health distress and those with unresolved trauma. As was discussed in chapter 1, traumatized people have a fight-flight-freeze response that is more easily triggered and amplified. Because of their trauma, they may be more inclined to "fight" to protect themselves; they may be hypervigilant for potential threats and perceive a display of dominance disproportionately. And when the central nervous system's fight-flight-freeze response is activated, it is subconscious and largely automatic.

The "National Use of Force Framework" was developed in 2000 and is used throughout Canada, including by the Toronto Police Service. This use-of-force policy consists of a progression from officer presence to using communication, to "soft" then "hard" physical control, to intermediate weapons, to lethal force. Officers are taught to advance through these stages based on *their perception* of whether the subject is non-cooperative, passively resisting, actively resisting, being assaultive, and if the officer perceives the subject poses a risk of serious bodily harm or death to someone.

When someone doesn't respond to police presence by becoming docile and compliant, then escalation tactics are used, including strong and forceful language and physically touching the subject. If the subject actively resists this, then "hard" control and intermediate weapons are authorized by this framework. If those don't subdue and the person is fighting back and the officer perceives a risk of bodily harm or death, deadly force can follow. This cycle progresses until the perceived "threat" is neutralized – or altogether eliminated.

But the assumptions of this use-of-force framework are fundamentally flawed – with potentially deadly outcomes – for a vast cross section of people that police regularly interact with, including people in mental health crisis, people with mental and neurological disabilities, those with unresolved trauma, people who are intoxicated with substances, and racialized people who have distrust and fear of the police. And when these incidents are subsequently reviewed by investigators, the use of force (including deadly force) by police seems typically to pass muster since it is interpreted as being simply in response to a perceived threat to the officer – even though the cascade of escalation may have been triggered by their initial and subsequent behaviour.

The Centre for Addiction and Mental Health (CAMH), along with family members of loved ones in mental distress killed during police encounters, have said enough is enough. In 2020, CAMH publicly called for the removal of police officers from being the frontline response to people in mental health crisis. Yet police forces across Canada continue to respond to people in mental health crisis, employing the flawed National Use of Force Framework. To make matters worse, police forces across Canada have recently been securing increased funding to hire more officers, perpetuating this dangerous model that isn't making our communities any safer. In reality, hiring more police officers actually undermines public safety for people experiencing a mental health crisis, those with unresolved trauma, and those living with mental disabilities.

"If people are traumatized by the people in their life that are supposed to take care of them, they'll have a lifelong distrust of authority figures, and a fear of them as well," said Dr. Maté. "I've seen it both ways. I've seen cops show up in a hostile kind of authoritarian, aggressive way, which only inflames the situation … I've often seen other cops who are more confident in themselves, perhaps more trauma-informed or just more or less attached to their role, and more in touch with their humanity, show up in a calmer, more patient, sometimes even humorous way, which diffuses the situation."

"Cops themselves never get this kind of training. And very often they themselves are traumatized. It's a difficult job that they have. And so their own traumas then tend to be brought into the situation to interact with the traumas of the people they are trying to control, and they've got the flame and the fuel."

Other mental conditions that have been linked to harmful police responses include autism, intellectual disabilities, brain injuries, and FASD. Perceived "non-responsiveness" or atypical reactions to police intervention have been mistaken by officers as intoxication, belligerence, non-compliance, resistance, or aggression. This then risks triggering the escalating use-of-force response by police that can lead to injury or even death.

For example, on the evening of July 27, 2015, Joshua Nixon, a twenty-three-year-old Indigenous man with autism, was walking home along some train tracks in Stratford, Ontario. He was wearing noise-cancelling headphones – a common and well-known tool used by people with autism to manage sensory overload. When police approached and asked him to identify himself ("officer presence"), Nixon kept walking. This perceived "non-compliance" and "passive resistance" was no doubt seen to justify escalation. The officer called for backup. As two officers grabbed Nixon's arms (a "soft" control use of force), he pulled away (interpreted now as "active resistance," seemingly justifying "hard" control). There was a struggle, where Nixon was forced to the ground. He was struck in the head by police and suffered a concussion. A photograph of his injuries provided by the family to the media shows Nixon with a bloodied and bruised head with his right eye blackened and swollen shut.

The SIU cleared the officers of any wrongdoing. No doubt, the National Use of Force Framework whitewashed the whole incident, ignorant of Nixon's Indigeneity, autism, and how his behaviour was completely misinterpreted by officers.

"It's pretty obvious just by the way that Joshua was wearing his headphones, the way that he speaks, and the way that he carries his body, that if you had any training or knowledge about people with disabilities, you would be able to spot that this person probably has autism or something that makes it difficult for him to communicate," said Jenaya Nixon, his sister. "And they didn't respect that. They just accosted him. They kept pushing him, they kept scaring him. And for what? Walking across the train tracks?"

———

A canine custody battle was the catalyst for a series of events that would eventually lead Nate, a thirty-six-year-old musician, to being imprisoned in a violent provincial detention facility and then left homeless and suffering from mental health issues.

"When we broke up, she kept the dog that I paid for," said Nate. "So, then we were arguing a lot and she reported it to the police, just to get me to leave her alone. And when I was drunk one time, I ended up just calling her or texting her, whatever it was, again and that's what gave me the [criminal harassment] charge."

"I've had really heavy drug and alcohol addiction in my life."

Nate was ordered to complete a large number of community service hours. But then the COVID-19 pandemic hit and everything shut down. Nate says the lawyers were sorting out what to do. He moved in with a new girlfriend, but they eventually broke up and he didn't have a permanent place to live. As a result, he missed a letter informing him of a new court date.

One day, as Nate was getting on public transit, he was randomly stopped by police and asked for identification. Since he'd missed a court date, they arrested him and took him to the police station. He was denied bail, he says because he didn't have a home to be released to. Studies have indeed found that those without a fixed address are more likely to be denied bail and held in custody – some finding it is "an almost guaranteed outcome." As a result, Nate spent four and a half months in a provincial jail. The conditions were harsh, including the conduct of corrections officers.

"They're really hard. They would be teasing people, they'd be making fun of them as they cried," said Nate. "Seven of us were left in the cell for twenty-eight days for the [COVID-19] quarantine, two of those people snapped and had to be brought down to the hole, which is where they bring you if you disobey things. One guy was crying hysterically, because he wanted to talk to his mother. And another guy – this was the second [stint] in a row of full lockdown we had – where he just came from federal. So he did, I think, 56 days straight of confinement and he just snapped."

"The one guy was crying. Basically, when they opened his cell to give him his food or something, he just walked out and just walked to the phone and then they called in one of their codes and then they came in and pepper-sprayed him and pretty much beat the shit out of him. And then brought them to the hole. They punished him. I think he received forty-two days in the hole, done straight."

"There was a couple of guys in with us that were just schizophrenic, just didn't know what they were doing," said Nate. "And none of these guards have any training for mental health and they don't care at all. There was a couple of guards stabbed when I was there. They would mock people a lot while they were in their cells, which I thought was wildly cruel."

———

"Others way before me have been talking about how criminal justice has become the asylum of the century," said Professor Adelina

Iftene at Dalhousie University's Schulich School of Law and Associate Director of the Health Law Institute. Efforts to "soften" the approach through so-called mental health courts are even seen by some as part of the problem. These specialized criminal courts were supposed to make the justice system more responsive to accused people with underlying mental health issues, but there is growing criticism that the court-supervised approach to mental health issues makes things worse.

"There's some evidence that mental health courts result in higher rates of new charges for infractions because you're expected to turn up on these dates and you expect someone with disorganization or disability to turn up and do things when they haven't got the other things in their life set up that they need to. So, we set them up to fail," said Dr. Simpson.

While data on the proportion of people who are incarcerated with mental health conditions is hard to come by – something alarming in itself – it is clear that people with mental health issues are disproportionately incarcerated. And this trend has been dramatically increasing in recent decades.

"About 30 per cent of the male [prison] population, about 50 per cent of the female [prison] population requires some sort of follow-up, psychiatric or psychological services," said Dr. Ivan Zinger, Correctional Investigator of Canada.

Since imprisonment has a devastating impact on mental health it only makes things worse. It not only exacerbates pre-existing mental health challenges but can also cause new mental health issues to emerge. In part, this is because incarceration replicates, intensifies, and perpetuates trauma. For traumatized individuals – who make up the overwhelming majority of people who are incarcerated – the prison environment can be profoundly triggering and retraumatizing, generating new traumatic experiences that compound previous unresolved traumas. The prison environment itself is harmful and traumatizing. In particular, for prisoners with complex and/or developmental trauma, the experience of being imprisoned can replicate prior abuse by a childhood caregiver or romantic partner: there is an authority figure (e.g., an abuser/parent/corrections officer) who wields power over someone (e.g., the abusee/child/incarcerated person) who is entirely dependent on them for basic necessities of life (e.g., food, shelter, clothing, protection), controls their activities and behaviours, and subjects them to harsh punishment and confinement.

People who are incarcerated may end up reliving their past childhood traumas through the experience of similar abuse, neglect, or other mistreatment by authority figures in the prison system – taken back in their minds to their three- or five-year-old selves – whatever age at which they were first traumatized. This can lead to revictimization "by perpetuating feelings of powerlessness and vulnerability," recreating the "helplessness and terror" that is emblematic of trauma.

The trauma of the prison environment can lead to extreme emotional, physical, and mental distress as well as damaging maladaptive coping behaviours (including self-harm, suicide, violence against others, and substance use). Often, neither people who are incarcerated nor corrections officers will know what is driving these behaviours – that it is an unconscious, automated psychological response to trauma. Instead, the behaviours are interpreted as noncompliance or aggression, which results in discipline and punishment, further fuelling the reproduction of early childhood trauma, and further exacerbating the situation.

The other side of the prison equation is the corrections officers who work there. "For the most part, jails are punitive," said Dr. Maté. "The guards are not trained [about trauma] in effect, the guards are often as traumatized as the prisoners are, so they inflict that trauma on the prisoners – their contempt, the lack of proper human interaction."

The criminal justice system is fundamentally flawed because its primary objectives cannot be met – and are in fact thwarted – by incarcerating people experiencing mental health distress and who have unresolved trauma. Denouncing people who commit crimes while in mental health distress is to ignore the role their mental illness has played in their conduct and its relationship to trauma. Deterrence is nonsensical when dealing with people in mental health distress, because of their underlying conditions. Additionally, in moments of crisis, we know that executive function/decision-making takes a back seat to survival responses of the brain (e.g., fight-flight-freeze), particularly when an individual does not feel in control of the stressful situation at hand. This phenomenon is compounded in traumatized individuals, whose "window of tolerance" for stress is narrower, thus making things potentially quicker to move to aggression. From policing through to corrections, instead of rehabilitating, the system is causing massive harm to people with mental health conditions and trauma.

———

Use of force by corrections officers, deaths in custody, and self-injury are all elevated risks faced by people with mental health issues who are imprisoned. Prisons are not the place for people who are already traumatized or have serious mental health issues to get better.

Use of force against people who are incarcerated includes using restraint equipment, physical handling/control, chemical or inflammatory agents (e.g., pepper spray), intermediary weapons (including tasers and batons), displaying or using firearms, and intervention by the Emergency Response Team. A major problem is how the system essentially punishes people for behaviours related to their mental health disorders – which incarceration aggravates – rather than seeking to help them in getting a diagnosis and receiving medically and culturally appropriate trauma-informed treatment, medication, and therapies in a supportive environment.

"Frustrating, violent, or impulsive behaviour that generally accompanies severe mental disorder such as bipolar or schizoaffective disorder may be interpreted by correctional staff as a threat to the safety of the prisoner themselves or other prisoners/staff, which may lead to higher rates of disciplinary violations and increased instances of segregation as a form of behaviour management," concluded a John Howard Society report.

Four in ten (41 per cent) use-of-force incidents in federal prisons involve at least one person who had a documented mental health condition, according to a report by Dr. Ivan Zinger. But even this likely vastly underestimates the true picture since there's a lack of reliable data from the Correctional Service of Canada (CSC) on mental health indicators.

"We continue to see examples of use-of-force incidents where the mental health elements at play are not adequately assessed, acknowledged, communicated, or factored into the interventions," said Dr. Zinger. For example, pepper spray is overused in federal prisons, something that is particularly cruel and traumatic for people who have serious mental health conditions and are traumatized.

Dr. Zinger informed Parliament about an example where a man who was certified under provincial mental health legislation was going through a health procedure. When the individual became "uncooperative," the prison's Emergency Response Team (ERT) "used two separate bursts of pepper spray, handcuffs and other forms of physical handling and, at one point, a shield to kneel the patient over a cement bench."

Dr. Zinger also highlighted concerns about the treatment of women in mental health distress or who are self-harming in prison, particularly Indigenous women.

"My Office investigated a case of use-of-force on a young Indigenous woman residing in the Secure Unit. She was self-injuring and experiencing mental health issues," said Dr. Zinger. "After she used her call button to ask for assistance, correctional officers arrived at her cell. She complied with their orders, was handcuffed and led to an interview room. There, she became very agitated and resumed injuring herself. Officers gave verbal orders from outside the room to stop, but they lacked keys to enter and the woman did not stop. When the keys arrived, the officers opened the door immediately and deployed pepper spray, which stopped her behaviour." The case highlighted how "security measures" are relied on to manage self-harm in prisons, rather than responding with compassion and following professional standards of therapeutic care for treating people who are self-harming.

Dr. Zinger also documented how random strip searches are particularly traumatic for sexual abuse survivors, who constitute a majority of incarcerated women. The conditions of incarceration also exacerbate mental health conditions.

"Overcrowding and double-bunking can increase stress, anxiety, and incidents of self-harming and suicidal behaviour," said Dr. Zinger. "Women's behaviours, many of which contribute to their maximum-security status, are often the result of untreated trauma and mental health issues. They would be better addressed with support rather than restriction and security."

Federally incarcerated people are also eight times more likely to die of homicide and suicide than the general population. A study by professor of criminology Thomas Gabor at the University of Ottawa of eighty-two deaths in federal custody in 2001–5 found six in ten were suicides, while about two in ten were homicides and two in ten were deemed "accidents." In 43.9 per cent of all of these deaths, mental health issues were considered significant.

"In one case, the failure of an inmate … to pick up his anti-depressant medication for three days was not shared with his case management team," found Dr. Gabor. The individual committed suicide soon after. "In another case in which an inmate committed suicide following an unsuccessful appeal of his conviction, there was no alert in the Offender Management System (OMS) despite a history of self-harm, suicide attempts (including one following a previous unsuccessful appeal), and a history of substance abuse."

Similarly, a study in the *Journal of Forensic and Legal Medicine* examined 478 male deaths in custody in Ontario between 1996 and 2010. It found that "[a]pproximately half of all deaths in custody occurred among those with a history of mental illness or substance use and those deaths disproportionately occurred in local police or provincial custody." Additionally, the study found that "the joint effects of a co-occurring history of mental illness and substance use were found to be statistically significant."

There are also disturbing cases alleging the involvement of prison guards in the death of incarcerated people. For example, Soleiman Faqiri, a thirty-year-old man with schizophrenia, was arrested in December 2016 for an incident with a neighbour. He was sent to segregation in Ontario's Central East Correctional

Centre (the "Lindsay Superjail") until a space opened up for him at a mental health facility. His family was not allowed to visit him. Within eleven days of arriving at Lindsay, he was dead.

"The coroner's report was very compelling," his brother Yusuf Faqiri told Global News. "At the time of Soleiman's death, the last few minutes of his life, both his legs and his hands were tied, he was pepper sprayed twice, he was in segregation the whole time, multiple guards were involved in his death, and the coroner's report said there were fifty blunt impact trauma bruises."

Soleiman's family wanted to see the guards held responsible. However, CBC News reported that the Ontario Provincial Police declined to lay charges "even after the province's chief forensic pathologist determined the guards' actions directly contributed to his death."

———

The isolation and separation caused by incarceration, as well as the conditions of confinement, directly lead to many people engaging in self-harm. A report commissioned for Public Safety Canada acknowledges that "[p]ersons who self-injure are usually seeking a form of relief from psychological pain, loneliness, depression, anger or in some cases an absence of feeling, furthermore, some persons self-injure in order to punish themselves." This can begin early in their youth.

"When you lock up a young person twenty-three and a half hours a day, seven days a week, in a room and especially I'm talking about the youth that are gang individuals. Where instead of opening the door and having interaction, they just slide food in a slot, like, how does that not damage your mental health?" said

Stan Tu'Inukuafe with STR8 UP. "I see a lot of people cutting and they're starting to cut, or a lot try, people try to hang themselves."

Tu'Inukuafe has spoken out in the media about a young Indigenous man named Curtis Mackenzie whom he used to visit in custody. Mackenzie had mental health and substance use issues. He had been abused physically and emotionally during foster care and his cousins introduced him to alcohol. Mackenzie also loved drawing and poetry. While incarcerated at one point, Mackenzie "was in solitary confinement for sixty days, somehow he got razors, and he cut off his nose and flushed it down the toilet," said Tu'Inukuafe. Mackenzie would later die by suicide at twenty-seven years of age on March 9, 2020, at Saskatchewan Penitentiary. The Congress of Aboriginal Peoples said that he had tried many times to get help.

A psychiatry professor at the University of Saskatchewan who knew Mackenzie publicly questioned why he was in a federal penitentiary instead of a forensic psychiatric facility for treatment. "[I]t's simply immoral to try to treat them when you're incarcerating them."

Beyond the impact on the individual while they are imprisoned, after they are released, there are other ongoing negative impacts on their well-being and on their families, communities, and Nations. These effects are especially pronounced for Indigenous people.

"I think you need to look at the person that's incarcerated and you need to look at the family and community that are left behind," said Dr. Shannon McDonald, acting chief medical officer at the BC First Nations Health Authority. "There is a particular sense of loss to be not only incarcerated physically, and socially limited, but to be incarcerated in a foreign system that isn't necessarily sensitive to those needs." But there are even more harms of imprisonment that come back to communities.

"There are higher rates of infectious diseases, sexually transmitted infections. There are issues of drug use and tainted drug supply coming into prison, and the risks of violent interactions with staff and fellow inmates in those situations. The mental health impact is huge. I think particularly of women, who may be separated from their children, often permanently as a result of their incarceration. There is a whole list of impacts that are directly against health and then indirectly against wellness that need to be considered."

It is sobering to hear that the average life expectancy for prisoners in Canada is sixty years, compared with the Canadian average of around eighty-two years. An audit of Ontario jails released in 2019 concluded: "Correctional institutions are not suited to provide appropriate care to the growing percentage of inmates who have possible mental health issues." Talk about an understatement.

———

The experience of being incarcerated for four and a half months hit Nate's mental health hard. He developed severe PTSD, had panic attacks, and felt dizzy. While he used to enjoy playing his music for crowds, now he isolates himself and views people in authority differently.

"It changed my view of police and authority figures from being protectors to just being villains in a way."

When Nate was released, he didn't have a place to stay. His life had been totally disrupted. In addition to his challenges with substance use and mental health issues from being imprisoned, he was now homeless, living in a tent along bike camping trails. He reflected back on his time in jail.

"All it did was just fuck me up," said Nate. "My view on jail over-all, it made me feel like most people are put there so our society can be perceived as a lot better than it really is. ... Because most people who are in there, I felt like, it's just because the other insti-tutions have failed them, now we're going to put them in one and that's going to only make their issues worse."

———

Our society disproportionately locks up people who are underedu-cated, unemployed, and poor. Six in ten (62 per cent) federally in-carcerated males were unemployed at the time they were arrested and "most have had difficulty finding legitimate employment or have never held a steady job." Grade 7–8 is the average literacy level of people admitted to federal penitentiaries in Canada.

"It's an insane amount of people who are illiterate, very low edu-cation, which was really strange," said Nate. "You see a lot of these guys who are big deals with different gangs, yet, when we could eventually get library books, they're taking out picture books be-cause they can't read."

Poverty, homelessness, and unemployment are deeply interwo-ven with the criminal justice system. People experiencing these so-cial disadvantages are subjected to inordinate police scrutiny and surveillance, and they're more likely to be denied bail. These phe-nomena have some insidious impacts that we have already seen, like the lack of access to justice for many individuals who plead guilty rather than hiring a costly criminal defence lawyer to give them the best outcome possible.

"Convicted persons with steady employment and stability in their lives, or at least prospects of the same, are much less likely to be sent to jail for offences that are borderline imprisonment offences. The unemployed, transients, the poorly educated are all better candidates for imprisonment," wrote Professor Tim Quigley in an article cited by the Supreme Court of Canada. Since these economic conditions are borne disproportionately by Indigenous people as part of the ongoing legacy of colonialism, Professor Quigley highlights the result: "our society literally sentences more of them to jail. This is systemic discrimination."

"One for the rich, one for the poor," said a criminal defence lawyer. "I think there's a perception – and I think it may be well founded – that you may be able to access justice, seek justice, and obtain justice if you're of a certain socio-economic status."

"Most of the people we see with serious mental illness in correctional systems, the driver of their offending is not acute symptoms of the illness. It's the poor housing; it's the poor function; it's the poverty; it's the co-morbid substance misuse; it's inability to safely negotiate into personal space, getting victimized and victimizing. That's the dynamic that occurs for the big numbers of people that we see," said Dr. Sandy Simpson.

Having a criminal record also makes life more difficult by putting up barriers for employment, housing, and travel. The impacts of incarceration are long-term and even generational.

"After an average of 14 years post release, most individuals were underemployed with a median income of $0. Of those who reported employment, the average reported income was $14,000," according to an analysis by Public Safety Canada. This figure falls far below the country's official poverty line, yet people with criminal records are not even mentioned in major reports by the National Advisory Council on Poverty. "We also found that barriers to finding gainful employment following incarceration disproportionately impacted women, Indigenous, and older individuals, with these groups fairing even poorer than men, non-Indigenous, and younger individuals with criminal records."

"The harms of incarceration are very real on individuals, families, and communities as well, and they cascade throughout the life course, they cascade throughout families and we know from the research that, in the long-term, incarceration has many substantial impacts in terms of mental health and wellness, employment, familiar relations, whatever it may be," said Professor Julius Haag, a sociologist at the University of Toronto.

One of the primary purposes for the corrections system set out in the federal *Corrections and Conditional Release Act* is "assisting the rehabilitation of offenders and their reintegration into the community." It will come as no surprise that research shows the criminal justice system has not only failed to achieve this objective but is fundamentally flawed because it actually perpetuates reoffending.

"The more you disrupt someone's social network – which of course incarceration is a profound experience of that – the harder it is for people to adjust," said Dr. Simpson. "And the net, and sometimes lifelong, effects on social integration, work, earnings, personal success are consequences of incarceration. There's plenty of evidence that if you get incarcerated once, you're much more likely to be incarcerated again. And in general, of course, we know that incarceration for minor offending increases risk of recidivism [reoffending] over non-incarceration approaches to minor offending."

In the lingo of criminologists, "incarceration for minor offending is a pro-criminogenic experience in its own right," meaning that imprisonment itself actually *increases* the likelihood of someone reoffending again and ending up back in custody. That's right, jails treat people in a way that all but ensures repeat business. Nowhere is this more pronounced than in people returning to custody for breaching release conditions – a topic we explored in chapter 2.

"The system literally feeds itself with breaches," said Michael Bryant, former attorney general of Ontario. "And I think, unintentionally and intentionally, police chiefs across Canada have facilitated this and enabled this system, and most police forces across the country grow year over year." This despite the fact that overall crime rates have declined in comparison with the 1990s.

Canada has a greater proportion of people in custody awaiting trial than any other G7 country, including the United States, by large margin. Two-thirds of people (67 per cent) in provincial and territorial custody are being held awaiting trial. In Ontario, this remand population constitutes 72 per cent of those in provincial custody – the highest rate in Canada. We know that people who are Indigenous, Black, poor, homeless, unemployed, and less educated, as well as those with mental health disorders or substance use, are more likely to be denied bail.

None of this is new information to those in authority. A report commissioned by the federal government involved a meta-analysis of fifty studies dating back to as early as 1958, involving 336,052 offenders. It found that the outcome of the $5 billion per year adult corrections system ($318 per day or $116,070 annually per federally incarcerated person) is a damning indictment: prison *increases* recidivism. The study's other top finding: "Prisons should not be used with the expectation of reducing criminal behaviour. On the basis of the present results, excessive use of incarceration has enormous cost implications."

CHAPTER FOUR

"Justice Is Not Blind": Indigenous People

"I'm an Indigenous treaty person from Treaty 6 Territory, Saskatchewan. I grew up in Saskatoon. I'm a Sixties Scoop survivor," said Angeline.

Beginning around the late 1950s, accelerating in the 1960s, and continuing for decades, thousands of Indigenous children were taken from their families and put up for adoption to non-Indigenous families across Canada, the United States, and overseas. This phenomenon is often simply referred to as the "Sixties Scoop." The Truth and Reconciliation Commission of Canada found that this caused Indigenous children to experience physical and sexual abuse; low self-esteem; substance use; lower levels of educational attainment; unemployment; and loss of Indigenous identity, language, culture, and spirituality.

"Cultural genocide" is how a 1985 Manitoba public review described the Scoops, saying they were done in a "systematic, routine manner." The main reason given for taking Indigenous kids from their families was "neglect," which, unlike physical or sexual abuse, had no clear criteria. In practice, neglect meant having parents who were Indigenous and poor.

This is due to the ongoing impacts of colonialism, which are many. Dispossession of land and resources. The death of a massive proportion of Indigenous populations in epidemics – whose initiation and severity were worsened by the intentional spread of diseases by settlers. The reserve system, which involved the forced relocation of Indigenous populations to small plots of largely unproductive land, while European settlers claimed, developed, plundered, and sold stolen land for their own financial gain. The residential school system that disrupted families, communities, and Nations. Assimilative and discriminatory laws, policies, and treatment. Chronic underfunding of a swath of public services for Indigenous peoples. And overt and systemic racism in economic development opportunities, education, child welfare, health care, and policing.

"My adoptive parents were white," said Angeline (whose pronouns are they/she). "I went into the foster care system when I was fourteen and aged out and yeah, that's the gist of it. I'm also a single mother." I asked Angeline to tell me about their experiences with the criminal justice system.

"Criminal justice system." Angeline paused for a few seconds. "I guess which parts would you like to know about?"

Angeline's hesitation about where to begin is understandable. For many Indigenous people, their entanglements with the criminal justice system as survivors and/or offenders, and their involvements with other state institutions, such as the child welfare system and youth criminal justice system, begin at birth and continue intermittently throughout their entire lives. But also like many Indigenous people, Angeline's over thirty-year journey is a remarkable story of resilience, courage, and survival.

"I guess my first interaction with the criminal justice system was when I was a child," recalled Angeline. "I was sexually assaulted by a neighbour when I was six and I was questioned by the police."

"And then, again, when I was fourteen years old, I cut off a piece of a cheerleader's hair at school because she made fun of my mukluks – my moccasins – and the police threatened to charge me, but they never did – I think to save face for the other girl. And that's when I got kicked out of home."

Angeline was handed over by their adoptive parents to the Saskatchewan child welfare system. While 16.6 per cent of the province is Indigenous, 86 per cent of "children in care" are Indigenous. Similar over-representation persists in other jurisdictions in what has been termed the "Indigenous child welfare crisis." Many "children in care" move at a dizzying rate through multiple foster care homes. For example, one study found that 16.5 per cent of children in care in Quebec typically have four or more such placements, with some having been forced to start over with a staggering thirteen sets of foster parents.

"I was physically abused when I was a teen, so I was like thirteen years old. This was shortly before I got kicked out of school and I got kicked out of my home. But my little sister witnessed against me and said that I was having a tantrum and that my adoptive dad was 'calming me down,' when in reality he choked me. He put his hands on my neck and was choking me."

Angeline turned to alcohol to cope. This brought them into contact with the criminal justice system again.

"I was in the drunk tank a few times when I was young, a teen."

One of the times that Angeline was charged as a youth, the Crown prosecutor voiced racist assumptions about their background.

"The Crown Prosecutor was talking about how I came from a good home just because I was raised by white people. And I was like, OK, you can't assume that I had a good upbringing just because I grew up with white people – I was physically abused in my adoptive home."

When Angeline became an adult, they reported the physical violence that they suffered by their adoptive father.

"But the police said, 'Oh, we heard that you were freaking out, and so you needed to be restrained.'" They did nothing.

Between the ages of sixteen and twenty-one, depending on the province or territory, youth who are in government care "age out" – meaning they're essentially kicked out of their homes and left to fend for themselves. That's what happened to Angeline.

"When I was in my twenties, that was when I was in an abusive relationship and I had a lot of contact with the police," said Angeline. "I had some charges for domestic violence, which was bullshit, because pretty much all of the stuff that I did was in self-defence."

"Dual charging" is when criminal charges are laid against both the perpetrator and victim in a domestic violence situation. Justice Canada acknowledges that "the over-representation of Indigenous women in the criminal justice system [is] in many cases linked to their criminal victimization (e.g., in instances involving dual charging policies in domestic violence cases)." In other words, when Indigenous women, girls, and 2SLGBTQQIA people (two-spirit, lesbian, gay, bisexual, transgender, queer, questioning, intersex, and asexual people) call the police for help when they are victims of violence, they put themselves at risk of being charged instead for defending themselves.

"Because I was in an abusive relationship, I always either dropped the charges or I never charged my partner, but he always charged me, and so he got off without a criminal record, but I had a criminal record for things that I didn't even do."

"I know it happens to other people, I know people who just won't even call the cops whatsoever when they get assaulted or anything happens, because they know that the police aren't going to help them or they're going to make it worse."

Angeline recently moved from their home in Treaty 6 Territory in Saskatchewan to another province. They told me that, in less than a year since their arrival, they have already been assaulted on four occasions. As before, the police declined to proceed with charges against the perpetrators.

"I was assaulted by someone on campus. There was video, there was a video camera, but I don't think that they investigated it properly. I claimed that the man assaulted me and they just didn't believe me. And then I was assaulted a second time in the hospital parking lot by a white woman and I had video evidence of that assault, I was holding up my phone, videotaping her and I showed the police officer and he's like, 'Oh, the Crown has no interest in charging this woman.'"

The third incident was when the COVID-19 pandemic's mask mandate was in effect. Angeline was shopping at a grocery store and saw a white woman not wearing a mask. Angeline told her to put a mask on.

"She had this big meltdown and there were other people in the crowd being like, 'wear your mask,'" said Angeline. "Then this dude comes up to me and shoves me and there's video evidence of that too – it's a grocery store. And all of these people saw it and no one tackled him. The security guard didn't tackle him. I've seen

Indigenous people who have assaulted people attacked by a crowd of whites in order to hold them down till the police come. But when it's a white male who assaults a person of colour, they're all like, oh no, just let them run away."

Angeline ran after the man, but they couldn't keep up with him. So, they called the police. They told the officer who arrived on scene what happened.

"The police officer drove me back to my vehicle in the grocery store parking lot and he's like, 'Oh yeah, I'll meet you at the front to get that video' and I'm like, sure, OK, because I needed to catch my breath and drink some water. And I sat in my car and then, when I went up to the front into the grocery store, the cop was gone. He never had any intentions of getting the video, he just dropped me off at my vehicle and drove away." Angeline never heard back from the police about the incident.

The fourth incident took place just a week before I interviewed Angeline in April 2022. They were driving with their son over a bridge. Angeline changed lanes, but a white man, driving behind them in what Angeline described as an expensive car, became enraged at them.

"He pulls up, right, and my windows are down, this guy, he pulls up right next to me and makes sure he goes the same speed as I am going and then he tries to spit on me through my window." Angeline followed him until he pulled into a driveway. Angeline parked their car to block his exit so that they could call the police. The other driver got out of his vehicle and began yelling at Angeline. Angeline asked two passers-by to be witnesses until police arrived.

"The cops come and, of course, they don't charge the guy," said Angeline. "I'm like, don't you guys chase down homeless people and attack them just because some white dude said 'that guy attacked me,' but I can't say this guy attacked me and you're not going to tackle him and drag him into the station, just because he's a white dude, because he drives a really expensive car."

Six police officers were on scene at this point. One got up close to Angeline and put his hand up in their face, signalling for them to be quiet.

"Don't fucking put your hand in my face," said Angeline as they responded by putting their hand up in the officer's face, like he was doing to them. The officer grabbed their wrist and twisted it around. His nails dug in, causing them to bleed and later swell (they took photos of the injury and went to hospital so it would be documented).

"Are you going to walk away?" demanded the officer. "Either you're going to walk away or you're going to jail."

"Go to jail for what?" asked Angeline, wondering what kind of story the officer was going to tell to justify bringing them in, after they were the one to call the police for help. Angeline's thoughts turned to their nine-year-old son, who was witnessing all of this from their vehicle. He was "crying and freaking out" after seeing the police officer grab his parent, surrounded by five other armed officers. If they were arrested, Angeline feared the police would also apprehend their son and put him into child protection.

Attempting to spit on someone is indeed an offence. However, the police never did charge the driver who tried to spit on Angeline. After the police left, Angeline saw one of the people they'd asked to be a witness beforehand. Angeline wanted to file a complaint against the police officer who assaulted them, but was concerned they wouldn't be believed. Unfortunately, the bystander didn't have his phone with him and hadn't recorded the incident. Angeline still plans on filing a complaint.

Angeline's experiences with the criminal justice system over the past twenty-five years have sent them a clear message. "The police were very convinced that I was always the perpetrator, regardless of how anyone else abused me. ... It doesn't really matter what I report, what evidence there is almost, it's like they're always going to turn it around and make it into my issue, because they know that I can't afford a lawyer."

Angeline has come to believe, like many other Indigenous people, that the system is not there to provide protection to everyone equally, and it is deployed against certain groups disproportionately.

"What the police in my mind are doing is creating their own crime statistics in order to promote their image of what crime looks like, so that they can get more funding and they continue to justify the violence they do to people of colour and to reinforce white supremacy." Angeline thinks back to the police officer who blamed them when they were choked by their white adoptive father at the age of thirteen.

"They had a witness for an assault against a child and they still didn't charge, because they said that me, as a child, was a threat to the adult, so the adult was justified in assaulting me. And then they can go out and say things like, 'Oh, Indigenous people commit this number of crimes and white people commit this number of crimes, so we are policing the right people.'"

"You end up not charging all of these white people, so that you can invent a reason to continue to be violent towards people of colour and allow white people to essentially do whatever the fuck they want to do and commit crimes without any kind of consequences."

Angeline has lost all confidence in the criminal justice system. "To me, cops are domestic terrorists, police officers are one of the most violent branches of government." They also expressed concerns about what information the police have about them. "I'm pretty sure that the police and the RCMP have some sort of thing on my file."

Despite all of what Angeline has been through, today they are attending university, working on completing their degree and being a parent. They are a survivor.

"One of the reasons why I pursued my education was in order to protect myself from these sorts of incidents, because it humanizes me to have an education," explained Angeline.

"What would you say to the police officers who failed you, if they were here right now?" I asked.

"I would say that they were criminals and that they should go fuck themselves and that they are the ones who broke the law and they should be in prison, because they're the ones who are promoting violence in the community and allowing whites to commit violence against people of colour. They're basically sanctioning it."

———

"There's this perception among Indigenous peoples, and I think it is founded, that there's this tendency of the justice system to exercise inordinate scrutiny on Indigenous peoples as perpetrators of crime, and yet be lax towards Indigenous peoples as victims of crime," said Professor David Milward at the University of Victoria's Faculty of Law. He is a member of the Beardy's & Okemasis First Nation in Saskatchewan and author of *Reconciliation and Indigenous Justice: A Search for Ways Forward.*

There are myriad reasons why many Indigenous victims of crime don't trust the criminal justice system to help them.

"We'll have victims who will say they don't necessarily want the person arrested," explained Jonathan Rudin, program director at

Aboriginal Legal Services in Toronto, Ontario. In other words, what the system is offering is not what some victims say they need. This inflexibility not only denies victims a role but with Indigenous people the settler legal system is also a foreign imposition. "We don't give agency to victims. We tell victims, 'This is what you should want.'"

For Indigenous mothers, a major concern when they or their children have been victimized is that, if they contact the authorities for help, they will be blamed for not protecting their children and have their kids taken from them. Given the lengthy and painful history of the residential school system, the Scoops and the ongoing Indigenous child welfare crisis, these are genuine concerns.

Angeline recounted an incident where they were in the midst of being assaulted by a former partner (who was white-passing) and tried to call for help. They recounted what happened next:

"I was phoning the police, he slapped the phone out of my hand and the phone hit my son," said Angeline. But the police didn't believe Angeline, concluding it was just an accident by their partner. But that didn't end the incident. The police then contacted child welfare investigators because Angeline's child had nevertheless been struck with the phone.

"They wanted to turn it against me," explained Angeline.

"We are penalizing victims. I mean people have their children apprehended because they are victims of violence," said Jonathan Rudin. This is particularly concerning given that Indigenous people are disproportionately impacted as victims of crime, particularly violent crime including homicides. Perhaps nowhere is this more pronounced than with the over one thousand Missing and Murdered Indigenous Women and Girls, as well as 2SLGBTQ-QIA people, which a national inquiry found to be a "deliberate, often covert campaign of genocide."

"Nothing is being set up according to the Truth and Reconciliation Commission, and nothing is being set up to help with the missing and murdered," said Elder Jerry Soltani. "You know, we've got missing and murdered right here in our own town. It's amazing. You know, as a territory I think we're 42,000 people now, but that's our entire population. What do you mean, these people are missing? Where did they go? What are you doing to help us find them?"

"The RCMP, we get rookies up here. Rookies. Rookies that don't know anything about working with the First Nations people."

———

Lana is a thirty-nine-year-old woman who had worked hard as an Indigenous activist to develop positive relationships with local police and the RCMP to address Missing and Murdered Indigenous Women and Girls (MMIWG). She had a good rapport with them and had even been working with a couple chiefs of police. That all changed one day in 2019.

Lana was driving with her boyfriend Travis in the passenger seat. He saw some people that he knew and asked her to pull over and pick them up. Lana didn't know who they were but obliged.

"We kept going and a police officer had seen us pick them up and followed us," said Lana. When she stopped at a traffic light, the police car's flashing blue and red lights came on.

"One of them had a gun in the backseat and told me that I couldn't stop," said Lana. "I'm like, oh my god, what am I supposed to do?" She was faced with an impossible dilemma: obey the man with the gun in the backseat of her car or obey the police officer with the gun in the vehicle behind her. But she could not obey both. "I was scared and I had adrenalin and it was just crazy."

"How do you deal in that type of circumstance, right? So, I kept going and he told me where to go."

Lana was in a police chase. At one point, a police helicopter was overhead tracking them as cruisers followed behind, their sirens blaring and lights flashing. "It was just a really long chase and by then the police were really upset."

As the chase took them outside of city limits, Lana noticed the police helicopter left them. It was then that her fear kicked into overdrive. She knew that the police helicopter would be recording everything that happened on video. Now that it was gone, she feared how the police would treat her and her boyfriend when they eventually caught up to them. Finally, out of options, she pulled over.

"I turned to my boyfriend. I told him, 'Shit, air support just left. That's the only thing saving our arse from being killed out here,'" said Lana. She and her boyfriend Travis said goodbye to each other – neither knowing if, or when, they would see one another again. "I was like, 'I love you and I don't know what's going to happen after this.' I was like, 'I honestly don't.'" The police officers approached Lana's vehicle.

"They asked me to get out first. I got out, they handcuffed me. The one police officer that handcuffed me, kicked me in the back of the head after I was handcuffed and I was wearing earrings and my earring went flying from my head."

The police's treatment of Travis was even more brutal.

"They asked my boyfriend to get out of the car and when he got out, a few of them surrounded him – I think it was eight police officers surrounded him – and they beat him and then they let the [police] dog go through the car. And then they let the dog go through the passenger seat side and they let the dog bite my boyfriend up and then they arrested him and they put them in a vehicle and they left."

"When we got to the police station, they were taking his mugshot and he was covered in blood from the top of his head down," said Lana. "He was covered in blood right to the bottom of his T-shirt."

"It's going to be OK, babe," said Travis. "You'll be OK. Don't worry about it, they'll let you out."

"I don't think that that brutal force was necessary," said Lana, recalling the incident. "We complied to their demands of us getting out of the vehicle in a timely manner and I don't think that that was necessary. Sure, when you're in a high-speed chase you build up adrenalin, but they're police officers. They should have training to deal with that adrenalin and training to deal with how you deal with people once something like that is over or comes to an end."

A total of over eighty criminal charges were laid against the five people in the vehicle, including Lana and her boyfriend Travis. She had a legal aid lawyer. Eventually everyone pled guilty until just Lana was left. The Crown prosecutor proposed Lana plead guilty to a series of driving offences for a two-year probation order as well as a weapons ban and driving ban. It meant she would have a criminal record too. She took the deal.

I asked Lana how it felt to have been assaulted by the police and witnessed what they did to Travis.

"I kind of expected it," said Lana, "working with the MMIWG, I've seen what the rapport with Indigenous people is. They [the police] have a bad track record with Indigenous people. ... I think I just kind of expected it when we got arrested, that shit, something's going to happen."

Lana has been unable to contact her boyfriend. Because they were co-accused and he was incarcerated because of the incident, they are under an order not to contact each other. "So, I honestly don't know what happened with him."

Lana tried to get a pro bono lawyer to take her complaint of police brutality forward, but to no avail. She says that she could clearly see the police dashboard camera recording Travis's beating, but says the police claimed there was no such footage available. "Because my charges were in the court system, they didn't want to touch it." She figures the limitation period for filing a complaint is up. She feels that the police "can still cover up whatever they want to."

As a result of the incident, Lana developed severe PTSD, including vivid flashbacks – "when I close my eyes and think about him, I see him full of blood still." Before she was eager to try and work with the police to help the missing and murdered. But now, she says, "I don't want anything to do with the police." And all because she just stopped to give someone a ride.

———

One in five Indigenous people in Canada (22 per cent) have little or no confidence in the police. An even higher proportion of Indigenous people (32 per cent) believe the police are performing poorly. Particularly lacking is "the ability of police to treat people fairly and be approachable and easy to talk to."

Indigenous people are significantly more likely to have contact with the police (45 per cent), compared with 36 per cent for non-Indigenous, nonvisible minority people. Furthermore, 7 per cent of Indigenous and Black people say they have been discriminated against by police, which is much higher than other visible minority people (2 per cent) and the rest of the population (0.6 per cent). Studies have also revealed that racialized people in crisis are even more likely to have force used against them by police than others exhibiting mental health distress. For example, in Toronto

"Black people were 1.9 times more likely to have force used on them [and] Indigenous people faced force 1.4 times more often."

What explains these discrepancies?

"Racism. We have to face it. It is systemic racism that is everywhere," said a non-Indigenous senior defence lawyer, who asked to remain anonymous. "We can smugly look at other organizations and say, 'who doesn't say there's racism in the RCMP,' but when we hold the mirror up to ourselves, to say the legal system suffers from racism, it's harder for us to own."

"What about judges? We have to recognize, of course, judges are racist, so are defence lawyers. Still, we have our biases and recognizing them is the first step." But not everyone or every institution is prepared to admit as much.

"Trying to suggest that there might be some bias that needs to be explored – I think it had a tendency to put people's backs up against the wall," said Professor Milward. "But at the same time, when Indigenous peoples are there in the justice system as alleged perpetrators, then all of a sudden the 'law and order,' 'throw the book at them' orientation manifests where, oh well, Indigenous experiences are dismissed as sob stories or lame excuses and the law should invoke full punishment and everything else."

"Anyone in the justice system knows that Lady Justice is not blind in the case of Aboriginal people," the late Chief Allan Ross of Norway House First Nation told the Aboriginal Justice Inquiry of Manitoba. "She has one eye open. She has one eye open for us and dispenses justice unevenly and often very harshly. Her garment is rent. She does not give us equality. She gives us subjugation. She makes us second class citizens in our own land."

"If you're Aboriginal, you're more likely to be stopped by police. If you're stopped by police, you're more likely to be charged and arrested,"

said Harold Johnson from the Montreal Lake Cree Nation in Saskatchewan. He speaks not only from personal experience as a former Crown
prosecutor and defence lawyer, but is backed up by reams of research
and findings from multiple commissions of inquiry. And he was just
getting started describing how Indigenous people face disproportionately negative outcomes at each and every stage of the system.

"If you are charged, you're more likely to be denied bail. If
you're denied bail, it's quite common for Aboriginal people to simply plead guilty to get their matter over with. If you do go to trial,
you're more likely to be found guilty. If you're found guilty, you're
more likely to get a prison sentence. If you're sentenced in Saskatchewan as an Aboriginal, your jail sentence is going to be twice
as long as a white person who's committed the same offence."

"You're more likely to be found a dangerous offender once
you're in prison [subject to an indeterminate sentence of impris-
onment]. You're more likely to be classified as a high-risk category
and serve your time in a maximum security. You're more likely to
be denied parole. 95 per cent of men and 97 per cent of women in
prison today experienced physical or sexual abuse when they were
children. For every year of incarceration, an inmate loses two years
of life expectancy. Those are the flaws in the justice system, they're
just not making things better, it's making things worse."

———

"We lived in the reserve," began Tracy. Along with her children,
she moved to the city where they encountered "a lot of systemic
racism" and faced "culture shock." It was not easy.

"We had no place. I was living in a vehicle, in my van," said
Tracy. "I had three boys at the time and Dylan would get onto his

bike, and he'd say, 'I'm going to go to the store.'" Dylan was her eldest son. He started spending more and more time away and fell in with the wrong crowd. So, Tracy moved the family again.

Tracy and her children began living in a tent in her mother's backyard in the city. But her efforts to protect Dylan weren't working.

"All of a sudden, one day the cops brought Dylan home and said they found him with a bandana and a knife. That was at the age of eleven. So, at that time, I was already afraid for him."

Tracy couldn't return to her reserve because they had become outsiders. As a young Indigenous boy, Dylan was already experiencing threats and violence from gang members.

"Many times, we had issues where my tires were slashed, or rocks were thrown at my windows," recalls Tracy. "I did what I could to move to another area, the same thing. Finally, my son told me, 'Mom, these gangs are after me because I didn't listen to them. ... I have to approach these gangs just like I'm friends with them.'"

"[I]n many cases Aboriginal youth become involved with gangs because they have nothing to live for," found a report commissioned by Public Safety Canada. Lack of educational opportunities and employment prospects, racism, and disrupted lives play a role – all of which are part of the ongoing legacy of colonialism.

Dylan got involved in schemes stealing vehicles and was caught by police. He began being incarcerated at a young age.

On one occasion, when Dylan was seventeen years old, Tracy says that the police violently arrested him for an arson that a judge later found he didn't commit. While in custody, he had a major mental breakdown. He suffered from anxiety and PTSD, which were triggered in prison. Tracy tried desperately to get him his medication – but to no avail. Dylan's mental breakdown grew worse.

"In the meantime, as he was sitting in the corrections, he was in the hole because he was freaking out. He hit the guards. Of course, the guards gave him shots back. They didn't let me see my son until after his bruises went away."

When Dylan finally came to court on the arson charges, Tracy spoke up on her son's behalf to the judge, "pouring my heart out, telling them that I did my best to keep Dylan home. And I know he did not commit no arson. The judge literally stood up and he put his thing down and he says, 'You are good to go. Let him out of that door. Open that door.'"

"And in no word of a lie, that door opened and he came running to me. That was the first time in my years of sitting in a court to see a judge tell that officer to let my son go in front of me. So, it was so heartbreaking to see and hear how the justice system can do a major fuck up and not even say sorry. It's bad to know how they think systemic racism is OK."

One morning, Tracy had a big breakfast with Dylan and his girlfriend. The couple had plans to move into a place together the next day. They were on their way to see a social worker to enrol in some programs. Dylan's phone kept going off. Suddenly, a vehicle with three people inside pulled up out back of Tracy's home, stereo bass rumbling. Tracy chased them off, telling them to leave. She took Dylan to pick up a social assistance cheque. He cashed it at a Money Mart and gave half of it to his mom.

"I'll see you after, like tonight," said Dylan. Tracy reminded him of his eight o'clock curfew that he was still subject to. She had signed release papers promising she would contact the police if he missed curfew, and she believed she would be on the hook.

"Oh, that's right," he said.

It was the last conversation she would have with her son.

When eight o'clock came and went, Tracy called the police to report her son had missed curfew.

As Tracy waited for her son, she kept seeing people on Facebook saying "prayers, prayers." Then there was news that a vehicle had been in a serious collision. Fearing the worst, Tracy went to the scene of the accident. A police officer stopped her.

"Who are you?" the officer asked. When Tracy told the officer her name, his face dropped.

"Nobody's allowed to come this way. So you've got to get back in your vehicle."

Tracy went home, but her son still wasn't back. She called the police, but they told her nothing. She called them again.

"It's OK, ma'am. We'll get back to you," the officer said.

Twenty minutes later there was a knock at the door. Two officers were standing there.

"We got some bad news," they said. "Your son is deceased."

"What?"

Dylan had died from blunt force trauma after a high-speed chase with law enforcement. During the pursuit, the police had fired their weapons.

"An Indigenous person in Canada is more than 10 times more likely to have been shot and killed by a police officer in Canada since 2017 than a white person in Canada," found a CTV investigative report in 2020.

While there was an inquest into Dylan's death, it wasn't mandated to find fault. There was no independent investigative body responsible for examining police-involved deaths in Tracy's province at the time. She believes that his being Indigenous and being in mental health distress contributed to his being killed.

"For that incident to be recorded, and for the cops to show me and then to see it in court, that broke my heart," said Tracy. "I'm still heartbroken because it could have been prevented where the cops should not have even shot. They could have just stood back."

Tracy also feels disrespected because, when she went to the scene where her son died, she wasn't allowed to practise her traditional ceremonies.

"I went to the scene over there, I could have did what I could to help my son," said Tracy, her voice growing quiet. "I know he was deceased. But I could have smudged my son. I could have did some prayers for my son. But they disrespected my culture by not allowing me to go and see my son, where he was killed. I feel they disrespected me and my son, our culture and the neighbourhood where they shot my son at."

———

"It is very rarely that people's first interaction with the criminal justice system happens at the age of 35. It does happen, but for most of our communities, there are people that are known to police from the time they're very young," said Dr. Shannon McDonald, acting chief medical officer of the BC First Nations Health Authority.

"And there hasn't ever been the intervention to say: 'What does this young person or what does this family need to provide them with more stability, more balance and the ability to function better within society, be it First Nations community or general population.'"

The disproportionate rates of incarcerated Indigenous youth are staggering and have been increasing. According to Statistics

Canada, while Indigenous youth are 8 per cent of the population, 50 per cent of admissions to youth custody were Indigenous teenagers (47 per cent for Indigenous males and 60 per cent for Indigenous females). This all but guarantees a greater proportion of Indigenous adult incarceration moving forward. It foreshadows an ever-worsening situation.

In 2019/20, the proportion of Indigenous youth admitted to secure custody was highest in Western Canada: Saskatchewan (88 per cent), Manitoba (83 per cent), Alberta (48 per cent) and British Columbia (47 per cent). When we break this down by gender, all female youth admissions to secure custody (100 per cent) in Saskatchewan and Manitoba were Indigenous teenagers.

In 2003, the federal *Youth Criminal Justice Act* came into effect. One of its goals was to reduce rates of youth incarceration. Professor Jamie Livingston, a criminologist at Saint Mary's University in Halifax, explained that while this legislation "led to a decline in non-Indigenous youth who are incarcerated, you see the proportions of Indigenous youth climbing."

What are some situations that may contribute to this early involvement in the youth criminal justice system and disproportionate incarceration of Indigenous youth?

"The pathway from child welfare – especially kids that have been moved around a lot – to youth justice, you might as well draw a red line on the road and say follow it," said Dr. McDonald. "And in incarcerating these kids, it just puts them on a pathway to more incarceration. ... Constantly herding young people into a system that dehumanizes them at very young ages is not useful and potentially extremely harmful."

"If kids are being abused physically, sexually, or verbally, and as they're growing up, these kids are trying to address those emotions.

And then when they start experimenting with marijuana or what-ever, they realize that, hey this actually makes me feel better, right, but they're not really addressing the root. ... And then it becomes a little bit more entrenched in their addiction, but they're not really addressing the trauma," said Stan Tu'Inukuafe with STR8 UP.

"You have some others, where yes, they're experiencing those type of things, but for whatever reason, they're deciding not to use drugs or alcohol. But because their parents aren't home and they're nine, ten, eleven and are looking after their siblings, they go out and steal food and bring it back to feed their siblings. But then they get caught and then they go in the justice system and then now they're around similar people like them and then they just, kind of, carry on."

CHAPTER FIVE

"Thrown in with the Wolves": Incarcerating Indigenous People

"How long do you think you've spent in your life in youth custody, provincial, federal? What's the total time? Have you ever added it up?" I asked.

Danny paused.

"No, I never really added it up. So, maybe about half my life. I'm twenty-seven right now. Yeah, pretty much half my life to the system."

Danny's Indigenous parents were both Sixties Scoop survivors. "So, they didn't get taught the right parenting skills, so it kind of went down on my generation. My parents both suffered from addictions and stuff like that."

"Even at a young age, I was taken from my family," Danny explained. "I went to the foster system for a while there, maybe like six months and that was a life experience there. It wasn't in a proper foster home. They were abusive, they locked us up in a room. But I was young, I remember bits and pieces."

Danny turned to an older sibling for support. He was a gang member. Danny saw that being in a gang meant having people around who would protect you and cared about you. "So, I looked up to that kind of lifestyle at that age, and I wanted to be someone like that."

Danny joined the gang at nine years old.

Since people under the age of twelve cannot be criminally charged, gangs sometimes involve young kids due to their impunity and impressionability. Plus, they're new recruits who will be loyal for the long run. Danny also started using drugs because they "make you feel better."

By age thirteen, Danny was facing his first set of criminal charges: robbery, use of a weapon, and aggravated assault. "They said that I went to school, my old elementary school, and I robbed someone for a hat and stabbed him for that." He denies he did it. However, he lost at trial and was convicted.

Danny spent several weeks in a youth detention facility and was placed on probation with conditions that he kept breaching, bringing him back inside.

"I was going against the system because I thought that system was going against me," said Danny. "It's a hard thing to get out of, with the conditions. They put conditions on people that they know that they're going to mess up on and it's just a cycle. It's a hard cycle to break out of, for a lot of people."

"I think it's set up to fail." It was a phrase I heard again and again from other people I interviewed about their experience.

To start with, Danny was required to abstain from alcohol, but at this point he was already addicted. He was also under a strict curfew and required to stay home at night. But his father became physically abusive when drinking. Danny's predicament was either to abide by his probation conditions by staying home and endure the violence there, or run away and be sent back to youth custody. Danny fled.

Danny would later go on to serve time as an adult in Saskatchewan's provincial corrections system, then federal penitentiaries in Saskatchewan, Alberta, and BC – including maximum security. But he said, looking back, that the worst experience of all for him was his time in youth detention in Saskatchewan.

"They do more hard time in the youth facilities it feels like. They lock you in the cell all day. ... You don't have really anyone to talk to. The youth facilities are pretty harsh. You'd rather do time in the correction or penitentiary than go back to the youth facility."

"It's really scary, you know what I mean? No one to talk to you about it. It's just scary. No one. Alone and no one to really open up to about."

When Danny turned eighteen, he would continue being institutionalized, but now in the adult corrections system.

"In the prison system, Saskatchewan, it's a whole different ballgame. I was in the max there and it's pretty crazy over there," said Danny. "I don't know how to put it. The system is they don't really offer help right off the bat. They just throw you in there with the wolves."

———

"Indigenous people are grossly over-represented in our correctional system and it's been going on like that for almost thirty years," said Dr. Ivan Zinger, Correctional Investigator of Canada. "Every year it gets worse. ... And the correctional outcomes are just terrible."

TABLE 1. *Over-representation of Indigenous People in Adult Custodial Admissions*

	Indigenous population	Indigenous custodial admissions
Alberta	7%	40%
British Columbia	6%	32%
Ontario	3%	14%
Saskatchewan	16%	75%
Manitoba	18%	76%
Quebec	2%	7%
Yukon	23%	65%
Newfoundland & Labrador	9%	25%
New Brunswick	4%	10%
Nova Scotia	6%	11%
Northwest Territories	51%	88%
Prince Edward Island	2%	3%
Nunavut	86%	95%

While 5 per cent of the Canadian population is Indigenous, Indigenous people comprised 17.6 per cent of federally incarcerated people in 2001. This has steadily climbed to 32 per cent in 2021. Dr. Zinger's conclusion is that it has been clear for years that "efforts to curb over-representation are not working" and "federal corrections seems impervious to change and is unresponsive."

Relative to their proportion of the population, there is massive over-representation of Indigenous people in adult custodial admissions in every Canadian province and territory, particularly in Western Canada and Ontario (see table 1 above).

"The Indigenization of Canada's prison population is nothing short of a national travesty," said Dr. Zinger.

Justice Canada's analysis confirms persistent and extreme levels of Indigenous incarceration, stating: "the rate of Indigenous male offenders remains eight times higher than that of non-Indigenous men. The number of Indigenous male offenders continues to increase while the number of non-Indigenous male offenders has decreased slightly ... the incarceration rate of Indigenous women continues to be much higher (12.5 times) than that of non-Indigenous women."

"So, what does that tell you right away?" asked André Poilièvre, co-founder of STR8 UP. "That's racism, definitely. There's no doubt about that."

Once incarcerated, Indigenous men and women have significantly worse outcomes in comparison with non-Indigenous people, according to a report by analysts from Dr. Zinger's office, entitled *Aboriginal Offenders: A Critical Situation*. Indigenous people are

- routinely classified as higher risk and have greater need for employment, community reintegration, and family supports;
- released much later in their sentences;
- over-represented in segregation and maximum security, which don't offer rehabilitative programs;
- disproportionately subject to use of force and self-injury; and
- more likely to return to prison for breaching conditions, including for administrative reasons, rather than committing new crimes.

This report reiterated the well-founded reasons for these outcomes, namely "systemic discrimination and attitudes based on racial or cultural prejudice, as well as economic and social disadvantage, substance abuse and intergenerational loss, violence and trauma." As discussed in chapter 4, these factors are directly linked to the ongoing impacts and intergenerational trauma of colonialism.

"This system is not worth saving. I don't think it's worth saving whatsoever. I think that all of the Indigenous peoples that Canada has incarcerated currently, to me they're almost like prisoners of war, I guess is what you could see it as because I believe that these people are victims to violent settler colonialism," said André Bear, a Nêhîyaw (Plains-Cree) writer and advocate of inherent and treaty rights.

"People argue the new residential schools are the jails, because that's where we put Indigenous people now," said a criminal defence lawyer.

"It is well known that Indigenous accused are pleading out," he added. Pleading out is when the accused pleads guilty, foregoing a trial. But why? "Number one: they're denied bail, so they're in for longer than their charges are worth. Plead guilty now and get out, or stay in custody to prove your innocence and stay longer. Are you going to stay in jail on principle? I understand if it's a sexual assault, you might stay in. But if it's mischief or assault, you plead out. Then the record accumulates and we're not going to let you out anymore. And it just self-perpetuates."

In addition to a flawed bail system and general lack of access to adequate legal representation, there are other mechanisms within the system that operate disproportionately to incarcerate Indigenous people. These include "tough on crime" policies introduced under former prime minister Stephen Harper's government, many continued under the subsequent federal Liberal government, including mandatory minimum penalties and restrictions on conditional sentences (e.g., serving a sentence under community supervision or "house arrest").

While the incarceration rates for Indigenous people overall in federal corrections surpasses 30 per cent, it is even worse when that is broken down by gender. In May 2022, Dr. Zinger announced that, while only 5 per cent of women in Canada are Indigenous, 50 per cent

of federally incarcerated women are Indigenous. "It's just terrible
and also correctional outcomes are so poor. Over the years, instead
of making it more gender-centred and providing a better response,
they have hardened the conditions of confinement. I'm especially
concerned about the security units, which are the maximum-security
units that were eventually built inside the five regional centres."

But the impacts of this over-representation of Indigenous people in Canada's prisons can only really be appreciated when we
hear the individual stories of those affected by it first-hand.

———

"Since I was twelve until about age thirty-nine, which I am now,
I've been in and out of jail for twenty-five years," said Courtney, an
Indigenous woman from Yukon whom we met briefly in chapter
1. She has served time in Yukon, Alberta, and British Columbia. "I
counted all my time up. It led to twenty-five years. I can't believe
it myself."

Before turning twelve, Courtney was already drinking heavily
and had multiple run-ins with the police. As soon as she turned
twelve, she was sent to juvenile jail. It was a co-ed institution, which
still exists today – sometimes even co-ed within the same unit.

"I was surrounded by boys because I was the only girl there with
all boys," recalled Courtney. "I had to put up with the boys' business, when they're being bad and stuff. I used to play a lot of sports
with them. They fed us pretty good there. They sent us a lot of
food: breakfast, lunch, and dinner, and snacks at night. So they fed
us like really good."

It was striking to hear Courtney describe receiving three meals
a day and a snack as something standing out as so positive about

her time incarcerated. It was a frequent theme among many people that I interviewed about spending time in prison, highlighting the poverty many experienced.

"Going outside to have fresh air was not allowed unless we were outside doing sports," said Courtney. "So, I was pretty secluded. Sometimes they'd lock me up in the rubber room when I got violent, like when I swear at staff or something, they would lock me up in the rubber room. And that was my experiences with the juvie jail."

"When I turned eighteen, I went to the adult jail and that was a different experience for me because the guys were all older and they were asking me for sex all the time because it was a mixed prison."

To pass the time, Courtney did a lot of artwork and eagerly awaited visits from her cousins and aunties.

When she was around twenty-one, Courtney says she started to lose respect for people. She began getting into fights with others behind bars. She spent time in several federal prisons, including maximum-security institutions. Often others would pick fights with her to see how tough she was. The fighting inevitably led to her being confined to segregation – or "seg" – again and again, one time for over eight months. It was an experience that significantly impacted her mental health.

"It was a hard time doing seg time there because it was just a little box and I'd hardly go out for fresh air. It was just like a little box, like a little bus stop. It was not very big," said Courtney. "I had a bad eating disorder at the time, too. I was bulimic and I was anorexic, so I was going through a lot of emotions, depression. I had suicidal thoughts. … I cried every day."

Courtney found ways to survive. "I ended up in seg most of the time and the only thing that got me through was my exercise and my artwork. And the writing. I wrote a lot of letters and diaries and stuff like that."

After release, she often ended up back in jail for breaching conditions that she abstain from drugs and alcohol – substances she'd been using since she was a child. She eventually dealt drugs on the street. When street-level addicted users/dealers like Courtney are caught, the higher-ups just find someone else to replace them and are rarely charged themselves. In addition to alcohol, she used cocaine and crystal meth. This led to multiple sentences of between one and six months.

"Like honestly, I'm an addict and I really crave drugs. Like I went on the methadone program but that didn't work for me. It just made me sleep."

Eventually, Courtney was sentenced to thirteen years imprisonment for robbery and put on a long-term supervision order, which imposes conditions upon release for up to ten years (such as abstaining from alcohol and other substances).

Serving time at a maximum-security federal prison for women was particularly hard for Courtney. That's when she tried to commit suicide by slitting her wrists, but was put into segregation right after returning from hospital. Courtney also described numerous negative encounters with prison guards.

"I got maced by a guard," said Courtney. "And he maced it right in my ears and right in my eyeballs and he kept it there for like over a minute and I was just burning, I was just swearing, and it took two hours to shower that mace out of my eyes and my ears. Then I was a little bit deaf in one ear for about a month. But that's the kind of stuff that happens. They go after me. Anyways, I would like to say don't go after me. Just figure out what I'm doing wrong and don't treat me so badly."

When I spoke to Courtney, she was out on parole at a halfway house. She has to check in every two hours, which she finds stressful. Courtney told me she suffers from anxiety and doesn't feel comfortable being around others. She described how she used to wander the streets in her spare time. While she enjoyed just being outdoors, it worried her that these walks place her in an environment that is potentially triggering for her substance use.

"It wasn't good for me to walk around too much because I might end up drinking or drugging and I'm trying to avoid that right now," said Courtney. "I haven't really seen the outside world."

———

The *Criminal Code* requires that, in crafting a sentence, "all available sanctions, other than imprisonment, that are reasonable in the circumstances and consistent with the harm done to victims or to the community should be considered for all offenders, with particular attention to the circumstances of Aboriginal offenders." The original version of this provision was adopted in 1996. In 1997, Indigenous people made up 12 per cent of those in prison – a proportion that the Supreme Court of Canada called "a crisis" when it was asked to interpret this provision in 1999. It was thought to be a watershed moment to address the disproportionate incarceration of Indigenous people.

In *R. v. Gladue*, the Court held that in sentencing Indigenous people, judges must consider: "(A) The unique systemic or background factors which may have played a part in bringing the particular aboriginal offender before the courts; and (B) The types of sentencing procedures and sanctions which may be appropriate in the circumstances for the offender because of his or her particular aboriginal heritage or connection."

In 2012, thirteen years after *Gladue*, the disproportionate incarceration of Indigenous people was again before the Court in *R. v. Ipeelee*. In the meantime, the proportion of federally incarcerated people who were Indigenous had ballooned to nearly 22 per cent. The Court conceded that its Indigenous sentencing guidance had "not had a discernible impact." However, this was largely attributed to judges failing to properly apply *Gladue*, so they provided some clarifications and reemphasized how important it was for judges to take a different approach to sentencing Indigenous people.

Despite this attempted course correction, the criminal justice system's efforts to do surgery on itself continue to have little "discernable effect," in fact quite the opposite. As mentioned above, the situation has only worsened in *Ipeelee*'s aftermath, with Indigenous people comprising 32 per cent of federally incarcerated people in 2021 – two and a half times what the Court in *Gladue* called "a crisis."

———

"I don't think we could talk about criminal justice in this country without talking about Indigenous people because who do we see in the courtrooms? As victims, as offenders, as accused persons, and who do we see in prison? Predominantly, it's my people. But then who do we see on the bench? And who do we see in the fancy suits? It's mostly not my people," said Métis-Cree lawyer Myrna McCallum. "I don't think you can talk about criminal justice and separate it from the Indigenous experience or decolonization."

"We end up having court systems that don't necessarily understand First Nation people," said Dwayne Zacharie, Chief Peacekeeper of the Kahnawà:ke Peacekeepers and past president of the First Nations Chiefs of Police Association.

In recent years, there has been a proliferation of so-called "specialized criminal courts" within the settler criminal justice system – drug courts (discussed in chapter 2), mental health courts (discussed in chapter 3), and Indigenous/First Nations/*Gladue* courts.

"These are courts that have been, that exist largely ... in relatively urban areas where there are either a large or a significant number of Indigenous people before the courts," said Jonathan Rudin, program director at Aboriginal Legal Services. "They are part of the existing court system. And they have greater or lesser amounts of support."

"When these things work best, the justice system participants know something. So, the judge will know something about Indigenous people and the justice system, and specific Indigenous circumstances and resources in the community. The Crown will have a different orientation. ... Defence counsel or duty counsel will know something, so it is a more informed process."

But there is also strong criticism from some Indigenous people about the proliferation of these so-called settler "Indigenous courts." To start with, most require a guilty plea.

"There was an announcement last summer, 'we're opening up another First Nations Court in Williams Lake,' and I'm like, that's nothing to celebrate," said McCallum. "We're not actually talking about an Indigenous court that is informed by Indigenous law, Indigenous customs, Indigenous practice, and created by community and brings elders in and all of that. Nope. We're talking about sentencing courts for Indigenous people."

"I think that it is really important that we don't celebrate that because that's an indication that you're still failing as a system that you're continuing to open up more of these courts. And two, call these places by their real names. They are not Indigenous courts, they're not First Nations courts, they're sentencing courts for Indigenous people or they are diversion courts for Indigenous people. That's really important because it feels, for me, so offensive when you're trying to present something to me like it's one thing, but it's not."

"You're selling another colonial court system, I mean, you're calling it by my name," said McCallum. "It's offensive. So yeah, pisses me off."

"So, some of the Indigenous courts that are established now in Ontario have Indigenous Knowledge Keepers or Knowledge Helpers who run those [sentencing] circles," said Rudin. "We have a traditional teacher who runs the circles. The judge says: 'You look after the circle. I'll do the sentencing, but you do the circle.'" In other words, in these courts, the judge appointed by the state makes the final decision on what the sentence will be, based on what the *Criminal Code* says. Even then, sentencing circles are rarely used in practice.

"Here in Saskatchewan, even though I would say that especially in the youth [system], 95% are Indigenous, there's not a lot of sentencing circles," said Stan Tu'Inukuafe. "We might have the option, but it's not being used."

"Like circle sentencing or sentencing circles; we have those. You know, I've been taught about them in university. In all my years – I graduated in 2016 and I went off and on since 2002 to do my degree – and I've never witnessed one of those," said Sherri Maier, a prisoner advocate and founder of Beyond Prison Walls Canada. "I've never ever witnessed a person who has went through them. They've asked for them, but they've never been able to get one, so what's the point of having it?"

Some scholars believe these specialized courts and unrealized promises of restorative justice through things like sentencing circles represent an attempt by the system to reform just enough to quiet criticism, but not enough to make any meaningful change. In other words, the system is evolving to survive without changing what it really is all about – a punitive, reactive, retribution-based system designed primarily around the idea of denouncing unlawful conduct and seeking to deter it through punishment. At its core, the settler colonial criminal justice system is uninterested in addressing root causes of criminality and victimization and remains diametrically opposed to Indigenous theories and practices of justice, which have been actively suppressed for hundreds of years.

Some argue that putting our efforts into reform – rather than radical transformation – props up a fundamentally flawed system, perpetuating its harms.

"What do you mean you're going to tinker with it to respond?" asked Professor Joshua Sealy-Harrington, citing the skyrocketing proportion of Indigenous incarceration. "Like, it is a ridiculous neo-colonial institution that is only set up for caging people whose lives we destroyed. ... And so, you know, what's the harm of tinkering? The harm of tinkering is letting that grotesque injustice continue."

———

"At the end of the day, the system takes them out of the community and into this foreign environment that's not conducive to any kind of rehabilitation," said Chief Peacekeeper Zacharie. "Lots of recidivism. The system does not rehabilitate anyone. It's just, they go away for a while, they go to prison, they come back, and I mean, they actually learn how to become real criminals in prison."

Even the Supreme Court of Canada has recognized that "Prison has been characterized by some as a finishing school for criminals and as ill-preparing them for reintegration into society." Yet it continues. The damage done to incarcerated people – not to mention their family members, loved ones, and community – is severe.

"People go into these institutions, and they come back more damaged in the sense that they've lost their ability to integrate again with our society, our community. You know, lots of addiction, even more, it's even worse when they come back because they've just, like it's a culture shock now to come back home," said Zacharie.

"The system is failing people in that it doesn't do anything. It's just like they've taken a vacation, but it's no vacation that you or I would ever want to do because, like, there's no fun in it, right?" said Zacharie. "To be in prison, it's all torture. You don't learn anything, and I mean, I do hear that there are programs for First Nation people, and lots of people now are starting to identify as First Nation and saying I want to be in these programs, or in this system. But at the same time Canada says, 'Well, there's no difference between somebody from the east or somebody from the west, you're all the same.' That's not the case. You can't paint everybody with the same brush and say like, you know, like there's no difference between a Mohawk person and a Cree person. It's not the same."

Among the intrinsic problems with the criminal justice system as it relates to Indigenous people is that it is using tools – punishment and incarceration – that are not only ineffective but exacerbate the underlying causes of criminality.

"*Gladue* was all well and good, but it's ultimately a tweak in Canadian law," said Professor David Milward. "So, certainly that might get some Indigenous persons out of jail. But at the same time, what's bringing Indigenous persons into the justice system to begin with? Poverty. Lack of education. Intergenerational trauma. If you don't deal with those things – a lot of the solutions for those have to be outside the justice system – you're just going to get your steady line of Indigenous persons going to prison."

Taking Milward's observation one step further: since things like poverty, lack of education, and trauma are what are bringing Indigenous people into the justice system to begin with, punishing them and imprisoning them actually makes each of these underlying causes worse, creating an ever-worsening positive feedback loop. Imprisonment takes people out of schooling and the workforce, giving them a criminal record that limits their opportunities and the stigma of being a convicted criminal – not exactly a poverty alleviation strategy.

The traumas of incarceration are vast. They include often harsh and over-crowded conditions of confinement, separation from family and friends, experiencing and witnessing violence by guards and between incarcerated people, death threats, gang rivalries, racism, reprisals, segregation, being under surveillance, drug withdrawal and overdose deaths for those with substance use disorders, limited access and denial of proper medical care, and countless other forms of violence and abuse that I was told about first-hand by people who had been incarcerated and that have been confirmed in independent investigative reports by the Office of the Correctional Investigator. Indeed, to really examine the traumas of incarceration would take an entire book on its own.

In short, the punitive criminal justice model – particularly the widespread use of incarceration – is a "cure" that is worse than the "illness." By failing to treat the underlying causes of antisocial behaviour and responding to the symptoms in a way that aggravates the problem, the system does great harm at tremendous cost to Indigenous people and others as well. Addressing the reasons for people's involvement in the criminal justice system as victims and offenders – and, as we've repeatedly seen, people who blur the lines between the two – is a necessary part of the way forward.

"I think that's fundamentally about the root causes," said professor of criminology Jamie Livingston. "This has all been spelled out in the TRC [Truth and Reconciliation Commission] and in the Missing and Murdered Indigenous Women and Girls report with recommendations about how to deal with the effects of colonialism, residential schools, the Indigenous kids in care, and all of those types of things that are at the root of all of these problems that lead to the over-incarceration of Indigenous people in our jails and prisons and youth correctional centres."

———

The harms done to Indigenous people by the criminal justice system are manifest and profound. The pervasiveness of incarcerated Indigenous people is so extreme that it has been called a genocide by Indigenous scholars such as Professor Pamela Palmater at Toronto Metropolitan University, a Mi'kmaw citizen and member of the Eel River Bar First Nation in northern New Brunswick.

Prisoners' Legal Services (PLS) agrees that the over-representation of Indigenous people amounts to genocide under international law. It authored a report setting out the rationale further: "it results in bodily and mental harm to a large proportion of Indigenous people; it prevents births within the group; it results in children being forcibly transferred to another group; and it inflicts destructive conditions on the group." Additionally, PLS says that these actions are intentional, as evidenced by the under-resourcing of Indigenous-led corrections options like healing lodges (discussed in chapter 7). PLS also submits that Indigenous over-representation in prisons is a crime against humanity, as it constitutes "a widespread and systemic attack involving 'imprisonment or other severe deprivation of physical liberty in violation of fundamental rules of international law' and 'torture' in many cases where solitary confinement is used."

The Correctional Service of Canada declined to be interviewed for this study. When I attempted to track down several individual corrections officers to participate, only one responded. This representative of the Union of Canadian Correctional Officers, whom I interviewed for over an hour, asking open-ended questions about the major challenges facing the criminal justice system, did not mention the words "Indigenous," "Aboriginal," or "First Nations" even once.

CHAPTER SIX

"The Usual Suspects": Anti-Black Racism

Julius Haag reached into his pocket for his wallet. He pulled out his ID and handed it to the officer. He'd done nothing wrong. The police officer evidently had no idea who Haag was – or what he did. Otherwise, he may have thought twice about randomly stopping him.

Haag is a sociology professor at the University of Toronto who researches the impacts on individuals and communities of policing and criminalization, including the experiences of Afro-Caribbean youth in the Greater Toronto Area. He also volunteers as a youth outreach worker in Toronto's Jane and Finch community (a high density, low-income area in the northwestern end of the city with a substantial Black community).

That day, Haag was once again experiencing first-hand one of the very policing tactics that he researches – carding. Also known as "street checks" or "community engagement," carding is a controversial practice involving the police stopping an individual for questioning and then documenting information about them without them being suspected of committing any particular offence. They're typically told to provide identification and may face a barrage of questions. In addition, information may be recorded about things such as their physical appearance and clothing. The data is then stored in vast police databases for "intelligence" purposes. Countless studies have found it amounts to harassment and surveillance of racialized communities, particularly Black people.

"In Toronto, I think we have probably the most thorough examination of it, but we see carding databases in other jurisdictions as well," said Professor Haag. "I'm talking about millions of cards now against people who were doing nothing wrong. People who were not suspected of involvement in a past criminal event or suspected for potential involvement in an ongoing criminal event. The vast majority of them were done for general investigative purposes. You know, more than nine out of ten."

Desmond Cole, award-winning author of *The Skin We're In*, shared that he has been carded by police at least fifty times in Toronto, Kingston, and throughout southern Ontario. Just one example in 2007 involved Cole walking his bike on the sidewalk on Bathurst Street in Toronto as he was about to enter his apartment. A police cruiser stopped, and the officer exited, saying, "It's illegal to ride your bike on the sidewalk." Cole responded, "I know, officer, that's why I'm walking it." The officer asked him for identification, which he then took back to his cruiser and sat behind his police computer for a few minutes. When he returned, he simply said: "Okay, you're all set."

For decades, a high level of secrecy, defensiveness, and obfuscation has surrounded these controversial policing practices. It took seven years for the *Toronto Star* to access police data on carding through Access to Information laws. When it finally published its findings that the data showed evidence of racial profiling and that Black people were more likely to be carded by police in these supposedly "random" stops, the Toronto Police Association responded with a $2.7 billion class action libel suit. If it had succeeded, it would have been one of the largest class actions in Canadian history – ahead of the $1.9 billion settlement for Indigenous residential school survivors. The lawsuit was eventually abandoned.

In Vancouver in 2018, the BC Civil Liberties Association and the Union of BC Indian Chiefs also gained access to a decade of data on "street checks" through Access to Information laws. It revealed that Indigenous women were nine times more likely to be checked by police than their proportion of the female population in the city. Indigenous men were eleven times more likely, and Black men six times more likely to be checked by police than their proportion of the city's population.

Vancouver Police Department (VPD) chief constable Adam Palmer's immediate response was dismissive: "The VPD does not control where crime falls along racial and gender lines. It is unrealistic to expect population and crime ratios to be aligned."

Such a response only fuels further cynicism and distrust. The Ontario Human Rights Commission's 2003 inquiry into racial profiling noted that numerous studies have consistently found racial profiling exists in the criminal justice system and that even the perception of racial profiling is problematic. It also found that the practice is ineffective and, ultimately, counterproductive.

"An unwillingness to discuss community concerns about racial profiling, a denial of its existence or an unwillingness to implement measures to monitor whether it may be occurring and to prevent it, further undermines public confidence," concluded the Ontario Human Rights Commission.

The Commission's inquiry found that the reality – or simply the perception – of racial profiling can have serious consequences such as unwillingness to cooperate with police, escalation of situations with police due to mistrust, wrongful acquittals due to bias against police officers, increasing hostility between profiled communities and police, and even civil unrest.

"We also know now from an emerging body of research that experiences with the police have the effect of what's been described as racial battle fatigue," said Professor Haag. "People who repeatedly experience a surveillance state in their neighbourhood, who repeatedly experience unwarranted and unprovoked contact with the police that they consider to be unfair or discriminatory. People who experience police harassment or even police brutality, this causes trauma, this causes stress, this causes anxiety."

———

In December 2020, two VPD officers were criminally charged for a 2018 incident involving alleged racism against Jamiel Moore-Williams, a Black former University of British Columbia Thunderbirds football player. One officer was charged with assaulting Moore-Williams, the other with assaulting him with a weapon. In Canada, a tiny fraction of cases involving allegations of excessive force and police brutality against Black people result in such charges and, of those, acquittals abound.

Moore-Williams was arrested for allegedly jaywalking on Granville Street. The cell phone footage posted online related to the incident is disturbing. In a civil lawsuit, he alleges that officers forced him to the ground, kicked him, and hit him in the head and body as well as tasered him multiple times. The citations against

Moore-Williams for jaywalking and obstruction of justice were subsequently stayed. But two of the six VPD officers at the scene were charged with assaulting him. They reportedly remained on active duty despite being charged.

In February 2023, Constable Jarrod Sidhu was found guilty of assaulting Moore-Williams with a weapon (a taser). The judge found that Moore-Williams had been respectful and non-threatening to the officers, did not pose an imminent risk of bodily harm to anyone, and that Sidhu's use of a taser was neither proportionate nor necessary. At the time of the guilty verdict, the VPD did not disclose whether Sidhu would remain on active duty. Charges against the other officer were stayed.

Police departments rarely, if ever, actively work with independent researchers to share data for racial profiling studies. In response to complaints about racial profiling, the Kingston Police Service worked with an academic expert to analyse data over a twelve-month period on all police stops. The study found that a Black person was 370 per cent more likely to be stopped than a white person, and an Indigenous person was 150 per cent more likely to be stopped than a white person.

In Montreal, an independent report commissioned by the city investigating police checks by the *Service de police de la Ville de Montréal* found that "Indigenous people and Black people were four to five times more likely than white people to be stopped by police. Indigenous women were particularly over-represented: they were eleven times more likely to be stopped by police than white women."

In Toronto, Professor Scot Wortley, a criminologist, and Professor Akwasi Owusu-Bempah, a sociologist, have done a "deep dive" on policing data in the city. Their analysis found that Black people are three times more likely to be stopped by the police multiple times than white or Asian people. But this is just the beginning. Among those stopped by police, Black people are again three times more likely to be searched. We see this cascading effect of differential treatment throughout the system for Black people as with Indigenous people. What explains these trends?

"Importantly, racial differences with respect to both direct and indirect police contact remain statistically significant after controlling for other relevant variables including age, income, education, driving habits, community-level crime, alcohol and marijuana use and criminal history," found Professors Wortley and Owusu-Bempah.

"These findings suggest that race matters. Indeed, black racial background appears to be a master status that attracts police attention and significantly contributes to police decisions to conduct street interrogations. To the police, young black males represent the usual suspects."

In *Policing Black Lives*, Robyn Maynard draws on several academic studies to explain that over-policing due to racial profiling creates a "self-fulfilling prophecy" because the "more that a group is targeted, the greater the likelihood that criminality will be discovered – particularly for those offences that are prevalent in society." A Montreal study found that "disproportionate over-surveillance, not Black proclivity for crime, is the leading factor in the disproportionate arrest of Black youth. Black youth experienced far more surveillance by police and security guards than white youth, and this over-surveillance may have accounted for almost 60 percent of their over-representation in the criminal justice system." This creates a "snowball" effect where arrests increase the risk of further charges, worsening criminal records, and increasing the likelihood of higher sentences and more restrictions – that can, in turn, trigger further charges if breached.

"Black people are not 'more criminal'; they are placed behind bars for crimes that, had they been white, would have been far more likely to have gone unseen and unpunished," writes Maynard.

In other words, the disproportionate involvement of Black people as suspects, accused persons, and offenders in the system is driven, in large part, by over-policing fuelled by systemic racism. Another major set of factors relates to social determinants of crime (such as poverty, inadequate housing, level of education, mental health, and experiencing violence), which often have their roots in ongoing legacies of colonialism, slavery, and segregation.

———

Back at the side of the road, Professor Haag waited for the officer to wrap up. "You know, I research carding," Haag told the officer, matter-of-factly.

"Won't you be surprised to see your name in the fucking cards," sneered the officer.

It didn't matter that he'd done nothing wrong. Haag was suspect simply for being racialized in public. That was enough.

Both Ontario and Vancouver have recently enacted measures purportedly to address racial profiling in police stops. It's fair to say there's good reason for a healthy dose of cynicism.

"While celebrated by some as the end of the discriminatory practice in the province, in reality, Ontario's ban on carding isn't really a 'ban' at all," wrote Professor Owusu-Bempah. "The regulations still leave room for creative circumvention: as long as an officer 'reasonably suspects [an offence] has been or will be committed' he or she can attempt to collect information." His pessimism – or realism – is shared by people in the community.

A 2019 Environics Research survey of Toronto-area residents found "significant racial differences with respect to levels of contact with the police and observed that rates of police contact have not been significantly reduced by the introduction of Ontario's street checks legislation."

In Vancouver, a 2020 VPD policy "overtly bans stopping someone based on identity factors such as race, sex, age or homelessness, and requires police to tell people being checked that their interaction is voluntary and that the subject can leave at any time." While some racial profiling is done intentionally and consciously, much of it is undoubtedly driven by unconscious bias, which is not going to simply go away because of such directives.

Additionally, the notion that telling "people being checked that their interaction is voluntary" and that they "can leave at any time" seems like a false safeguard. Are we to expect that individuals from the marginalized groups mentioned in the VPD policy would feel completely free to walk away from an officer or group of officers who stops them to question them? The idea would be laughable, if it weren't such a serious matter. I would personally think more than twice about simply walking away from a police officer who stopped me for questioning, even if they told me the encounter was voluntary. The power imbalance, physical dominance, and legal authority held by the police just seems too great to overcome by mere words of reassurance that someone can leave whenever they wish.

But I've never been carded. I don't expect I ever will. Quite the opposite. When I was pulled over for speeding once, I was cordial, and apologized for it, and got off with a warning. The officer even gave me some helpful advice that there was wildlife on the highway ahead, so best to slow down. "Thank you, officer." And I was on my way. Service with a smile. No wonder studies find that white people don't tend to see racial profiling as a major problem because it doesn't affect them. In addition to not being carded, I also never got "The Talk." Not that talk. The other talk.

"We know from the research that the harms of the police and attitudes towards the police are intergenerationally transmitted," said Professor Haag. "They're transmitted both directly and vicariously, they're transmitted through witnessing the police practices in their neighbourhood. They're transmitted through hearing about them from friends and they're transmitted through what has broadly been described as 'The Talk' where parents or older siblings, primarily in Black communities, tell their children or their young siblings what to expect when you come into contact with the police, how to comport yourself, how to end these interactions safely."

"Over time, these cultural scripts and cultural norms around police and attitudes towards the police become embedded within community settings and they lead to this larger climate of legal cynicism where the law and its agents, the police, are deemed to be illegitimate."

As a middle class white kid growing up in Calgary, I received a totally different message about the police. I became aware of this disparity when Professor Haag told me about "The Talk" many Black kids receive. Instead, I was told the police were there to help and if you haven't done anything wrong, you don't have anything to worry about. If I have an encounter with the police, I expect they're going to believe me and not mistreat me. In other words, I received a completely different "talk" than what Professor Haag was describing.

The intergenerational trauma of discriminatory and violent policing against Black people also seriously undermines our society.

"It creates suspect communities," said Professor Haag. "It creates entire communities where everybody in the community – by virtue of their appearance, their religion, who they spend time with, where they socialize, things of that nature – the entire community is considered to be risky or suspect. And in that context, people are made to feel outside of our society. And that has very, very serious harms."

"Why would somebody choose to help the police in those situations if they can't expect fair treatment on a day-to-day basis from the police?" asked Haag. "This is a contradiction – of over-policing in terms of the harassment in daily surveillance of them, and then there's the under-policing that, when we need help from the police, they're unwilling, they're uncaring, they're uncooperative, or they treat us as if we don't matter or they're uncaring about the concerns of the community."

———

One in five Black people in Canada (21 per cent) have little or no confidence in the police, according to Statistics Canada, which is double the proportion of white people who have lost confidence in the police. And 58 per cent of Black people born in Canada believe the police are performing poorly, especially when it comes to "the ability of police to treat people fairly and be approachable and easy to talk to."

Public opinion about anti-Black racism in policing continues to deteriorate. An Environics Research survey conducted in 2019 for the Canadian Association of Black Lawyers found that the perception of police discrimination against Black people has increased over the past twenty-five years. The majority of respondents perceived that the police treat Black citizens worse or much worse than white citizens.

It's also notable that 7 per cent of Black and Indigenous people say they have been discriminated against by police, which is much higher than other visible minority people (2 per cent) and the rest of the population (0.6 per cent).

Black scholars and activists also speak of a palpable fear of the police that exists in Black communities stemming from the risk that interactions between Black people and police are more likely to lead to the use of force. In an Ontario study by Professor Scot Wortley at the University of Toronto, Black people were found to be five times more likely than white people to be subjected to police use of force and eleven times more likely than white people to die as a result.

Troublingly, there is no systematic data reporting of police-involved shootings by race in Canada. Many police forces do not even keep race-based data, so we do not know the full nature and extent of police killings of Black people in Canada. This lack of transparency represents a massive failure of public accountability regarding the use of deadly force by the state. This is particularly alarming when we read studies that find police are four times more likely to pull out their weapons during arrests of Black people.

It was not until June 2022 that the Toronto Police Service finally released its own race-based use-of-force policing data, after being compelled to do so by provincial law. It revealed that among the 1,224 people subjected to use of force by police in 2020, 39 per cent (482) were Black, while 10.2 per cent of the population in Toronto is Black. In use-of-force incidents when an officer thought someone had a weapon, police drew their firearms almost half the time someone was Black (48 per cent) but only 33 per cent of the time when they were white. In use-of-force incidents when officers thought someone was unarmed, Toronto police drew their firearms 2.3 times more often against Black people than white people. They also found disproportionate rates of strip searches against Black and Indigenous people. Notably, the Toronto Police acknowledged that they could not explain these disparities by any reason other than race.

An Ontario Human Rights Commission report in 2020 also found Black people in Toronto are twenty times more likely than a white person to be fatally shot by police, six times more likely to have a police dog used against them, five times more likely to be tasered, and four times more likely to be pepper-sprayed.

"Our own analysis of our data from 2020 discloses that there is systemic discrimination in our policing," conceded James Ramer, Toronto chief of police. "That is, there is a disproportionate impact experienced by racialized people, particularly those of Black communities."

"Police violence in Canada against Black and brown and Indigenous people is outrageous. And people just don't think about that," said Professor Joshua Sealy-Harrington. "The average person doesn't think about it; people in power certainly don't think about it, because they're not experiencing it and they're not thinking about it and they're constantly comparing to the United States."

Professors Sealy-Harrington and Haag each emphasized that "Canadian exceptionalism" about anti-Black racism – the deeply ingrained assumption that Canada isn't racist, or at least not in comparison with the United States – is pervasive and an obstacle to change. Afterall, wasn't Canada the land of freedom for enslaved African American people using the so-called Underground Railroad?

Like many Canadians, I was never taught about our country's sordid two-hundred-year history of slavery, including Indigenous and Black slavery in New France and British North America, and the practice of indentured servitude (a practice akin to slavery) even after Black enslaved people were freed.

Speaking of "'The Usual Suspects,'" the standout quote from that 1995 movie was "The greatest trick the devil ever pulled was convincing the world he didn't exist." The same can be said of racism. While many Canadians know the name George Floyd, I strongly suspect that the vast majority of white people probably wouldn't recognize the names that Robyn Maynard compiled of just some of the Black people in Canada who have died during encounters with the police, including Lester Donaldson, Michael Wade Lawson, Sophia Cook, Raymond Lawrence, Tommy Anthony Barnett, Hugh Dawson, Duane Christian, Jermaine Carby, Kwasi Skene-Peters, Anthony Griffin, Presley Leslie, Fritzgerald Forbes, Marcellus Francois, Trevor Kelly, Rohan Wilson, Quilem Registre, Alain Magloire, and Bony Jean-Pierre. I fully admit that I didn't know any of their names or stories. I'll provide just one synopsis of what happened from this list of Black lives lost.

"In 2014, the police were called on Alain Magloire, a forty-one-year-old Black homeless man in the midst of a mental health crisis, because he was wielding a hammer in distress. He was first hit by a Montreal police squad car, rolled over the hood of the car, and was then shot four times by the Montreal police." Magloire's killing by police highlights how deadly police encounters result when racism, homelessness, and mental health challenges converge. And it isn't an isolated incident.

"George Floyd is obviously a pivotal historic moment in global dialogues around police violence and racial hierarchy, but we have a lot of stuff in our backyard," said Professor Sealy-Harrington. "That exceptionalism really undermines the ability for Canadians to grapple with the fact that we do live in an extremely unjust and unquestionably racist and colonial society."

———

Black people are grossly over-represented in the criminal justice system at every stage. There is strong evidence they face "over-charging." They are 3.7 times more likely to be charged with a criminal offence than their proportion of the population would suggest, with Black males being 7.3 times more likely to be charged. Black people are the subject of more charges where the police have wide discretion, such as obstruction of justice, failure to comply, or disturbing the peace.

Upon arrest, Black people are significantly more likely to be denied bail – held in custody while awaiting trial – even when other factors were considered. If released, the conditions (i.e., rules they have to follow or face further penalties) that are placed on their liberty are stricter. In terms of sentencing, Black people have also been found to be sentenced more harshly in comparison with white people, even when the latter had more serious criminal records. Black people are more likely to be sent to maximum-security prisons. They are less likely to be granted parole (early release from prison). As with Indigenous people, the injustice at every single step of the criminal justice system against Black people is staggering.

Black people in Canada are disproportionately imprisoned and have been for a very long time; this disparity has been widening. From 2005 to 2015, the number of Black people incarcerated increased by 69 per cent in federal penitentiaries – more than any other group. While Black people represent 3 per cent of the general population, 8.1 per cent of federally incarcerated people were Black in 2019–20.

A major driver of mass incarceration of Black people in North America is the "war on drugs" – stringent criminal penalties against drug users and traffickers. Tougher mandatory minimum penalties for drug trafficking have disproportionately been given to Black people. In Canada, 42 per cent of people convicted of drug trafficking were Black. Conservative "tough on crime" penalties disproportionately affected Black people, as the proportion of Black people convicted of drug trafficking grew from 33 per cent to 43 per cent between 2007 and 2016.

The first study considering data on the incarceration of Black people in provincial jails in Ontario was only published in 2021, and it relied on data from 2010. It found that "incarceration is heavily concentrated among young Black men who come from economically marginalized neighbourhoods. The American experience shows us that concentrated incarceration has negative consequences at the individual, family and community levels, including social problems relating to poverty, mental health, education, employment and civic involvement."

The study concluded that "Black men were five times more likely to be incarcerated than White men and Black women were almost three times more likely to be incarcerated than White women." This translates to at least one in fourteen Black men (eighteen to thirty-four years of age) being held in custody in provincial correctional facilities.

The researchers also confirmed the over-representation of Black people in the Nova Scotia corrections system. Black men are also held for longer in provincial custody and transferred to federal prisons in greater proportions, compared to other men. The experience of Black people in prison, along with Indigenous people and people of colour, is egregious.

"My investigation of race and involvement in use-of-force incidents in federal penitentiaries is deeply troubling," said Dr. Ivan Zinger. "We found that racial background was uniquely associated with the over-representation of Black, Indigenous, and Peoples of Colour (BIPOC) in use-of-force incidents. Regardless of risk level, security level, age, sentence length or gender, identifying as an Indigenous or Black incarcerated person was associated with a greater likelihood of involvement in a use-of-force incident."

Among almost ten thousand documented use-of-force incidents in federal prisons, Dr. Zinger's analysis found that 60 per cent were against BIPOC persons, who represented 44 per cent of federally incarcerated people. In his report, Dr. Zinger also called on Canada to join ninety other countries that have ratified the 2006 United Nations *Optional Protocol to the Convention against Torture and Other Cruel, Inhuman or Degrading Treatment or Punishment*, which would require Canada to open up all places of detention to independent national and international inspections. To date, Canada has refused.

———

Not only are Black people overpoliced and over-incarcerated, they are also underprotected when they are victims of crime. This is especially concerning given that Black people are disproportionately victims of violent crime. For example, in 2007, while Black people represented 7 per cent of the population of Toronto, 40 per cent of the city's murder victims were Black. Racism in the criminal justice system and distrust of police keeps victims of crime isolated and vulnerable to further harm.

"People engage in a rational calculus when they decide [whether] to involve the police in their problems," said Professor Haag. "And for a variety of reasons. It could be mistreatment at the hands of the police, it could be vicarious knowledge of mistreatment from other people. They may decide as the victim of a crime that it's just not worth it to contact the police."

In some instances, rather than being supported, Black victims of crime are themselves treated with suspicion of wrongdoing by the system. For example, a young Black woman that Professor Haag interviewed for his research was herself the victim of gun violence – the shooter mistook her for someone they were targeting. She'd been shot through no fault of her own. She was a victim. How did police respond?

"The police detectives who questioned her tried to allege that she was a gang member and she precipitated her own victimization as a result," said Haag. "From a victim's perspective, what I hear informally and what I hear through conversations through my research from people is that it's just not worth it to call the police. 'They never arrive on time. They never take my complaint seriously.'"

Haag explained that this crisis of confidence in the system can contribute to a further cycle of violence when people don't see any recourse within the system.

"Where people are unwilling to involve the police, people are more likely to take the law into their own hands, they're more likely to do those things to protect themselves from victimization in the neighbourhoods, to seek redress in ways that might even involve violence."

———

"For racialized folks, for me, the starting point is that this was a system that was never designed for racialized people, and Black folks in particular," said Brandon Rolle with Nova Scotia Legal Aid. "If you look at the history of the justice system in Nova Scotia, Black folks have been treated as property. And that's how we started in the justice system."

"It is a little-known fact that Black people were considered 'property' well into the 1800s here in Canada," wrote Justice Michael H. Tulloch. "It is within this historical context that the Black communities' relationship with the police was formed and initially defined."

Justice Tulloch is the first Black judge to sit on the Court of Appeal for Ontario, appointed in 2012. It's notable that during the almost 150 years of the Supreme Court of Canada's existence, there has yet to be a Black judge on our country's highest court. In fact, it only had its first person of colour appointed to the bench in 2021 (Justice Mahmud Jamal, who was born in Nairobi, Kenya, into a family originally from India) and first Indigenous person in 2022 (Justice Michelle O'Bonsawin, who is Franco-Ontarian and an Abenaki member of the Odanak First Nation).

"I do think that the existing system, as structured, will continue to disadvantage racialized persons by the very nature of its mandates," said Professor Haag. "And I think that that is something that is linked to the mandate of policing systems in the western context that they are, you know, to borrow a phrase from Richard

Ericson, they're designed to reproduce order and they're designed to reproduce the existing order. They're designed to maintain the status quo."

At first, Haag's warning sounded to me a bit like a conspiracy theory. But the more I heard and learned about how the criminal justice system is causing massive harm while perpetuating itself, and proving stubbornly resistant to any deep and meaningful changes, the more I began to see he was right. The system's reforms have been superficial and performative. "Too little and too late," as Harold Johnson said. Just enough to keep serious challenges to the status quo at bay. Perhaps nowhere is this more evident than with how the system has simultaneously tolerated and thwarted initiatives for Indigenous-led policing and corrections.

CHAPTER SEVEN

"An Alien System of Law": Suppression of Indigenous Justice

The Mohawk Council of Kahnawà:ke decided it was time to take a stand. Their allies had become exploiters.

One hundred sixty-five years earlier, the Mohawk (Kanien:-keha'ka) Nation, which is comprised of eight communities, including Kahnawà:ke, had played a decisive role in repulsing two attempts by the United States to invade Canada. In 1813, they halted an American army advance towards Montreal by the Chateauguay River. And at the 1814 Battle of Beaver Dams, Kahnawà:ke joined Akwesasne, Kanesatake, and Six Nations to "beat the American detachment into a state of terror."

However, once the Kanien:keha'ka alliance had outlived its usefulness, the Canadian state was quick to turn on it. The Mohawk Council of Kahnawà:ke records this history: "Within less than a hundred years, repressive government legislation, such as the 1876 *Indian Act*, would ravage a thousand years of our political growth, social development and economic prosperity. The *Indian Act* and subsequent government policies suppressed our Traditional government, attempted to 'civilize' and assimilate us into mainstream society, prohibited the use of our language and the practice of our culture, diminished our land base, determined who is eligible to be an 'Indian' based on a legal definition, and removed our authority to determine our own affairs." But concerted efforts by the Canadian state to assimilate them and destroy their way of life have not succeeded. In 1979, a rock quarry on Kanien:keha'ka traditional territory became a flashpoint.

"For the longest time the community of Kahnawà:ke was exploited by the province, the feds," said Dwayne Zacharie, Chief Peacekeeper of the Kahnawà:ke Peacekeepers. "They take land, they build highways, they build bridges, the seaway came through, they expropriated lots of land. And some other companies had, for example, quarries and that type of thing. So, they were taking natural resources from the community. And the Mohawk Council said enough is enough now. We want the quarry closed, like we don't want our natural resources being exploited anymore."

The quarry was like an open wound on the land. The Mohawk Council of Kahnawà:ke ordered the Amerindian police – which had been jointly established with the province of Quebec – to close the quarry.

"Didn't happen. And they said, all right, enough is enough and then the entire service was fired, terminated. And after that they said we need to have our own thing, our own police service, our own law enforcement body, that understands what it is that our community needs."

That's when the Kahnawà:ke Peacekeepers were created.

"Our community wanted to have something different and more in line with the needs of the community ... commensurate with the needs of what Kahnawà:ke said law enforcement should be, and that is true community policing."

From 1979 until 1995, the Kahnawà:ke Peacekeepers provided law enforcement duties to their community without any support from the federal or provincial governments. In the 1990s, they played an important role in the Mohawk Resistance at Ka'nehsatà:ke (also known as the "Oka crisis"), a seventy-eight-day standoff between Mohawk land-defenders and settler forces that was triggered by plans to expand a golf course onto Kanien:keha'ka burial grounds.

"Kahnawà:ke was one of those communities that closed its borders down in solidarity to our sister community [Ka'nehsatà:ke], which is about a forty-five-minute drive from here," said Zacharie. "So, we closed all the highways, roadways, seaway, Mercier Bridge, and that, like I said, it disrupts about a hundred thousand commuters a day. And that was closed for seventy-nine days, and the entire community was surrounded by the RCMP, the SQ [*Sûreté du Québec* – provincial police force], and the Canadian military."

"At the time, the Kahnawà:ke Peacekeepers were kind of tasked with safety and security of everybody on both sides," explained Zacharie. "They were tasked with *Ratinatanónhnha'*, which means 'they guard the town.' Trying to keep the military and the other police services like, for lack of a better term, calm and relaxed; trying to keep people in the territory, calm and relaxed; so, it didn't precipitate like some kind of all-out war. Because people on both sides had armed themselves." What Zacharie described reminded me of the traditional role of UN peacekeepers in blue berets standing between two opposing sides, their presence designed to quell the threat of violence.

Four years later, in 1995, the Mohawk Council of Kahnawà:ke signed an historic agreement with the Government of Canada and Government of Quebec, which finally officially recognized the

Kahnawà:ke Peacekeepers as the law enforcement authority for the territory. Zacharie described the significance to the community of no longer being policed by non-Indigenous people who don't understand or live in the community they're policing.

"We understand our community because we're from here, we live and work here. And we're the only First Nation police service in this country that's made up entirely of First Nation people."

"People call us for anything," said Zacharie. "'I got a flat tire.' 'My basement's flooding,' you know, 'What's the number to this restaurant?' Like I know it seems small, but you know what, there really is no call too small for what we do. And if somebody was to call here and we'd say, 'Sorry, call somebody else,' we've lost their trust forever cause they're calling us for help, no matter what it is. And at the time when they're calling anyone – no matter what the call is – that's the most important thing in the world to them."

"To this day, people look at us and say, 'Well, you're peacekeepers and this is what you're tasked with doing.' And it's hard for them to understand that at this moment, we also enforce the *Criminal Code of Canada*."

Zacharie explained that having lived and grown up in the community means there are real relationships with people, and trust that is built up over time. "I live here, I work here, I grew up here. People know where I live. People come to my house every single day, you know, like five o'clock in the morning people are knocking on my door," said Zacharie. "People know who I am, they know who my kids are, they know who my parents are, they know my entire history of my whole life. I can't go anywhere without people going, 'that's the Chief Peacekeeper.'"

The Kahnawà:ke Peacekeepers' approach to enforcing the law in their community stands in stark contrast to the experiences of

Indigenous people encountering settler police forces that I shared earlier. Indigenous peoples have been calling for greater involvement and recognition of their inherent right to provide safety and justice for themselves. But Indigenous-led policing and corrections initiatives have been stifled and starved of funding.

"On a year-to-year basis the government goes, hmm, do we still need them? They do know they need us, but they still haven't yet recognized us as an essential service," said Zacharie. "And for the longest time, that's what the government has done. We didn't have the resources, we didn't have infrastructure, maybe some of the First Nation policing departments didn't have training. Some of the officers didn't have the tools that they needed. Some guys, they would have to trade off bullet proof vests or remove their duty belt and say, all right, you're the next shift, here's the firearm. Like they don't even have stuff that's assigned to them, they can't afford it."

As a result, while some on-reserve Indigenous communities manage their own police departments, most are policed by the RCMP, the Ontario Provincial Police (OPP), or *Sûreté du Québec*. Additionally, over half of First Nations people and two-thirds of Métis people live in urban centres policed by municipal settler forces.

While the cost of funding Canada's 68,718 police officers in 2018–19 was $15.7 billion, during the same period, the First Nations Policing Program (FNPP) received a mere $149 million (covering 60 per cent of First Nations and Inuit communities) for 789 officers in Indigenous self-administered police forces and 450 RCMP officers. On a per officer basis, the FNPP is grossly underfunded. The total FNPP budget is just 0.9 per cent of the total policing budget in Canada, and only 1.1 per cent of police officers in Canada are in Indigenous self-administered police services, despite Indigenous people comprising around 5 per cent of the population.

Public Safety Canada even concedes that policing in Indigenous communities has been chronically underfunded, despite disproportionate rates of victimization and crime, which also negatively impacts the "physical and mental wellbeing" of officers. This discriminatory funding of Indigenous policing has recently been successfully challenged in the courts by the Pekuakamiulnuatsh Innu First Nation.

"The First Nations Policing Policy is a means to implement the inherent right of Indigenous peoples to self-government by providing First Nations with access to police services that are professional, effective, and culturally appropriate," ruled the Court of Appeal of Quebec in a December 15, 2022, decision. "By refusing to fund the appellant's police department to ensure that the services provided are equal in quality to those offered to non-Indigenous persons, the respondents breached their duty to act honourably."

"There's a lot of articles that are out there that talk about how First Nation policing was set up to fail and for the most part it was. We just continued to exist because we just say, well, we're not giving up without a fight, and we're not going anywhere because what we do is important," said Zacharie.

Chief Peacekeeper Zacharie is being humble – Indigenous police forces have done far more than just continue to exist. Public Safety Canada's own assessments have found that Indigenous communities with the FNPP experienced "a 26% decrease in incidents of crime from 2004 to 2014, with a 25% reduction in incidents of violent crime." Additionally, it found that Indigenous communities feel safer with their own self-administered policing. That they continue to be denied adequate funding cannot be justified in light of their proven efficacy and the ongoing breaches of trust by settler police forces vis-à-vis Indigenous people.

Indigenous-led police services are still currently operating, however, within the framework of the *Criminal Code* and corrections legislation. Some also enforce their traditional laws, such as restrictions on alcohol and other substances in the community, and laws pertaining to gambling, hunting, fishing, and trapping.

"And I mean at the end of the day when you look at some of the things, it makes sense, right – homicide, and impaired driving, and all of that stuff. It's important for us to enforce those laws because it has a huge impact on our community and the well-being of our community. But at the same time people don't like that *Criminal Code of Canada*."

"It's like big brother, it's like the government is saying, 'This is how it's going to be, and this is what you're going to enforce.'"

———

Similar to Indigenous police forces, Indigenous-led corrections services are also being short-changed. Under the 1992 *Corrections and Conditional Release Act*, the federal government can enter into agreements with Indigenous governments, who would provide correctional services to Indigenous people, and these services would be funded by the federal government – a substitute to traditional prisons. Correctional investigator Dr. Ivan Zinger said that such Indigenous-led correctional facilities "yield a much better outcome."

Their priorities and focus are very different from traditional penitentiaries. For example, the Eagle Women's Lodge in Winnipeg, Manitoba, run by the Indigenous Women's Healing Centre, follows a holistic approach focusing on "self-identity, self-esteem, the intergenerational cycle of violence, grief and loss, as well as intergenerational trauma," in addition to educational and employment skills. Residents "are given the opportunity to heal, grow and reconnect with Indigenous culture through activities, support and ceremonies offered by Elders/Spiritual Advisors." There's also an emphasis on greater time with family and community support to encourage reintegration into the community upon release. In other words, addressing what we've seen are underlying causes.

"There's a need for that in the community, that cultural component," said Renzo Caron, provincial director of Indigenous justice centres with the BC First Nations Justice Council. "There's that need to be, hopefully, a rehabilitative healing site too ... perhaps dealing with the underlying issues such as trauma."

However, only ten such healing lodges have been established. Four are operated by the Correctional Service of Canada (CSC) and the remaining six are run by Indigenous Nations. Altogether, the ten healing lodges have a maximum capacity of just 439 people. In 2019–20, there were 6,027 Indigenous people imprisoned in the federal corrections system, meaning only a fraction (7 per cent) could be accommodated in a healing lodge – and only 3 per cent in an Indigenous-led healing lodge. This isn't even including the much larger number of Indigenous people in provincial/territorial custody who are ineligible to attend one of these federally approved healing lodges.

The category of people who are allowed to attend a healing lodge is highly restricted. "CSC basically only allows the very low risk to go there," explained Dr. Zinger.

"If individuals are in healing lodges, the reason they get there is because they want to kind of connect with their culture. But a lot of times they're unclear on how they even access the healing lodges while they're in an institution," said Stan Tu'Inukuafe, co-founder of STR8 UP.

Tu'Inukuafe explained some of the benefits of Indigenous-led corrections: "there's a much more respectful environment in terms of human dignity. There's a much better relationship between employees and residents and much better targeted attempts at resolving underlying issues that many offenders are struggling with, which a lot of it is substance abuse and a lack of financial resources, a lack of skills. ... [I]t's more responsive to the unique needs and spirituality of Indigenous people."

Healing lodges have a notably higher level of success for Indigenous people not ending up back in prison due to breaching their conditions. They help disrupt the revolving door prison cycle, at least in the earliest stages, for Indigenous people. The Auditor General of Canada has concluded that "Indigenous offenders released from Healing Lodges were more likely to successfully complete their supervision (78 percent) than those released from other minimum-security institutions (63 percent)."

Despite their proven benefits when compared to traditional penitentiaries, an investigation by the Correctional Investigator of Canada found that Indigenous-led healing lodges are being chronically underfunded in comparison to the CSC-run healing lodges. Similar to Indigenous-led police forces, this discriminatory underfunding has slowed their growth and risks undermining their successes.

"It was about sixty-two cents on the dollar that would have been provided to operate healing lodges if it was an Indigenous community who had the contract as opposed to CSC," said Dr. Ivan Zinger. "They're so badly funded and struggling and they need more." It's clear that Indigenous-led policing and corrections have been sabotaged from the very beginning.

———

"We feel that we are victims of an alien system in law that has been imposed on us as Indian people," said Chief Louis Stevenson of Peguis First Nation, the largest First Nations community in Manitoba with a population of just over ten thousand. "The devastating and tragic results are borne out in the negative statistics of our people involved in a Canadian system today."

Prior to the arrival of European settlers in the Americas, Indigenous communities had been governing themselves since time immemorial. Each had their own unique laws and practices to address harm and wrongdoing within their communities as well as between communities and Nations.

Settler colonialism ("a system which seeks to erase and replace Indigenous peoples in order to ensure the permanent use of land for settlers") supresses and disrupts Indigenous laws and legal orders. As Harold Johnson explained in *Peace and Good Order: The Case for Indigenous Justice in Canada*, the colonial criminal justice system was weaponized to advance settler colonialism. It utilized the criminal law and state officials, including the police, Crown prosecutors, and judges, to do so.

"Everything that has been done to Indigenous Peoples has been legal," wrote Johnson. "To say that law and justice have failed Indigenous Peoples in Canada is a vast understatement. Law and justice appear to be the tools employed to contribute to the forced subjugation of an entire population."

"Indigenous-police relations are directly tied to a history of colonialism," acknowledged Justice Michael Tulloch of the Court of Appeal for Ontario in an independent review of policing for the Government of Ontario. "Often the face of colonialism was that of a police officer, beginning with the North-West Mounted Police, and continuing through to modern police services. Police officers came to Indigenous communities to enforce discriminatory laws and take away Indigenous children. Due in part to this unique history of oppression, Indigenous peoples today are less likely to engage with the police or police oversight bodies."

The history and ongoing legacy of the federal *Indian Act* is a paradigmatic example of how Canada's criminal justice system has repressed Indigenous peoples and their legal orders. As Sir John A. Macdonald, Canada's first prime minister, stated in 1887, "the great aim of our legislation has been to do away with the tribal system and assimilate the Indian people in all respects with the other inhabitants of the Dominion as speedily as they are fit to change."

"I want to get rid of the Indian problem," said Duncan Campbell Scott, deputy minister of the Department of Indian Affairs, speaking to amendments to the *Indian Act* in 1920. "[O]ur object is to continue until there is not a single Indian in Canada that has not been absorbed into the body politic and there is no Indian question and no Indian Department, that is the whole object of this Bill."

"From an Indian perspective, this legislation represents nothing less than a conspiracy. Examined as a whole, it exhibits a clear pattern founded on a conscious intent to eliminate Indians and 'indianness' from Canadian society," wrote St'sùkwanem (Joe Mathias), a hereditary Chief of the Sḵwx̱wú7mesh Úxwumixw (Squamish Nation), and lawyer Gary R. Yabsley. "The consequences of this legislation in terms of the loss of economic well-being, political power, cultural integrity and spiritual strength are immeasurable."

Indigenous peoples have actively resisted the oppression of discriminatory laws and policies, including the *Indian Act*. The legislation compelled "Indian" children to attend residential schools and criminalized Indigenous parents and guardians who did not surrender their children to residential schools. Jail time was also used to prohibit Indigenous religious and legal ceremonies, festivals, and dances, including the potlatch. It was punishable by a fine or imprisonment to provide funds for a lawyer to represent an Indigenous group.

Canada's "justice system" played a pivotal role in all of this, something not forgotten by Indigenous peoples. This painful ongoing legacy irredeemably taints the Canadian criminal justice system for many Indigenous peoples.

———

Our constitution declares itself to be the "supreme law of Canada, and any law that is inconsistent with the provisions of the Constitution is, to the extent of the inconsistency, of no force or effect." So, what exactly is the legal basis for Canada's legal order, including its criminal justice system?

"To understand the nature and purpose of Canadian criminal law, it is necessary to understand its sources," reads *The Federal Prosecution Service Deskbook* (2005 edition). It then goes on to explain how Canadian criminal law is the law of the land because Canada was either "unsettled territory," conquered by England, or ceded to England by another colonial power. Tellingly, the latest version of *The Federal Prosecution Service Deskbook* omits this content, despite previous assertions about its necessity. Nothing replaces it to explain the legal basis for the criminal justice system.

In *Canada's Indigenous Constitution*, Professor John Borrows, Loveland Chair in Indigenous Law at the University of Toronto Faculty of Law, persuasively dissects four alternative potential legal justifications for the "reception" of settler law to the exclusion of Indigenous laws that were operating throughout the country at the time, including the three ones mentioned in the previous version of *The Federal Prosecution Service Deskbook*. Borrows considers the potential justifications under the common law of colonialism that prevailed at the time – yes, there were laws purporting to justify colonialism. In other words, Borrows assesses these claims on their own terms.

First, the doctrine of "discovery" was used to justify the colonization of much of the Americas, backed by several edicts issued in the 1400s by Catholic papal authorities. The idea being that, if land is *terra nullius* – Latin for "barren and deserted" – it is lawful for the "discoverer" of that land to claim it and govern. But, as Borrows points out, at the time of asserting British sovereignty, North America was in fact neither vacant, nor treated as such by the British or French, who entered into treaties and formed economic, political, and military alliances with Indigenous peoples. The Royal Commission on Aboriginal Peoples found the doctrine of discovery to be "factually, legally and morally wrong" and the Truth and Reconciliation Commission of Canada has called for it to be "formally repudiated by all levels of Canadian government" and faith groups. In response to ongoing calls from Indigenous leaders, on March 30, 2023, the Vatican issued a statement repudiating the doctrine of discovery.

Second, the doctrine of occupation operates to justify the exercise of jurisdiction based on effectively occupying the lands at the time sovereignty is asserted. However, as Borrows notes, the Supreme Court of Canada itself has conceded: "When the settlers came, the Indians were there, organized in societies and occupying the land as their forefathers had done for centuries." So this doctrine doesn't apply either.

Third, an analogy could be made to the doctrine of prescription (or "adverse possession"), meaning that with the passage of time, Indigenous nations have acquiesced to Crown sovereignty over their lands and peoples. In this analogy, the Crown is like a squatter who uses another person's property notoriously and without their complaint and, after a long period of occupation, thereby gains a right to possession. Again, Borrows dispels this illusion: Indigenous peoples have persistently objected to assertions of Crown jurisdiction over their lands and the denial of their right to self-government.

Finally, the doctrine of conquest – the notion that Indigenous peoples' lands were the fruits of some military conquest, where the victor's law prevails. Conquest was only justified if national security or rights were threatened. As Borrows explains, the Supreme Court of Canada has recognized that "Canada's Aboriginal peoples were here when Europeans came, and were never conquered." Rather, early Indigenous-Crown relations in parts of Canada included so-called friendship treaties borne of peaceful negotiations. And, as we saw at the outset of this chapter, Indigenous peoples like the Kanien:keha'ka Nation were actually powerful military allies in fending off foreign invaders bent on conquest.

After dismantling these myths, Borrows concludes that Indigenous legal traditions were "not extinguished" with European contact and settlement – rather, they retain their force today. In other words, Indigenous peoples have inherent rights to self-government and self-determination in matters including criminal justice, and any changes to this must be through agreement on a nation-to-nation basis. Borrows explains that such treaties create an inter-societal framework for relations and "without treaties, the so-called reception of the common law remains an act of forced dispossession."

———

The settler colonial criminal justice system does not, and cannot, adequately serve Indigenous peoples, no matter how many tinkering reforms are made. A wolf may dress up like a lamb, but it will still behave as a wolf when free to roam among the flock.

The disproportionate incarceration of Indigenous people has only grown in the last thirty years, despite untold hours of continuing legal education for lawyers and judges; efforts to "Indigenize" the system with Indigenous judges, lawyers, and Elders; the amendments to the *Criminal Code* discussed in chapter 5, clearly stating that incarceration should be a last resort for Indigenous people; and repeated decisions by the Supreme Court of Canada insisting that sentencing judges take it all much more seriously.

"We've failed Indigenous peoples and, as a result, failed ourselves and the legal system that we purport to ensure does a good job and is part of our society," conceded a senior criminal defence lawyer, who asked to remain anonymous. "There has to be something very significant that needs to happen to ensure effective change because all of the things we've tried to this point have failed."

"The fundamental difference between how First Nations would maintain peace and good order and how Canada has administered it is that First Nations would apply principles of redemption, whereas Canada relies upon deterrence," wrote Harold Johnson. He emphasized that punishment – even severe sanctions – doesn't deter people. Indeed, a massive body of scholarly research confirms that more stringent penalties do not deter people from committing crimes.

Indigenous police forces tasked with implementing settler laws find the system wholly unsuited to their communities, traditions, laws, and way of life.

"Like, I see people from our community all the time. They get arrested, they get charged, and sometimes it's by us, for sure," said Chief Peacekeeper Zacharie. "So, we charge somebody with a crime, whatever it is. First Nation people, like they want to atone for what they've done, but they get mixed up in this whole system, this whole quagmire of legalese and they end up getting a lawyer, then the lawyer says, 'Don't say anything, don't talk, don't plead guilty – plead not guilty.' They end up in this whole system and that's not the way of our people, you know what I mean? We have a different system here."

Chief Peacekeeper Zacharie's observation is relevant not only to Indigenous people and their involvement in the system, but to all of us. As we will see in chapters 8 and 9, the system has chronically failed victims of crime (Indigenous and non-Indigenous alike) because it treats them as outsiders at best – and mere pieces of evidence at worst. Zacharie rightly observes that Canada's settler criminal justice system, with its fixation on "due process" rights for the accused, is inherently antagonistic towards relationality and restorative justice efforts in which victims play an integral role and stand on common ground with the person who harmed them.

For the vast majority of offences, the very first piece of advice any criminal defence lawyer is likely to give to a suspect or accused is "Don't say anything to the police." Make the state prove its case. Why did these rights emerge? Two main reasons are relevant to this discussion: (1) the adversarial nature of the system and (2) the punitive nature of the system with harsh punishments.

First, the settler criminal justice system is adversarial at its heart – conflict permeates its every aspect. The role of the Crown prosecutor "is to lay before a jury what the Crown considers to be credible evidence relevant to what is alleged to be a crime," while defence counsel's "duty is to protect the client as far as possible from being convicted." While both sides have duties towards the "proper administration of justice," they are undeniably in conflict with one another. This helps explain why efforts to make the system "more restorative" have largely failed to go beyond pilot projects or small-scale initiatives. For the vast majority of people who commit offences – Indigenous or non-Indigenous – the system is the antithesis of restorative.

"*Gladue* or restorative justice programs, like I said, they're tweaks. They're just kind of small things that don't fundamentally alter the Canadian system itself," said Professor David Milward. "And the Canadian system is fundamentally committed to punishment through incarceration. And the idea is hopefully at some point we can get to Indigenous legal orders where they provide different ways of accountability and responsibility and community safety."

In contrast to the adversarial, state-centric, and punitive approach of settler criminal law, Indigenous laws and legal orders tend to focus on relationality, healing, and restoration when harm is done. This may involve a vast array of dispute resolution processes and traditional practices that bring the person who was harmed and the person who caused harm into a setting where they are equal participants, often along with other members of the community. It is seen as advantageous if those involved have some knowledge of the people affected. And as we will explore in chapter 18, Indigenous peoples have diverse and rich practices of fostering accountability, and healing based on their laws, customs, culture, language, and spirituality. As Chief Louis Stevenson said, the settler system couldn't be more "alien" in comparison with Indigenous approaches to justice. And it's not like the settler system is even working.

A second reason why due process rights (like the right to remain silent and proof beyond a reasonable doubt) emerged in the settler system is because, if the Crown was successful in proving its case, the accused would be liable to severe punishment. The rights of the accused were developed by judges during an era in English law when hundreds of offences were punishable by death (including "pickpocketing more than a shilling, the theft of shipwrecked goods, or falsifying an entry into a marriage registry"). Torture was, for some time, an accepted tool in judicial proceedings. The last hangings in Canada took place in 1962 and the death penalty was formally abolished in the *Criminal Code* in 1976. Other penalties included lashing (which was only formally abolished in Canada in 1972) and penal transportation (a practice whereby convicts "were removed from the place of conviction to an overseas colony or border region, where they were subjected to forced labor" for a fixed period of time). Author Resmaa Menakem has even linked the historical trauma of hundreds of years of draconian European punishment, torture, and inquisitions with the transmission of trauma globally through colonialism and slavery.

To mitigate the harshness of these punishments, which typically left little or no discretion to sentencing judges, the common law developed a range of due process doctrines, such as the right to remain silent and the related privilege against self-incrimination. There's also the presumption of innocence and related requirement that the Crown prosecutor prove the guilt of the accused beyond a reasonable doubt. To protect the accused from the harshness of ordained punishments and the imbalance of state authority, we also have the common law maxim that it is "better ten guilty persons escape, than that one innocent suffer."

Today, every single offence in the *Criminal Code* – and literally tens of thousands of other federal, provincial, and territorial offences – includes the prospect of imprisonment, even for minor offences like shoplifting, selling a pair of counterfeit sunglasses, and graffiti. The fixation on punishment and incarceration runs deep. In 2019, without any compelling reason, Prime Minister Justin Trudeau's government succeeded in increasing the default summary conviction penalty in the *Criminal Code* from six months to up to two years imprisonment. Imprisonment is threatened over and over.

Would such expansive due process rights be required if criminal prosecutions did not terminate in exposure to such harsh sanctions? Could we not imagine greater recourse to Indigenous justice as well as restorative justice approaches for non-Indigenous people that also foster recovery, rehabilitation, and healing for both people who cause harm and those who suffer it?

Could we imagine a different way of achieving accountability and healing? Indigenous peoples are already doing just that.

The ground beneath the system has become entirely unsettled. These ideas are rarely, if ever, uttered. It is heresy in judicial chambers, law firms, law schools, Parliament, the media, and public discourse to question such dogma. But, at one time, it was also heresy to say that the earth is round. Indigenous peoples are saying that. Canada needs to listen to them.

At this point, we have seen and heard how the system is failing Indigenous people, Black people, and people of colour, as well as people with unresolved trauma, substance use disorders, mental health conditions, and those experiencing poverty and homelessness at every turn. All of this policing, prosecution, and punishment is supposedly responding to the harm caused to victims of crime. So how well is the system helping the very victims that it purports to protect?

CHAPTER EIGHT

"Nobodies": Victims of Crime

"Why don't you leave him? What are you stupid?"

Skye couldn't believe what they'd just heard. Wasn't this person supposed to be helping them? After all this was a counsellor with the crime victims' assistance centre at the courthouse. It wasn't the first time – or the last – that Skye would feel mistreated and humiliated by the criminal justice system. Like many survivors, it had taken them years to get to the point of being able to file a police report.

"I had been in a very abusive domestic relationship where I was being beaten and raped almost daily for five years," said Skye (they/she), who was in their early twenties at the time the abuse began, and identifies as nonbinary. "The neighbours kept calling the police."

Time after time, the neighbours would call 911 after hearing sounds of violence reverberate through the walls. The police would show up, again and again, but as Skye explained, "For the most part they didn't seem to care very much."

Researchers cite myriad reasons why many survivors of intimate partner violence are unable to leave, ranging from the coercive control exercised by the abusive partner through to threatened or actual physical, sexual, or emotional violence; a lack of financial resources; self-blame for their partner's behaviour; fear of the repercussions of reporting; and the stigma or shame of leaving their partner. Many also cite "love" for the abusive partner as a reason for staying, although this may also be related to "traumatic bonding" (similar to Stockholm syndrome in the context of hostage takings), which describes emotional attachment developed through a combination of power imbalance and intermittent abuse. It can replicate toxic patterns experienced during childhood victimization.

For over three decades, the Supreme Court of Canada has rejected the myth "that battered women are not really beaten as badly as they claim, otherwise they would have left the relationship." As Justice Claire L'Heureux-Dubé explained in another case, experiences of domestic violence are quite simply "outside the common understanding of the average judge and juror," and it is vital to "overcome the myths and stereotypes which we all share."

"What would have helped you?" I asked Skye about their many encounters with the police coming to the doorstep.

"I needed to be assured that there was some safe place to go, or there was some way to get better. I guess a plan. If one person had maybe brought up the website of a women's shelter and they were nice to me and said, 'The people here are really nice, I know them. And this is kind of what goes on here. There's rooms here, you can stay there for a while and they help you learn how to take care of yourself, get a job, stand up for yourself better.' If they'd shown the reality of what could be, I would have had an option I think."

Skye's situation eventually reached a breaking point. The physical, emotional, psychological, and sexual abuse became intolerable. They had no one else to turn to, so despite their trepidations, they contacted the police to file a report. What followed was a blur. "I was too upset to really process what was happening at that point."

To make matters worse, Skye didn't have anywhere else to go – they had also suffered horrific abuse in their family as a child. So, they continued living with their abuser. He pleaded not guilty. Then the lethargic process of moving towards the trial began. It was at that time that Skye met the courthouse counsellor and things got worse, beginning with their abuser not being kept separate from them.

"He was allowed to sit outside the counsellor's room at the courtroom and kind of intimidate me before I went in."

Once inside the counsellor's office, Skye's hopes of support and compassion were quickly dashed. Rather than supporting them, the counsellor seemed focused on another objective – probing whether she thought Skye could withstand the crucible of cross-examination at trial. But her "methods" – if there was any meaning behind them at all – were insensitive, harmful, and counterproductive.

"She would basically bring up everything that was really terrible that was going on until I was like crying, and then she'd be like, 'Oh, you don't look like you're ready, we're going to postpone it.' I didn't even get the option to say yes, I want to, or not. They just kept on postponing it."

An infamous presentation to lawyers at a 1988 continuing legal education conference in Ottawa laid bare a controversial defence strategy known as "whacking" victims. It seeks to intentionally undermine and intimidate or, in the words of one defence lawyer, "destroy" victims by subjecting them to humiliating and prolonged cross-examination. In retrospect, "whacking" appears to be a toxic by-product of an adversarial system run amok, where victims are viewed as enemies to be dispatched with "slice-and-dice" tactics. Despite protestations by prominent defence lawyers that "whacking" victims is a thing of the past, recent research demonstrates that it remains a serious concern, and I heard examples of it first-hand from victims during interviews for this book.

Like many victims before and after them, Skye was seen as a piece of evidence to be consumed by the system – not a person who suffered great harm and was deserving of care and support.

"So, they kept postponing and the court decided to send us to a psychologist together since we were still living together," said Skye. What advice did he give to Skye about how to interact with their abusive boyfriend? "He told me to try not to make him so mad."

Skye promptly stood up and walked out. Their response to the psychologist's gaslighting was taken as evidence of Skye's "unwillingness to cooperate" – a finding that disallows victims from receiving any support through criminal injuries compensation funding in some jurisdictions. The charges against Skye's boyfriend kept getting postponed until court staff eventually just stopped contacting them.

———

One in five Canadians are victims of crime every year, according to Statistics Canada. This includes 8.3 million criminal incidents, including violent crimes such as physical assault (1.5 million incidents), sexual assault (940,000 incidents), and robbery (220,000 incidents), in addition to other offences, including break and enter, theft of motor vehicles (or parts), theft of household or personal property, and vandalism.

If criminal victimization were a game of chance, the odds are stacked against the most marginalized members of our society. Women experience violent victimization almost twice as frequently as men. Indigenous people are seven times more likely to be victims of homicide than non-Indigenous people.

Young people (fifteen to twenty-four years of age), women, nonheterosexual people, Indigenous people, people living with disabilities, people who had adverse childhood experiences, people who use substances, people experiencing homelessness, and those with lower incomes are disproportionately subjected to violent victimization. Where these identities and experiences intersect, there are even greater levels of criminal victimization. We see this in striking terms with missing and murdered women.

"The missing and murdered women were members of one of the most marginalized groups in Canadian society," wrote Wally Oppal, commissioner of the BC Missing Women Commission of Inquiry. "As a group, these women shared the experience of one or more disadvantaging social and economic factors: violence, poverty, addiction, racism, mental health issues, intergenerational impact of residential schools and so on. A disproportionate number of the women were Aboriginal."

Oppal found that the marginalized status of these women, many of whom were in the survival sex trade, meant that they were treated as "nobodies" by much of society, even though they were valued members of their community, with friends and family who loved them.

———

Statistics Canada acknowledges what criminologists have long known: the majority of criminal incidents go unreported to the police. Only one in three criminal incidents are reported to police in Canada. Indeed, only one in five people who experience criminal victimization report it directly to the authorities (with other cases coming forward in other ways).

One might assume that it's just "petty crime" that is going unreported. Not so. Strikingly, only 6 per cent of sexual assaults are reported to police.

"This figure is consistent with results from other self-reported surveys conducted both before and after the #MeToo movement, which have found that sexual assault is much less likely than other types of crime to be reported to police, and that police-reported sexual assaults represent a fraction of all sexual assaults in Canada," wrote Adam Cotter with Statistics Canada. "When controlling for other incident characteristics, the odds of sexual assault being reported to police were about 80% lower than for other violent crimes."

Canada has one of the highest rates of underreporting of crime in the developed world. While Canada has comparable average rates of criminal victimization among thirty peer countries, it significantly lags in those incidents being reported to police: Canada ranked twenty-fourth out of thirty on that metric. Why have the vast majority of victims of crime in Canada opted not to report it to police?

"Many victims who did not report a violent incident to police cited concerns about the police or the criminal justice system as reasons why," according to Cotter. Among the reasons for underreporting, half of victims (49 per cent) didn't want the hassle of police involvement, 37 per cent didn't believe the offender would be adequately dealt with, 32 per cent feared or didn't want to go through the court process, 15 per cent were concerned about bias by police, and 13 per cent cited previous negative encounters with the police.

Looking at the data for crime reporting by women, additional reasons that stand out for not going to police include shame or embarrassment (34 per cent), concern that they wouldn't be believed (25 per cent), and apprehension that going to the authorities would bring shame or dishonour on their family (19 per cent).

As we heard in detail in chapters 4 and 5 (focusing on Indigenous people) and chapter 6 (focusing on Black people), the police have been chronically unresponsive and unsafe for these Nations and communities, instead perpetrating harm and violence against the very communities and groups of people that they are supposed to "serve and protect."

"One of the things that we hear from police constantly is they have difficulty soliciting cooperation from people in different communities when it comes to solving serious crimes," said Professor Julius Haag. "The police fundamentally require the cooperation of the public to do their job. The extent and nature of crime in society is far too broad and too complex for the police to have any hope of detecting or even solving serious crimes without the cooperation of the public, but their very actions on a day-to-day basis, the very character of neighbourhood level policing in so many communities has fundamentally compromised their ability to develop affective positive relationships with the very communities where they're seeking to solve serious crime. So, the harms are far reaching."

Marginalized people who disproportionately experience criminal victimization appear to be less likely to report their victimization to police. For instance, while women are twice as likely to be victims of crime than men, they are half as likely to have an incident of violent victimization reported to police. In short, those most victimized by crime are least likely to seek help from the system.

Victims of violent crime were two and half times more likely to express little or no confidence in police, compared with people who were not violently victimized. As we saw at the start of this chapter, that was certainly Skye's experience with the police, courthouse counsellor, and psychologist they encountered. The system not only failed to give them the protection and support they desperately needed, it did tremendous harm by shaming and blaming them for being abused, only to abandon them. The system left them out in the cold to fend for themselves.

Victims of crime in Canada have effectively given up *en masse* on the criminal justice system. They are "voting with their feet" as it were – demonstrating their lack of faith in the system by walking away from it or ignoring it altogether.

———

"I decided at that point that being beaten and raped was easier and felt better than being treated like shit by the people who were supposed to be helping," said Skye. "I felt like less than nothing."

"I would say it was more traumatizing than the actual event. I completely lost faith in the world. I thought the world was a terrible, awful place. I thought I'd never get help for anything. I thought that my life was over. I thought there was no chance of me ever getting out of there. I thought if I ever did try to ask for help again or if I told anybody, I would be treated even worse again. It prevented me from taking care of myself. It prevented me from treating my PTSD. It prevented me from working. It prevented me from being able to go to the people that were supposed to help me, including doctors," said Skye. "So, I very much suffered for a very long time because of this."

After enduring five years of daily abuse compounded by the betrayal and abandonment of the criminal justice system, Skye felt hopeless. Their encounter with the system was a traumatic reproduction of the helplessness and terror they first experienced being abused by their mother as a child, then by their boyfriend as a young adult.

"It felt like there was nobody in the world who would help me because nobody ever had, and when I did go for help, I was treated so badly. It was just devastating."

Yet through it all, Skye has shown incredible resilience. As they reached a point where they couldn't handle life anymore, they somehow made one last desperate plea for help. But this time, Skye reached outside the criminal justice system that had failed them. They started looking on their own for someone – anyone – who could help them start to address all of the ways their mental health had suffered from years of being abused.

Skye knew that part of what was keeping them from being able to move forward with their life was that they had been living since childhood with ADHD (attention deficit–hyperactivity disorder), a neurological disorder that causes difficulties with paying attention, impulse control, and hyperactivity. Researchers have found a significant association between childhood trauma and moderate to severe ADHD.

"I begged a stranger for help, someone who was an ADHD coach," said Skye. "I told her I couldn't afford help, my life was just in ruins, I didn't know what was going on. I just cried and cried in her office. She helped me find someone who stayed with me for years who helped me for at least three hours a week. She's still helping me and never asked for anything in return. And she could be charging me $200 per hour."

"No matter how much I struggled, she just stayed with it. She never abandoned me, she never let go. And because of that, I'm okay. She taught me everything I needed to do to get a job and schedule and now I'm in school."

Skye is studying psychology and aced her last two assignments. Their life today is totally different than before. They've done a lot of healing already. "I work at a health food store. I like to volunteer. I like to do yoga. I like to eat healthy food, but I also like to eat a lot of junk food," Skye said laughing. "I'm generally a very happy person."

"I'm incredibly lucky. That's one of the reasons I'm here talking to you. I'm okay, but most people who have been through what I've been through are very much not okay, or they're dead."

Skye isn't exaggerating. A year before we spoke, Skye was supporting their sister-in-law who was also in an abusive relationship. Skye was determined to help her. They knew how cruel and heartless the system could be towards victims. But history was destined to repeat itself. Skye had changed. But the system hadn't.

"My sister-in-law went through the same thing where I saw her offender sitting in that same room staring at her, intimidating her before she went in to a counsellor who did the exact same thing to her and then dismissed me when I was trying to make sure she would actually go to court," said Skye. "She was extremely dismissive and rude to me in front of my sister-in-law."

The harm to Skye's sister-in-law by her mistreatment at the hands of the criminal justice system and lack of support for her needs as a victim of crime was overwhelming. "She never got over it. She couldn't handle the fact that her offender pleaded not guilty, just as mine did. She couldn't handle the fact that she went to court and nobody did anything about it. And she committed suicide."

———

"Victims are so much left out of the system," said Kimberly Mann, executive director of the Collaborative Justice Program in Ottawa. "They have no information about what's happening."

Mann recounted how her charitable organization, which works with both victims and accused people, has contacted victims to offer their services only to discover that no one had even bothered to tell them that someone had been charged. This lack of communication can be paralysing as victims seek to make sense of what has happened to them, to come to terms with it, to feel safe, and to begin healing.

"Why did he kick in our front door? Why? Like what was he thinking? What was going on for him? Why is he drinking so much? How does he feel about it now? Is he laughing at us? Did he choose us? Did he target our house? Why us? Why did he come to our house?" said Mann, explaining that in the wake of experiencing criminal victimization the minds of many victims of crime swirl with questions that the system doesn't help them answer. "You know, who can answer those questions? Nobody except the offender." But the accused has a constitutional right to remain silent. And if they do speak, what they say can be used against them. Not exactly a model for honest dialogue, vulnerability, accountability, and openness to promote restoration.

So, what role do victims have in the process?

First, just because an incident is reported to police doesn't mean that criminal charges will actually be laid, or any other process will be used to address the complaint. A complaint may be disbelieved, ignored, or not taken seriously. There may be insufficient evidence to pass the threshold for approving charges that must be proven beyond a reasonable doubt – this standard is so high that an accused person is to be acquitted even if the judge or jury believes they are only likely guilty. The claim may also simply be deemed "unfounded" or not in the "public interest" to proceed.

Even if charges are laid, a substantial number are withdrawn or stayed – meaning they go nowhere. There's no trial or resolution. Nationally, an average of 35 per cent of charges are stayed or withdrawn, but this figure reaches as high as 46 per cent in Ontario.

Among the reasons that charges can get stayed is unreasonable delay, infringing the right of the accused under section 11(b) of the *Canadian Charter of Rights and Freedoms* "to be tried within a reasonable time." Under the Supreme Court of Canada's test in *R. v. Jordan*, this means that charges in provincial court are presumed to have unreasonable delay if they take longer than eighteen months from charges laid to the actual or expected end of trial, or thirty months for charges in superior court.

I heard from Jessica (whom we met in chapter 1) about the devastating impacts on her when charges against her ex-partner for repeatedly sexually assaulting her child were stayed due to unreasonable delay.

"This poor guy who raped a twelve-year-old girl, his rights are being violated. So that really was a sucker punch to the stomach," said Jessica. "So, it's just a rug was pulled out because nobody prepared us for this happening. I'm Indigenous. OK. I cut my hair to my ears that day. I'm in therapy. ... I was suicidal for about three days. I was also homicidal for three days. I thought of many ways I was going to go and kill him. Because, again, more loss of power."

If charges aren't stayed or withdrawn, the vast majority (upwards of 90 per cent) still don't make it to trial. They are resolved through plea bargains struck between defence lawyers and Crown prosecutors, without a judge or victim present.

"The process largely takes place behind closed doors and there is, therefore, no opportunity for meaningful victim participation," wrote Professor Simon Verdun-Jones, a criminologist at Simon Fraser University, and researcher Adamira Tijerino. They note that since 1987, calls to involve victims in the plea negotiation process have been ignored, even though the outcome can have profound personal implications for victims.

This situation worsened with the Supreme Court of Canada's 2016 decision in *R. v. Anthony-Cook*. It decided that when the Crown prosecutor and defence make a plea deal, the trial judge should approve it absent exceptional circumstances (i.e., where it "would bring the administration of justice into disrepute or is otherwise contrary to the public interest"). This, of course, means that victims are sidelined in sentencing involving plea bargains. The Court said that without this approach, "our justice system would be brought to its knees, and eventually collapse under its own weight."

In short, we're told that justice takes time and money, both of which are in short supply, so compromises must be made. The *Anthony-Cook* decision does an end run around the so-called *Canadian Victims Bill of Rights*. This 2015 federal legislation recognizes that victims have a range of rights in the criminal justice system but offers no real recourse if they aren't respected. For instance, victims have the right to participate in sentencing by presenting a victim impact statement that is supposed to be considered in determining the accused's sentence. But sentencing judges have complained that "years after the *Victims Bill of Rights* came into effect, the Crown continues regularly to ask this Court to sentence offenders without victims having been informed of their right to be heard." Some judges are "troubled" by how the *Anthony-Cook* decision binds them from having the discretion to "meaningfully [address] gendered violence" against Indigenous women at sentencing.

Furthermore, only a tiny fraction of criminal incidents make their way through the gauntlet to trial where a victim can ever hope to be heard: the incident must first be reported or otherwise identified by the police, an investigation has to happen, charges have to be laid, those charges must not be stayed or withdrawn, and there must be no plea bargain. Even then, the formal role of victims at trial remains largely limited to that of being a witness (restricted to responding to questions asked by lawyers) and, if the accused is found guilty, to provide a victim impact statement at sentencing if they wish, describing the "the physical or emotional harm, property damage or economic loss suffered." No more, no less.

How many incidents actually make it through the entire system? It varies by offence, but the most extreme is with sexual assaults. "Less than one percent of the sexual assaults that occur each year in Canada will result in any form of legal sanction for those who perpetrate these violations of another's sexual integrity," according to Professor Elaine Craig at Dalhousie University's Schulich School of Law in Halifax.

Only 14 per cent of Canadians have a great deal of confidence in the criminal courts, and "people who reported having contact with the criminal courts were more likely to say that they do not have very much confidence in the courts." Rates were even lower for women who had contact with the courts as well as people from marginalized or historically disadvantaged groups, such as people with disabilities, bisexual people, and people with no university diploma. Indeed, as we will explore in the next chapter, for the few victims that manage to see the inside of a courtroom, many experience it as a site that is harmful and hostile.

———

Savannah had gathered with her family in her father's home to mourn the loss of her uncle. It was a tragic occasion, but she was with people she loved. Everything changed that day when her cousin sexually assaulted her for the first time.

After Savannah's father died in the winter and she could no longer bear her cousin's abuse, she decided to leave her family and community in Yukon.

"I'm going to suffer this trauma for the rest of my life," said Savannah. "Who is going to pay for it? Who is going to take care of me? Who is going to comfort me?"

Jerry Soltani is the resident Elder at the Fetal Alcohol Syndrome Society of Yukon (FASSY). FASSY supports people, including Savannah, with fetal alcohol spectrum disorders who are in contact with the criminal justice system. After police charged Savannah's abuser, he kept missing his court dates. Savannah's greatest fear is that he will abuse someone else. Elder Soltani kept trying to find resources and support for Savannah.

"There is nothing for her. I have researched everything that I possibly could for this young lady. She is twenty-three years old, beautiful First Nations girl, very talented. She's gone to university, she is extremely eloquent."

Because her fear of her abuser was so great, Savannah made the painful decision to uproot her entire life, leaving her home, her family, and her Nation to move across the country. Yukon is a very small place in terms of population, where it's often said that everyone knows everybody else. Savannah was left to fend for herself as the system fixated exclusively on her abuser. Savannah was fortunate to have a supportive partner.

"You know what, let's go, let's make a clean break, let's move clear across the country," said Savannah's partner. "I know you don't have family, I know you don't have any of your traditional things here, but let's just go and make a new life."

Savannah and her partner were able to buy a little homestead and they're working to make it liveable for themselves. She has also been trying to stay sober, not going back to alcohol to numb the pain. It's been ninety days now – a big milestone for anyone in recovery.

"She has a chance," said Elder Soltani, "she has a partner that's very supportive. You know, she has family that, while she's living far away, were still all very supportive of her."

Not everyone is able to flee the abuse. Yukon, the Northwest Territories, and Nunavut received the worst grades for victim support among the thirteen provinces/territories in a criminal justice report card that I co-authored in 2018. This is all the more worrisome because they also have higher crime rates when compared with the rest of the country.

"A lot of people, especially in our communities, they don't turn in an abusive spouse or abusive partner because they know that there is no help," said Elder Soltani.

———

Victims like Savannah bear the direct impacts of crime. The physical, emotional, mental, economic, social, and spiritual harms and losses are tangible and intangible, short-term and enduring.

Lost income, lost productivity, unemployment, missed schooling, health care expenses, counselling expenses, moving costs, stolen or damaged property, and money lost due to theft or fraud. Being injured or having your property damaged or taken are just the tip of the iceberg. Often the deeper, enduring wounds are harder to see.

An overwhelming proportion (87 per cent) of victims of violent crime reported being emotionally impacted by it. Not surprisingly, many people who survive violent crime experience symptoms consistent with PTSD, including hypervigilance (feeling perpetually on guard or startling easily), avoidance (trying to not think about the traumatic experience and avoiding triggering situations), feeling numb or detached, nightmares about their experience, and intrusive thoughts about it. But the impacts of primary victimization caused by the perpetrator are, unfortunately, just the beginning for many victims.

CHAPTER NINE

"Do No Harm or Injustice": Secondary Victimization

The police had Melissa's apartment surrounded. They'd been tipped off that her ex-partner Jake (a high-risk offender out on probation) had broken into her home. Jake was legally barred from contacting Melissa since the last time he assaulted her. This time he was high on meth and came demanding ten dollars for another hit. Melissa told him she didn't have the cash and tried to leave.

He came at her.

"No, you're not!" said Jake enraged.

"He grabbed me by my hair, punched me in the face, punched me in the eye, dragged me to the bedroom," recounted Melissa. There was a thick blanket on the floor. "He tried to stomp on me, he stomped on my head. And then I was like, OK, I'm done."

Jake had often threatened to kill Melissa. She thought this was the end. But as she rolled over, he saw what he had done to her.

"Oh, shit, what did I do to you again?"

"Just leave me alone," said Melissa as she eased her body off the floor and into bed. Jake got her something for her face, then went into the other room. Melissa didn't know it, but Jake had also brought a machete with him. It was laying on her kitchen counter.

Melissa quickly used her phone to contact a friend, sending a photo of her face through a messaging app.

"Look, this is what he did."

"He's going to kill you."

"I know."

Melissa's friend anonymously called the police, giving them her address.

"OK, cars are on their way. Don't worry, the police will be there in a few minutes."

Suddenly, Jake was back. Seeing Melissa on her phone, he grabbed it from her.

She told herself help was on the way. She just had to hang tight.

Minutes later, the police kicked down her apartment door. Melissa was staring down the barrel of a gun.

—

"Victims of crime and their families deserve to be treated with courtesy, compassion and respect, including respect for their dignity," reads the *Canadian Victims Bill of Rights*. "It is important that victims' rights be considered throughout the criminal justice system." This legislation was supposed to be a major reform to help victims but has proven hollow for many.

People like Melissa who experience criminal victimization are supposed to have rights under the *Canadian Victims Bill of Rights*, including to information, protection, participation, and restitution, as well as the right to file a complaint if these rights are infringed. However, as noted in the previous chapter, there's no actual enforcement if these rights are violated. This puts victims in a vulnerable position. Their "rights" are effectively subject to the whims of individual police officers, prosecutors, courthouse staff, victim support workers, judges, and corrections officials. Melissa was about to find out first-hand the consequences of having "rights" without a remedy.

———

"Oh, I love you so much," said Jake. "What did I do? I fucked up. I love you."

Melissa watched as an officer arrested her ex-partner and took him away. There were three police cruisers and two ambulances outside. Police officers had covered the pathways around Melissa's apartment and her balcony in case Jake tried to flee.

The ordeal was over – or so she thought.

"This time, they literally had everything that they needed and would have wanted to get him in as a dangerous offender," said Melissa.

Jake had spent most of his adult life incarcerated and had a lot of underlying issues. Like thousands of other young Indigenous kids, he had been taken from his family and community in the Scoops. From there, a series of foster homes, into the youth justice system, and then straight into the adult corrections system, including doing time in the notorious Kingston Penitentiary, known for rampant violence and poor conditions, which operated from 1835 to 2013. The system had failed him too. The first time Jake was charged with assaulting Melissa, she wanted to try and help him. "I found he fell through the cracks," she said.

"I arranged for him to try and get into detox and to try and get in with an Elder and everything was good," said Melissa. "But the 'no contact' order that we had kind of screwed that all up because we were going to enter couples counselling and all that kind of stuff. With the 'no contact' order, you couldn't do that. So that was the end of that. That's when I realized, you know what, this isn't going to go anywhere. I don't want to take any more risks with this kind of lifestyle."

"I just left," said Melissa.

Now Jake had been arrested a second time for violently assaulting Melissa. She was wary of the system but knew that as a victim of crime, she too was supposed to have rights.

But almost immediately, Melissa could tell that the police and Crown prosecutors had an agenda that did not seem to include her best interests. The night the police broke her door down, she gave them a statement about what had happened. When the interview concluded, they left without fixing the door.

"I literally had to sit there when this whole incident happened the whole night with my door pretty much wide open," said Melissa. "Like it wouldn't close. It wouldn't latch. So, if somebody walked by, the door would swing open again."

The next morning, Melissa went to work with two black eyes. "I was working in a law firm. So, like, I looked really stupid." She also experienced internal bleeding for months after the incident, having to go to the hospital repeatedly.

At night, Melissa would have recurring traumatic nightmares of the police pointing guns at her in her bedroom. She slept on the couch rather than her own bed. "I couldn't sleep on the couch forever. I had to get over it. But yeah, I wake up sometimes."

As Jake's scheduled trial got closer, Melissa submitted her victim impact statement to the Crown prosecutor in charge of Jake's case. She dreaded having to appear in court. She felt harassed by police insisting that she give a "better statement" about what happened. She stopped going to the door if the police came by.

"I was avoiding them because I didn't want to go. They got to the point where they harassed me at work and served me at work," said Melissa. She was issued a subpoena legally compelling her to testify at Jake's trial, or *she* could be arrested and brought to court by police. But that wasn't all. At the time, Melissa didn't have a valid driver's licence. She alleges that the police used that to threaten her.

"We know you shouldn't be driving. So be careful on your way home," said the officer, according to Melissa. "Make sure you're at court."

"It's almost like they went harder after me than him. I felt like I was the person that was, like, the perpetrator."

Melissa resigned herself to testifying at Jake's trial. A few weeks before it was scheduled, even though he was under a fresh "no contact" order, Jake called her from jail, taunting her.

"Oh yeah, bitch. I'm going to court today."

"No, you're not. Your court is not for like two more weeks, three more weeks."

After she hung up the phone, Melissa called the courthouse to check.

"Yeah, he has court today."

"So I freaked out because I didn't know, because, in my *Victims' Bill of Rights*, they're supposed to be notifying me of this, they're supposed to be allowing me to go," said Melissa. After more calls and more confusion, Melissa found out that the Crown prosecutor assigned to her case had gone on vacation and her victim impact statement – that she had sent him twice – was missing.

"Oh yeah, he's taking a deal," said the new Crown prosecutor assigned to the case after Melissa managed to track him down. Based on the *R. v. Anthony-Cook* decision discussed in the last chapter, Jake's behind-closed-doors plea deal was as good as done. Melissa wasn't notified about the negotiations or consulted about her views and she, of course, wasn't present for it. There was no evident consideration of how it would impact her safety or how the crime had affected her as the victim of it. She was treated like an interloper.

Melissa went to the courthouse for Jake's sentencing hearing anyway. She wanted to share how Jake's violent attack had affected her, even though it wouldn't have any impact on what happened.

"I went to court and they read it," said Melissa. "It was like a big joke for them all. It was a joke for my ex, he laughed about it."

Melissa has reason to believe that Jake was given a reduced six-month sentence in jail because he gave the police information that was valuable to them. "He always ends up giving more information, being a rat."

Jake had previously told Melissa: "I'm going to get a deal. I'll evade that one too, you dumb bitch."

"And he thinks it's funny, he's always getting away with everything," said Melissa. "He joked once, he's like, 'I'd probably get away with murdering you too. Nobody would care.'"

A friend helped Melissa write a complaint to the provincial minister of justice and a letter to the newspaper describing how she'd been treated. Neither responded.

"They gave me $6,500 for counselling. But I mean, does that make up for it? Yeah, it helps. But I don't know, it was a shitty experience," said Melissa. "I just don't expect anything from them. I've lost all hope. If it would happen to me again, they wouldn't do shit."

"They're supposed to be there to protect the victim. They act like they care about the victim. Maybe they do certain ones," said Melissa. "It's window dressing."

Melissa's experience wasn't defined by the "courtesy, compassion and respect" promised by the *Canadian Victims Bill of Rights*. Looking back, she believes that the high-risk offender's unit failed her, and that Jake should never have had the opportunity to viciously attack her. Melissa says that she and others had previously warned the unit of their suspicions that Jake was breaching the conditions of his parole order before the violent attack she endured, which could well have killed her. Her security was not a priority. Her rights to information, protection, and participation were infringed. And when she complained about it, she was ignored.

"They put me through hell," said Melissa. "I went through hell, but they didn't do anything about it." Like Savannah in the last chapter, Melissa also had to leave her home and life behind when the system failed to support and protect her. Despite what she's endured, Melissa doesn't consider herself a victim now, but a survivor.

———

In the 1970s, researchers began examining victims' experiences with the criminal justice system. Until then criminologists didn't consider victims much at all. The results were shocking.

"These early studies showed that victims were more dissatisfied with their treatment in the criminal justice system than offenders," according to Professor Joanne Wemmers, a criminologist at the Université de Montréal who specializes in victims of crime. "In other words, individuals who had come to the police seeking assistance following a crime were less satisfied than individuals who had been stopped involuntarily by the police."

Unlike physicians, criminal justice professionals have no equivalent to the Hippocratic Oath that binds them to "do no harm or injustice." The term "secondary victimization" or "second injury" emerged to describe persistent empirical findings that victims of crime felt they were victimized a second time through their ill treatment by the criminal justice system and other institutions. It's what Skye (in the last chapter), Melissa (in this chapter), and numerous other victims of crime described to me in vivid terms.

Wemmers notes that victims who experienced trauma from their primary victimization by the perpetrator are particularly susceptible to secondary victimization. This secondary victimization can be cumulative, becoming more pronounced as the case proceeds through the system.

"The trial process can be particularly upsetting for victims," writes Wemmers. "Criminal justice workers' responsibility to build a strong case for the state leads them to place the state's interest ahead of victims' interests."

"We do a lot of harm to complainants who come forward," said Myrna McCallum, a Métis-Cree lawyer who has experience as both a criminal defence lawyer and Crown prosecutor. "They're just another matter, another person with a story to tell to help the prosecutor get the conviction or to get the matter through the trial process."

"We're very paternalistic in telling people, 'This is what you get' and 'this is what you don't,' and 'this is how it's going to be.' We're not usually accustomed to asking questions or even saying, 'What don't I know that I should know? What do you need?' We don't prioritize seeing people, hearing people, connecting with people, prioritizing their safety as they go through processes which are really terrifying."

In her book *Putting Trials on Trial: Sexual Assault and the Failure of the Legal Profession*, Professor Elaine Craig documents in

clinical detail the innumerable ways in which sexual assault survivors have been horrifically mistreated, damaged, and abused by
the system. Sexual assault survivors described their experiences on
the witness stand as "punishing," "brutal," "shocking," "horrible,"
and "traumatizing." One woman who underwent three days of being cross-examined by defence lawyers asked for a bucket so that
she could vomit because of how distressing the ordeal was for her.

Craig explains these are not anomalous incidents, noting it is now
well established that the process is traumatizing and harmful to many
victims, despite numerous law reform efforts to make the system
more "progressive." She notes this is amplified by the fact that, as with
Melissa, "in some cases women are *forced* to perform this potentially
traumatic role in the criminal justice system."

"There are so many cases of sexual assault it would make your
head spin," said a senior defence lawyer, who asked to remain
anonymous. "Do you want to go to court where the onus is on
the Crown beyond a reasonable doubt, so if there's any doubt, he
gets the doubt? Do you want all details in open court, in a public
forum? And he's not asked any questions by the victim in court.
Everything is going to be exposed. People say it feels like being
raped a second time."

"Sometimes it's worse going to court. The judge didn't say he
didn't believe me, but given the standard you just can't convict.
That's cold consolation to go to court, bare their lives, and in their
eyes the other person walked free."

The *Canadian Victims Bill of Rights Act* gives victims appearing as
witnesses the right to request "testimonial aids," which can include
measures like excluding the public from proceedings, testifying behind a screen, having a support person with them, testifying outside
the courtroom by closed-circuit television, giving their evidence by

videotape, and not allowing the accused to personally cross-examine them. However, each measure has its own legal test that a judge must apply in deciding whether or not to grant it. So once again, whether victims are supported or not in the system is often highly discretionary. It largely depends on the particular judge.

Wenda Bradley, executive director of FASSY, witnessed this first-hand. She was contacted by victims' services because they needed specialized support for a male sexual assault survivor who was significantly affected by FASD to testify at trial.

"They were very upset to be going to court," said Bradley. "Number one: a lot of community pressure. Number two: a lot of shame and guilt about the significant charges that they were the victim of."

Bradley tried to help by arranging for the complainant to visit the courthouse beforehand and see the courtroom. It was clear that he was in so much distress that he wouldn't be able to testify. Bradley asked about whether he could testify by closed-circuit video – something allowed under the *Canadian Victims Bill of Rights Act* – so that he could testify under oath but not have to do so in the intimidating courtroom environment, with the accused staring at him. Where a witness has a mental disability and may have difficulty communicating their evidence, the *Criminal Code* says that the judge or justice "shall" allow this, unless it would "interfere with the proper administration of justice" – meaning there's a strong presumption it would generally be granted. But it wasn't that straightforward for the victim Bradley was trying to support.

"I had to actually be in court discussing with the judge and the Crown and the defence that this person is not going to do well here," said Bradley, "because they just can't handle being in front of their perpetrator as well as they cannot handle telling their story in a way that's going to get out what you need to hear."

"The judge said to me, 'What do you expect this person to do?' And I said, 'I expect him to break down and cry.'"

The judge disregarded Bradley's assessment, despite her independence and specialized knowledge, and instead ordered the complainant to be brought into the courtroom. Bradley watched helplessly as things played out just as she told the judge they would. The complainant had a total emotional breakdown, overwhelmed by the shame, fear, and humiliation they felt.

"At that point then, they allowed the person to leave the court, which was very upsetting," said Bradley. "We didn't have to go there, right? Because we knew that – I knew that was going to happen. And I had told the courts."

"When this person has the guts to come forward," said Bradley, "and then was actually more of a victim afterwards because of that. Which is not an uncommon story."

I heard similar stories from other victims directly about their experiences of having to testify: "I had just one of the worst days of my life. I was crying so much. I was dry heaving. And he smirked at me. So that was not fun. I have found through this process, the accused has a lot of rights. And I just can't name one right that I had as a victim."

"The secondary victimization endured by victims means that we cannot continue to offer up victims for the greater good," argues Professor Wemmers.

———

There are also serious questions to be asked about how judges and juries assess the testimony of witnesses, including victims, who have experienced trauma. For this project, I interviewed dozens of professionals as well as dozens of people with lived experience as either survivors and/or people who committed offences. There was a striking difference between the two groups.

Frequently, people with lived experience who had endured significant trauma, particularly those who disclosed a range of adverse childhood experiences (ACEs), were unable to answer open-ended questions, and they often told their stories in a disjointed and non-sequential way – circling back a few times to discuss the same events, and using slightly different ways to explain them. Sometimes they would correct something they said earlier or phrase it differently. Small details would change. I recognized these as consistent with research on the impact of trauma on memory (as discussed in chapter 1). But under the glare of the courtroom lights, these observations that I made would be pounced on by defence counsel and viewed with great suspicion by a judge or jury – inconsistencies are dissected with great precision and typically viewed as indicia of a lack of reliability, if not overt lying. Without a trauma-informed approach, traumatized victims who *are* telling the truth are prone to be discounted, discredited, and disbelieved by the system – and retraumatized in the process.

Some interview participants, including Melissa, talked about how difficult memory retention was for them in relation to the traumatic events they were expected to testify about.

"Like, as a domestic violence victim or anybody, even as a witness to anything, they drag it so long. How do you remember anything from that?" asked Melissa. "Because by the time I was assaulted to the time they went to court was like over seven months. It's close to a year. How am I supposed to remember anything?"

————

The crisis of confidence with the criminal justice system related to victims of crime is endemic and terminal. It is baked into its historical origins and underlying philosophy. This is the reason that no amount of tinkering or platitudes, education or training have – or can – overcome it, despite forty years of a vigorous international and national victims' rights movement. It is why, in this book, I simply refer to the criminal justice system as "the system" – it has taken on a life of its own, quite independent of the various actors that play their role in it.

Canada's common law adversarial criminal justice system is, of course, not indigenous to Canada. Rather, as we have explored earlier, it was imposed as part of settler colonialism from imperial Britain, which imagined crime as being "against the State" – not the victim. Rather, "the victim is a *witness* to the crime against the state."

This cornerstone of deeming a wrong perpetrated against a victim as instead being a "crime against the state" is pervasive, unquestioned, and almost a millennium old in English law. The phrase appears over two million times on Google and in well over a hundred reported Canadian judicial decisions from 1887 to 2019.

"A crime is not a wrong against the actual person harmed, if there is one, but a wrong against the community as a whole," reads *The Federal Prosecution Service Deskbook* (2005 edition). This authoritative guide for all federal Crown prosecutors sets out the orthodox view of the matter in stark terms. Generations of judges, law professors, lawyers, and law students have drunk this Kool Aid, most without likely having had a passing thought to question the inherent contradiction it poses – or its implications. First, where did it originate in English law?

Historians explain that in medieval England around the twelfth century, there was a consolidation of authority in the hands of the King by a series of rulers, including Henry II (1154–89) who classified a number of serious offences that had previously been dealt with as wrongs between citizens as "crimes" under the king's jurisdiction. It appears to be partly a power grab, and partly about maintaining order. "Thus, crime ceased to be a private affair between families, and the state increasingly became a stakeholder in criminal justice."

The effect of this shift was to monopolize state authority to sanction wrongdoing. "Little by little, the criminal justice system came to focus on the relationship between the state and the offender, while the victim became a mere witness to the crime," according to Professor Wemmers.

In practical terms, this also meant that any money that may previously have been paid as restitution from the person who caused harm to the victim instead became a fine paid to the state, leaving the victim without redress. With the subsequent creation of professional police forces and prosecution services, the adversarial criminal justice model had just three players now: the judge, the Crown, and the accused. Victims were largely unseen and unheard. Not able to speak unless spoken to. Having no say over whether or how charges against the accused would proceed. And no say in how they were evaluated or disposed.

Indeed, to this day in Canada, criminal proceedings are brought in the name of *Rex* (King in Latin) or *Regina* (Queen in Latin), depending on who is the current monarch of Canada. While no one within the system appears to question any of this – doing so would be akin to figurative judicial treason – some judges have begun to express great unease about the troubling irony of how the system excludes victims.

"The criminal justice system is frequently experienced by victims as alienating, confusing, and stressful," wrote Judge Anne Derrick of the Youth Justice Court of Nova Scotia. "Despite their intimate experience of harm and loss, victims have felt excluded, relegated to looking on as the case proceeds."

It's time that we seriously question this central tenet of the system: that crime is committed by individuals against the state, and not against victims. While the state has a legitimate interest in certain criminal matters, this should not be to the exclusion of victims' legitimate interests as a general principle. Criminal wrongdoing *is* overwhelmingly committed against victims and should be conceptualized and addressed as such.

When I interviewed victims of crime for this book, they frequently described in graphic detail the harm that they experienced. Horrific incidents of violence, including being hit, kicked, sexually assaulted, exploited, and nearly choked to death. Recurring nightmares. Some had to change their names and move far from their abusers. Others tried to commit suicide, lost their jobs, and were unable to perform the most basic daily tasks – leaving bed to briefly take out the garbage was all that they could muster in a day. Just hearing their stories brought me to tears more than once, affected my sleep, made me feel a sense of hopelessness, and caused me to doubt that things could ever change. I heard them in their own words describe their pain and loss.

How dare we tell them that these things were not done against them, but "against the state." It is not only factually wrong, but unethical, invalidating, dehumanizing, and a form of state-sponsored gaslighting to do so. It denies their lived experience. It appropriates their suffering to justify punitive measures against the perpetrator that the victim may neither desire nor support.

If there is to be any way forward in redressing these wrongs, then they must first be understood for what they are and have always been: personal wrongs against victims themselves. In part 2 of this book, I will outline one way we could reimagine our approach to criminal justice. For now, as a matter of principle, it is necessary to consign the notion that crimes are simply a wrong against the state to the dustbin of history. As we observed earlier, this is also an impediment to a revitalization and resurgence of Indigenous justice.

Moving from history to legal theory, in her book *Victimology: A Canadian Perspective*, Professor Wemmers bluntly recognizes that "[t]raditional legal theories are unable to accommodate victims." She explains that classical justifications for why we punish people who commit crimes fall into one of two main camps: retributivism and utilitarianism. Retributive theory is backward-looking, seeking to administer proportional punishment for wrongdoing, while providing due process rights to ensure fairness to the accused. On the other hand, utilitarian theory is forward-looking, aiming to deter, incapacitate offenders, and rehabilitate the offender to reduce future criminality. Neither "recognizes victims as persons before the law."

"In retributive theory, victims are considered objects to justify punishment. Utilitarian theory is indifferent to victims' needs and interests, focussing on the collective interests of society," explains Wemmers. The consequence of this is stark and felt in profound ways every day. "The inability of criminal justice theories to accommodate victims is consistently used to justify victims' exclusion from criminal justice procedures."

"Legal theories that fail to accommodate victims are incomplete and unacceptable in the current context," concludes Wemmers. "[W]e need to develop new models that respect the human rights of victims and recognize them as persons before the law."

CHAPTER TEN

"Perfectly Designed"

Every indictment must be proven with evidence, including the indictment against the criminal justice system that has been brought forward in the preceding chapters. You have heard the eyewitness testimonies of people whose lives have been profoundly impacted, in some cases catastrophically, by the criminal justice system. Their testimonies have been corroborated by expert testimony from a wide range of leading academics and professionals. It is also supported by countless peer-reviewed and governmental studies along with the findings of coroner's inquests and federal and provincial commissions of inquiry, spanning over six decades. All of this evidence is on record. You have also heard from informants from inside the system, including police, Crown prosecutors, defence lawyers, and corrections staff.

Absent from this list of witnesses are the people who have been killed during their involvement with the criminal justice system, directly or indirectly. Those who died by suicide because of how they were treated by the system. Those who died by homicide because the system didn't protect them from their abusers in the community or other incarcerated people. Those who died during encounters with police and corrections officers. Those who died in "drunk tanks." Those who died of a toxic contaminated drug supply in the community, in custody, and upon release from custody. These people are not here to give their testimony.

Instead, you have heard surviving family members and friends tell how they witnessed the system materially contribute to, or directly cause, the death of their loved ones. And we have the evidence of coroners, criminologists, and public health experts demonstrating that these are not isolated incidents.

The legal test in Canadian criminal law for whether an individual or group acting together is responsible for causing harm is whether their conduct was a "significant contributing cause" of the harm. When considering the system, you have heard strong evidence that it has clearly been a significant contributing cause of countless deaths and other harms.

The evidence in this case is tens of thousands of pages long. In all, over seventy witnesses came forward with their testimony – many more wanted to share their stories but didn't get the opportunity because of funding, space, and time constraints.

This evidence tells us how people who use substances are harassed, arrested, displaced, and criminalized. How the system causes harm by punishing people for their addictions, many of whom are using substances as a way to cope with the unresolved trauma in their lives, particularly childhood trauma. How criminalizing people who use drugs contributes to stigma, using alone, and using faster – all of which increase the risk of death. How people are dying in custody when they need medical intervention and treatment.

How a toxic cocktail of street drugs is widely available, but a safer supply isn't. How conditions of release requiring that they abstain from the substances they're addicted to sets them up to fail and punishes them for having a clinical diagnosis. How being imprisoned worsens their underlying trauma and isn't conducive to recovery. How incarceration dramatically increases their risk of dying from unregulated drugs and is like a death sentence for many.

This evidence tells us how people with mental health disorders are disproportionately in contact with police and substantially more likely to die during police encounters. How standard police use-of-force protocols directly contribute to these killings. How police are then absolved of any wrongdoing and carry on as usual. How police have beaten people with autism who didn't respond to police displays of dominance because of their disability. How being incarcerated causes people to develop new mental health disorders while, at the same time, exacerbates existing ones. How people who have self-harmed were pepper-sprayed and locked in segregation rather than treated with care and given support. How the isolation, violence, and sorrow of prison causes self-harm, substance use, and suicide.

This evidence tells us how people experiencing homelessness and poverty are disproportionately in contact with police and incarcerated. How they are disproportionately denied bail for not having a home and receive little to no help to improve their education or employment prospects while in custody. How being imprisoned and having a criminal record further raises barriers to economic advancement for themselves, their families, communities, and Nations. How some breach their conditions or commit new crimes just to go back inside for a dry place to sleep and three meals a day, despite the harms and violence that come along with it.

This evidence tells us how the system has been weaponized against Indigenous peoples to supress their laws, languages, and cultures, dispossessing them of their lands and taking their children – first in residential schools under penalty of imprisonment, then the Scoops, the child welfare system, and the criminal justice system. How they are disproportionately victimized by crime, yet underprotected, as shown by the over one thousand Indigenous women and girls who have gone missing and were murdered. How they are treated with overt and systemic racism by each branch of the criminal justice system and disproportionately incarcerated in ever increasing degrees. How they are subjected to higher levels of punishment, violence, and deaths at every point in the system.

This evidence tells us how Black people have been subjected to constant surveillance by police and stopped without cause. How they have been disproportionately pepper-sprayed, tasered, and shot by police. How they have been disproportionately incarcerated in increasing measure and subjected to greater use of force, facing discriminatory outcomes throughout the entire system, with no other explanation but racism.

This evidence tells us how victims of crime were treated with indifference, disrespect, disdain, blame, shame, intimidation, and judgment and were even charged themselves when they sought help.

In all of this evidence, you have heard credible and serious accusations about how the criminal justice system traumatized and retraumatized people. How it has afflicted already marginalized people and communities. How it has precipitated mental health disorders. How it has caused serious bodily harm and killed people. How it is racist. How its actions may even amount to crimes against humanity and genocide.

When a person commits a criminal offence, it is no defence for them to point to all of the times that they didn't do those wrongs or that they were otherwise a "good person." For example, it is no defence when someone commits a sexual assault that they donate to charity and help old people cross the street every now and then. By the same measure it uses to judge people, the system is entitled to be judged too for the harm it is continuing to cause.

———

"Every system is perfectly designed to get the results it gets." This simple but powerful idea explains the pervasive and insidious nature of the problems plaguing the criminal justice system. It is undeniable that the criminal justice system is causing massive harm – that's the first part of proving this indictment, and I've discussed that above. But is the criminal justice system at fault for the harm it has caused? That's the second part of proving it.

In a wide range of circumstances described in this book, the criminal justice system has intentionally or knowingly caused harm (e.g., compelling Indigenous children to attend residential schools), been deliberately ignorant in causing harm (e.g., police "drunk tanks"), recklessly caused harm (e.g., incarcerating people with opioid use disorder and also releasing them without support; allowing "whacking" of sexual assault complainants in court-rooms), or negligently caused harm (e.g., police "welfare checks" and use-of-force protocols). In criminal law, each of these are morally blameworthy levels of fault. The harm of the system cannot be described as accidental, with no fault to be borne. Nor is it justified.

At a minimum, the evidence reveals the system as a whole is either deliberately ignorant to the massive harm it is causing (which

is deemed in Canadian criminal law to be equivalent to knowledge) or reckless as to the harm it is doing. The Supreme Court
of Canada describes deliberate ignorance as "an actual process of
suppressing a suspicion," and describes recklessness as "knowledge
of a danger or risk and persistence in a course of conduct which
creates a risk that the prohibited result will occur." Given what is
now known – and has been widely known for decades – about the
harms the system is causing, there can be no doubt these standards
of fault are met.

Having proven an indictment, the next question is sentencing. Can the system change its ways and reform? Or does it need
to be put away where it can no longer hurt anyone else? The record shows that the system has been incapable of change, despite
countless attempted reforms, and the problems with it are chronic,
terminal, and only getting worse. That's because, as we've seen,
the system is making them worse. The evidence is clear that the
serious allegations about the system are not a case of a few "bad
apples." They are systemic and embedded in the very DNA of the
criminal justice system itself.

Throughout part 1 of this book, I have shown how the unquestioned fundamental design features of the system are at the root of
much of the harm that it causes, including (1) crimes conceived
as a wrong "against the state"; (2) the reductive nature of the system, which distils the offender's behaviour to a single moment in
time to be proven and then punished; (3) the adversarial model of
adjudication; (4) extensive due process rights of the accused and
requirement of proof beyond a reasonable doubt; (5) the legally
and morally unjustified imposition of the system on Indigenous
peoples and active suppression of their laws; (6) a persistently
punitive, retributivist philosophy based on denunciation and

deterrence, while giving mere lip service to rehabilitation and restoration; and (7) widespread availability and use of incarceration.

Despite the fact that childhood trauma and intergenerational trauma are key risk factors for both victimization and offending, the evidence shows that the system is woefully and deliberately ignorant of how trauma affects victims and people who commit offences, as well as the substantial overlap that exists between these two categories. By failing to identify, acknowledge, and appropriately address trauma, the system triggers and retraumatizes people while at the same time piling on fresh trauma that leaves many individuals more broken than before they encountered it. Furthermore, the system responds to anticipated maladaptive coping behaviours like substance use as criminally blameworthy and punishes traumatized people, which not only fails to help but further exacerbates pre-existing unresolved trauma.

From cops to courtrooms to corrections, we have seen how the failure to acknowledge and properly address trauma has had devastating impacts on individuals and society as a whole. Failing to recognize trauma and attendant mental health conditions has led, in turn, to excessive use of force and fatalities in policing and corrections, truthful witnesses being systematically disbelieved in courtrooms, a "revolving door" of imprisonment that leaves people worse off than when they entered, and worse public safety outcomes.

For Indigenous peoples and Black people, this is all in the context of the system's indelible taint stemming from its role in propagating the ongoing historical traumas of settler colonialism (including criminalizing Indigenous laws, spirituality, customs, and language as well as its enforcement and coercive role in residential schools, the Scoops, and the ongoing Indigenous child welfare crisis) and its role in slavery, segregation, discrimination, and racism against Black people.

None of this is amenable to resolution through more training or education of justice system practitioners, new programs or pilot projects, amending a section here and there in the *Criminal Code*, or yet another "landmark" decision by the Supreme Court of Canada promising to fix things. All this has been attempted and failed over and over and over again.

As we've seen, the reason for the persistence and acceleration of these challenges, despite reform efforts over the decades, is complex. But it can be distilled to a simple answer. It is the astute observation about how systems function that I mentioned above: "Every system is perfectly designed to get the results it gets." In other words, the criminal justice system is perfectly designed to get the devastating results we are seeing from it. If the system tried someone who caused the extensive, repeated harm that it itself has done, it would declare them a "dangerous offender" and lock them up without an end date. The system collectively has caused vastly more cumulative harm than anyone it has ever prosecuted.

The vast majority of people whom I interviewed (both the criminal justice professionals as well as people with lived experience) believe that a total overhaul of the criminal justice system is necessary – that the system is not going to improve through mere reform. Some of them have decades – even a lifetime – of experience trying. Others spoke of how they tried to change the system, but it ended up changing and damaging them instead.

But what would we do without this criminal justice system? Can we leave it behind? Are we as a society like an abuse victim who keeps being harmed by the system but keeps being told by the abuser that they'll change, with the cycle repeating over and over?

Do fear and familiarity keep us constrained? Maybe we need to see that a better future is possible.

Or are you, like me, among the privileged in our society who don't experience these harms at all? Do we simply sit and watch while someone else is being harmed in front of us, in the name of the state we belong to, using our tax dollars to do it, and do nothing? Our approval of the system, voting for "tough on crime" measures, silence, inaction, and/or funding of the system make us complicit in its harms.

This was me and more. I'm done with it.

I unreservedly apologize for my role in perpetuating the criminal justice system and supporting "tough on crime" laws and policies earlier in my career, especially in 2012–13 when I was on leave from my job as a law professor to advise Conservative prime minister Stephen Harper. He is responsible for his decisions. But I am responsible for the advice that I gave – and didn't give. I deeply regret these past actions and now recognize these laws disproportionately impacted marginalized communities – without making Canadians any safer – including Indigenous and Black people, people with mental health and substance use disorders, and people who are experiencing poverty, homelessness, and unemployment.

I know hearing this may lead to different reactions from different people. Some may be angry – on both sides of the divide – and I won't tell you not to be.

I am committed to using the time that I have left working to make amends and towards a different, more compassionate, and evidence-based response to harm in our society. I hope this book (and author royalties that are being donated to non-profit organizations that help survivors and people who have committed offences) will be a small part of beginning to make amends. In my teaching, research, and public advocacy, I plan on continuing to raise these concerns, listening to those who've been affected, and giving them platforms to speak out. I know that more is needed.

Harold Johnson inspired me with his *mea culpa* for his role in the system, and I saw the power his transformative message had on students. I'm grateful for his example and hope it helps others to do the same. I know at least two federal prosecutors, for example, who have quit their jobs because they concluded it was ethically wrong to perpetuate the war on drugs and ongoing criminalization of people who use drugs. Maybe this is how change starts – yes, in the streets, but also in people examining their own hearts.

There has been very little space in criminal law research about what a new vision for criminal justice would even look like. But as I found, there are people thinking about it – and quietly doing it – already. It's an exciting moment and an important one that I will devote the rest of this book to talking about. At a minimum, this promises to be an interesting thought experiment.

But maybe we can be more ambitious. Maybe by showing a different way is possible, it will help spark a vital national conversation about very different, better ways forward, hastening the decline of a faulty criminal justice empire that has stood for centuries, and allowing something better to emerge.

I think the time has come to begin that conversation in earnest. We will now turn the page (literally and figuratively) on our indicted criminal justice system, and I will sketch out just one vision of what a reimagined approach to addressing harm could look like.

PART TWO

A New Vision for Criminal Justice

CHAPTER ELEVEN

A New Vision

It's far easier to tear down than to build up. Far simpler to criticize a movie, a song, a meal, or a painting than to create these things. Articulating a new vision for criminal justice is an incredibly daunting exercise. After all, we're talking about a staggeringly complex web of inter-related issues and considerations affecting millions of people and involving billions of dollars, where the stakes are exceedingly high and will profoundly impact people's lives, communities, and Nations.

The deconstruction of the system in part 1 of this book was so extensive that I questioned whether it was even possible to envision something new. Where to even begin. Things got much easier when I realized it's not up to me to figure out this multidimensional puzzle – that would be precisely the wrong approach. Like everything else in this project, I began by listening to all of the people who shared their stories and expertise with me.

"The justice system is a huge machine, it's been around for over one thousand years," said Harold Johnson. "People believe in it, people believe that punishment works. Whenever the Conservatives get in, they rely on 'tough on crime' legislation. They get lots of support, people believe that stuff. But it's a belief. And you can't change belief with evidence. So, rely more on evidence-based approaches, put ideology and belief aside."

Our approach to criminal justice "needs to be completely overhauled in terms of the philosophies of wellness and healing versus that of incarceration and punitive," said André Poilièvre, co-founder of STR8 UP. "The road that we're on right now is the wrong road. It's not working."

"We're in the time of pushback, and that's where calls for defunding, decolonizing, abolishing criminal justice systems come from," said Dr. Jamie Livingston, a criminologist at St. Mary's University. "The idea is to give this power back to communities."

"Substance abuse, there's another big thing too. They got to give leniency on that shit," said Matthew, an Indigenous man who survived a shotgun blast only to be incarcerated. "Give a guy a break on that. You may fuck up once or twice just because he has an addiction. But don't send them back to jail and shit."

"Our system isn't working, so why are we still following the same ways? Something needs to be done. Change is always good, you know. And they tell these offenders: 'Well you need to change your life.' OK, well then change the system that is drawing them away. Change the system that wants them to change," said Sherri Maier, a prisoner advocate and founder of Beyond Prison Walls Canada.

When I stepped back from analysing all of the data from all of the people I'd interviewed, along with a dozen research memos exploring various aspects of the criminal justice system written by my student research assistants, the core elements of a new vision for criminal justice began to emerge.

What I will be describing in this part of the book is just one possible vision for a new approach. By describing it, I want to show what else is possible so we can one day move past the pain, futility, and loss of the status quo. And I hope that will spur others to begin similar exercises about what could be. That's the main purpose of this book: to get us to engage with the crucial project of reimagining criminal justice in Canada.

———

A new transformative justice vision for Canada is what I am proposing here in order to contribute to conversations around reimagining criminal justice. I'll start by explaining what I mean by a "new transformative justice vision" and then outline the seven core aspects of this vision, which will each be discussed in the following chapters. First of all, what is transformative justice? And what is "new" about this transformative justice vision?

"Transformative justice" was the original name that I independently came up with for this new approach because of the idea, introduced in chapter 1, that "trauma that is not *transformed* is transmitted." Transforming trauma should be our main objective when harm occurs: transforming the trauma of people who have been harmed as well as those who caused them harm and their communities.

But I soon found that "transformative justice" was actually first coined by the late Ruth Morris (1933–2001), who authored *Stories of Transformative Justice*. Morris was a Quaker and global spokesperson for abolishing prisons and other justice system reforms. When I then read her book, published in 2000, I was struck by how it resonated with what I'd been hearing in my research too.

Transformative justice, as she described it, is very much the starting point for me.

"Transformative justice includes victims, offenders, their families, and their communities, and invites them to use the past to
dream and create a better future," wrote Morris. "Transformative
justice recognizes the wrongs of all victims, and recognizes also
that sooner or later, we are all both victims and offenders. But it
doesn't use that truth to excuse the harm to any current victims."

"Transformative justice sees crime as an opportunity to build a
more caring, more inclusive, more just community. Safety doesn't
lie in bigger fences, harsher prisons, more police, or locking ourselves in till we ourselves are prisoners. Safety and security – real
security – come from building a community where because we
have cared for and included all, that community will be there for
us, when trouble comes to us. For trouble comes to us all, but trouble itself is an opportunity."

In other words, transformative justice makes us strive to understand what is really going on, rather than focusing narrowly on a
single incident at one moment in time. We don't do this to deny accountability, but to enhance our understanding of who is accountable – and in what ways – along with what is needed for healing.

My proposal for a new vision for criminal justice has enough
core similarities with Morris's description of transformative justice that I felt it was fitting to call it a "new" transformative justice
vision.

What makes my approach "new" is the way that it builds on
Morris's work by explicitly incorporating a trauma-informed approach, an emphasis on revitalizing Indigenous justice, a more detailed accounting of decriminalization, and a focus on investing in
social determinants of crime and victimization (which is broadly

consistent with Morris's distributive justice approach). This also distinguishes it from other versions of transformative justice, particularly those in the US, both to reflect the Canadian context and that transformative justice can apply in both formal and informal settings.

With the core philosophy of transformative justice, as I use the term, described, I'll now briefly introduce the seven key aspects of this new vision.

A New Transformative Justice Vision

1 **Healthy Kids and Communities**
   Proactively intervening to prevent and mitigate adverse childhood experiences, and supporting investments in social determinants of justice to prevent and reduce harm in our society.

2 **Decriminalizing People**
   Decriminalizing people who use substances, have mental health conditions, and are experiencing poverty and homelessness; and reinvesting in treatment, housing, income support, education, and employment opportunities that are trauma-informed, evidence-based, and culturally appropriate.

3 **Transforming Trauma**
   Adopting a trauma-informed perspective and trauma-services approach to transform harm to healing and growth, both for people who were harmed and people who caused them harm.

4 **Real Safety**
   Achieving safer communities through 24/7 non-police mobile crisis teams, community-level governance over police services, and enabling people who have been harmed to obtain civil

emergency protection orders and longer-term protection orders. This means a reallocation of resources away from policing towards non-police responses that are better equipped to deal with a wide range of community needs.

5 **Peacemaking and Accountability**
Creating restorative justice opportunities – involving people who were harmed, people who caused them harm, and the community – to be the primary approach for resolving conflict; if restorative justice efforts are unsuccessful, ensuring accountability through a conflict resolution process.

6 **Rehabilitation and Healing**
Abolishing traditional prisons and jails; significantly expanding and improving community-based alternatives to incarceration that would support rehabilitation and healing. Only separating people from society as a last resort where there is a significant risk of harm to the victim or public that cannot be managed under community supervision, or the harm done was so egregious that it shocks the conscience of society. Separation from society would be in secure rehabilitation and healing centres with an emphasis on these objectives – not punishment.

7 **Indigenous Justice**
Recognizing and supporting the revitalization of Indigenous laws and legal orders, and affirming the inherent right of Indigenous peoples to self-government and self-determination in criminal justice matters.

In the chapters that follow, I'll elaborate on each of these seven components of a new approach, highlighting real-world examples of successful initiatives and programs that illustrate how it could look in practice. They're just a handful of examples from many that give us an exciting glimpse into a new way of addressing harm in our society – one that offers greater healing, accountability, and safety.

The overarching philosophy behind transformative justice is that much harm can be prevented and, when it does occur, be transformed into healing rather than cause further harm. We can proactively address the factors that we know lead to people harming others to reduce its occurrence and build healthier, more resilient communities.

But we know that some harm will still occur. When it does, the objective is to support healing for people who are harmed and for the people who caused them harm and, if and when they're interested and able, to support restoration between them. There's also a role for people to be accountable, but not in strict, punitive ways. For people who have caused harm and continue to pose a significant risk to the safety of others that cannot be managed by any other alternative approaches in the community, or where the harm they have caused shocks the conscience of the community, only then will they be separated from society for a period of time in an environment that supports their own rehabilitation and healing.

I asked many people: "If you could reimagine criminal justice, what would it look like?" This answer seemed like a good place to start.

"I have sat and thought about this lots, I have talked with lots of my friends. 'How do you break it? Where?' You know?" said Elder Soltani. "So maybe it's like spring cleaning. You spring clean your house, you pull everything out of the drawers, all the nooks, the crannies, the closets, the basement, the drawers, everything. You wash it all out, you smudge it, and then you put things back. Whatever is older or you don't want any more, you donate, you get rid of, you recycle, whatever. Maybe that's what needs to happen here."

CHAPTER TWELVE

Healthy Kids and Communities: Preventing Childhood Trauma and Investing in Social Determinants of Justice

"I had been abused since childhood. My mom was incredibly abusive," said Skye, a survivor of intimate partner violence.

The adverse childhood experiences (ACEs) that Skye experienced were "a key risk factor" for them being subsequently victimized, as we explored in chapter 1. We heard in chapter 8 how Skye was treated horribly by the system, including by throngs of police officers who didn't seem to care, a victim counsellor who shamed them by asking "Why don't you leave him? What are you stupid?", and a court-referred psychologist who victim blamed them by telling Skye not to make their abusive ex-boyfriend "so mad."

Reflecting back on the entire ordeal, Skye shared their insights on how things could have been done better, including how the system could have dealt with their abuser. Like Skye, their ex-boyfriend was abused as a child, paving the way for harming others later in life.

"It would have made me a lot happier if my boyfriend had gotten – whether or not he used it – it would have made me a lot happier, if he'd gotten constructive help," said Skye. "That would have meant better support as a child. It would have meant having more resources at school for him so that he could do better in school. More emotional help. I know his mom was abusive. Abuse is like a thing that's learned, right, so it is passed down."

Skye doesn't support punishment as the main response to harm, but instead wants people who cause harm to rehabilitate and get healing from their traumas, addictions, and mental health issues.

"I think a lot of people assume, a lot of the time, that people who are survivors or who are victims of crime – however you identify – that the public just assumes that they want the offender to go to jail," said Skye. "In general, if we take the time to be careful and show love rather than punishment, then it will work a lot better. Punishment doesn't work. Revenge doesn't work. They serve to look like they're doing something, but the result is that it creates more violence, it creates more anger, and it doesn't resolve any issues about what the victim or survivor has gone through. ... It is allowing our government to carry out revenge on our behalf. It usurps our role as victims and it is just not useful."

Skye wants to see harm addressed by "programs that rehabilitate and teach people socialization and how to take care of yourself and how to interact with others and how to recognize faulty behaviour patterns. Better mental health care."

"Women have been treated horribly by our criminal justice system and offenders have been treated horribly by our criminal justice system," said Skye. "And we're all just humans and we need to work together to solve this issue rather than make it an 'us-versus-them' thing. And we need to stop letting a government who is unwilling to take care of us to take our roles."

———

How can we proactively prevent and reduce harm in our society? What evidence-based investments can we make that will reduce the chances of people being harmed or causing harm to others?

First, we need to invest in early childhood development, prevent childhood trauma as much as possible, and mitigate its harmful effects when, unfortunately, it does occur. According to Harvard University's Center on the Developing Child, decades of neuroscience and behavioural research demonstrates that investing in early childhood development "is a foundation for a prosperous and sustainable society."

Second, we must invest in social determinants of justice, including housing, education, and employment. While these are the right things to do in any event, they are also strategies to reduce the likelihood *both* of someone becoming a victim and/or perpetrator of harm. These actions would also significantly reduce criminal justice, health care, and social services costs. Investing in kids, housing, education, and employment can yield massive benefits.

The research is clear that, by helping children and their parent(s) today, we prevent harm tomorrow. This should be something everyone can get behind. A new transformative justice vision would proactively support evidence-based programs and interventions that prevent and mitigate ACEs. Some jurisdictions, like Washington State, have enacted ACEs reduction laws. Scotland has endorsed the 70/30 Campaign "to reduce child abuse, neglect and other adverse childhood experiences (ACEs) by at least 70% by the year 2030."

"We were constantly alleviating symptoms – that goes for governments, and it goes for charities. Always responding to the symptoms, but not tackling the root causes," said George Hosking, founder of the UK's WAVE (Worldwide Alternative to Violence)

Trust – the organization behind the 70/30 Campaign. "I realized that, if we could only formulate strategies that tackle root causes, we could make significant differences to levels of child abuse."

Hosking's organization evaluated four hundred interventions from around the world that could help address violence, narrowing the list down to forty-two that were the most promising – a key criteria for effectiveness being the "earlier the intervention the better."

For example, the Nurse-Family Partnership (NFP) is an empirically grounded program designed to promote well-being by supporting "at risk" low-income, first-time mothers as well as prevent early childhood trauma. Recall from chapter 1 that the basic architecture of the brain begins before birth, and myriad adverse childhood experiences may affect disadvantaged families.

The goals of the NFP are to improve pregnancy outcomes, nurture early childhood development, and support family economic self-sufficiency. The NFP involves a two-and-a-half-year commitment by participating families and a Registered Nurse trained in the program. Home visits begin by twenty-eight-weeks gestation and last until the child is two years old, with an average of thirty-three total visits during that time. Each visit takes sixty to ninety minutes and the nurses support twenty to twenty-five families. Support is given in areas including fostering emotional attachment, non-violent parenting, contraception, childcare options, career choices, and help with planning the mother's future.

Randomized controlled trials found that families participating in the NFP "are less likely to abuse or neglect their children, have subsequent unintended pregnancies, or misuse alcohol or drugs; and they are more likely to stop needing welfare support and to maintain stable employment."

When the children in this program reached fifteen years of age, researchers compared their outcomes to those of control group families who hadn't participated. They found the children in the NFP program experienced 79 per cent less maltreatment, 56 per cent fewer arrests and 81 per cent fewer convictions.

The investment in early childhood development has been shown to not only be effective, but also generate a return. The Rand Corporation estimated the NFP saves US$2.88 in public expenditures for each $1.00 of investment, with other studies estimating even greater net returns. The Washington State Institute for Public Policy estimated a net return of US$18,000 per family participating.

McMaster University has adapted the NFP to a Canadian context and successfully piloted it. This has expanded to British Columbia with 739 participating mothers.

The Roots of Empathy (ROE) program is another example of a scientifically proven early childhood development initiative for kids between three and fourteen years of age. ROE aims to "break the intergenerational cycle of violence and poor parenting" by fostering empathy, enhancing emotional literacy, reducing bullying and aggression, promoting pro-social behaviour, and preparing students to be responsible and responsive parents themselves.

The ROE program is quite simply beautiful. A parent brings their two-to-four-month-old infant into the classroom with a facilitator for nine monthly visits, allowing students to get to know them and see the baby grow and develop. The students join in celebrating infant milestones, like rolling from back to front, crawling, starting to talk, and sometimes even celebrating the baby's first birthday. Healthy attachment forms through emotional connection. Students have an additional eighteen visits with the facilitator.

The ROE program even ties into other academic programming. For students whose lives at home are enveloped in violence and trauma, it can be a particularly powerful experience.

"Students use maths skills to measure, weigh and chart the development of their baby. They write poems for the baby, and read stories that tap emotions, such as fear, sadness, anger, shyness. School children on the program learn to relate to their own feelings, as well as recognize these same emotions in others."

Being immersed in the life events of a helpless, innocent newborn and witnessing the love, compassion, and intimacy this child has with their parent does something profound and incredible.

"Babies are 100 per cent accepting, and they don't judge," said Mary Gordon, founder of ROE. "Their superpower is that they can make you love them. With the help of an instructor, children observe the most powerful relationship in the lifespan. The research calls it the attachment relationship between a parent and a baby."

"They learn about what the baby's feeling. The children fall in love with the baby. And they learn a lot about love from the baby and they learn about all their feelings. And then they learn how to have those same feelings for other people."

Evaluations of the ROE program found that participating children demonstrated significant improvements in emotional knowledge, social understanding, and pro-social behaviour with peers as well as decreased aggression with peers and bullying. The program has spread to New Zealand, the United States, the Republic of Ireland, England, Wales, Northern Ireland, Scotland, Norway, Switzerland, Netherlands, Costa Rica, and South Korea.

There's something deeply moving and poignant about starting the conversation of how we envision a new approach to criminal justice with an initiative where children spend time with babies.

TABLE 2. *Preventing Adverse Childhood Experiences*

STRATEGY	APPROACH
Strengthen economic supports to families	• Strengthening household financial security • Family-friendly work policies
Promote social norms that protect against violence and adversity	• Public education campaigns • Legislative approaches to reduce corporal punishment • Bystander approaches • Men and boys as allies in prevention
Ensure a strong start for children	• Early childhood home visitation • High-quality childcare • Preschool enrichment with family engagement
Teach skills	• Social-emotional learning • Safe dating and healthy relationship skill programs • Parenting skills and family relationship approaches
Connect youth to caring adults and activities	• Mentoring programs • After-school programs
Intervene to lessen immediate and long-term harms	• Enhanced primary care • Victim-centred services • Treatment to lessen the harms of ACEs • Treatment to prevent problem behaviour and future involvement in violence • Family-centred treatment for substance use disorders

At a broader policy level, the US Centers for Disease Control and Prevention has generated a list of priority areas for preventing ACEs based on decades of research (as summarized in table 2 above).

Parents who are living with unhealed traumatic experiences need supportive therapies, counselling, and other supports to prevent trauma from being passed down to their children. Preventing ACEs is not only important for kids today (who will grow up to be healthier adults that are less likely to be harmed or to harm others), but also for their children and grandchildren too, given what we know about the intergenerational effects of trauma.

———

"To end the cycle, we need to change the environment in which families operate," said Dr. Robert Maunder and Dr. Jonathan Hunter, psychiatry professors at the University of Toronto. "The changes that are required are big: effective treatment for mental illness and addiction, livable incomes, support for parents who need to work and parents who need to stay home, well-resourced day care, education that helps parents to tune into a child's world and respond with sensitivity."

A new transformative justice vision would also make these evidence-based investments in social determinants of crime and victimization. Research clearly shows us that certain socio-economic disparities are significant predictors of crime, so these are important areas for supporting individual people too.

"Long-term unemployment and having only a basic education, in particular, were the most robust predictors of offending," concluded a massive Finnish criminology study that found this to be true for all categories of offences (including violent offences, property offences, driving while intoxicated, and so on). "These associations held after controlling for previous criminal involvement as well as other social characteristics, whereas the effect of low income on crime was primarily attributable to prior involvement in crime." Educational achievement is linked to employment prospects and income earning potential.

Providing meaningful education and work opportunities to people who have commited offences reduces recidivism and is far more cost effective than the ongoing revolving door of criminal justice. These interventions make us all safer. Recall in chapter 3 that the average literacy level of federally incarcerated people is grade 7–8 and that most were unemployed at the time of their arrest. There's significant unmet potential here. Many people I interviewed who had been incarcerated expressed the desire to improve their lives and found that time in custody had only made things worse. We have a massive population of people sitting in prison getting worse when they could be getting better, gaining further education, learning a valuable skill or trade, and filling needed jobs on release.

Canada is facing a critical shortage of workers, exacerbated by an aging population. Economic migration is not able to keep up with the need. As of April 2022, there were nearly one million job openings across Canada. Job openings in demand include trades like mechanics, welding, electrical engineering, painting, masonry, and manufacturing. The Business Development Bank of Canada says 64 per cent of businesses are experiencing stifled growth due to labour shortages. The Conference Board of Canada has said the shortage of trained workers cost the economy $25 billion in 2020. This is contributing to inflation as companies compete over scarce workers.

Training, educating, and empowering those who come into contact with the criminal justice system could also be part of a solution to our labour shortage. But there are currently numerous obstacles to this occurring.

For one, the current stigma attached to wrongdoing means that even properly qualified individuals with a criminal record may be passed over for open positions. Only some provinces and territories have legislative provisions which generally prohibit discrimination by potential or current employers based on someone having a criminal record that is unrelated to their employment. Even fewer bar discrimination on the basis of criminal convictions for which a pardon has been received. Both of these prohibitions should be enshrined in human rights legislation across all jurisdictions.

Investing in education and skills training for people who have been harmed and who have caused harm, particularly in areas with pathways to employment, is a good idea for many reasons. It will reduce victimization and crime, is cost effective, and will generate substantial economic gains for individuals, businesses, communities, Nations, and the economy as a whole. Everyone benefits.

A lack of housing security is another social determinant of crime and victimization – it makes people more vulnerable to being victimized and more likely to harm others. Researchers explain that Housing First "is a recovery-oriented and complex intervention to ending homelessness in individuals with mental health problems." People experiencing homelessness are given stable, long-term housing as quickly as possible and then provided with supportive services after. In other words, the strategy is first to house, then to support, rather than the other way around. Housing can help people stabilize in safety so that they can get help with mental health and addictions issues and begin to work on their unresolved trauma once they're ready.

Studies have found that Housing First "is strongly successful in improving housing retention and reducing services usage (e.g., emergency shelters, emergency health services, and criminal justice system)." There have already been some Housing First projects in Canada and they have worked. A Canadian study found that the odds of being victimized reduced by 18 per cent over a two-year period for Housing First participants. But it is not a panacea – researchers have found that people who are homeless and have mental health issues with significant ACEs will also need specialized treatment for trauma.

A Swedish study, which specifically looked at the role that housing instability plays in offending, found "a significant increase in criminal convictions from the year of eviction until the end of the period studied, two to three years later. The pattern was similar for men and women." In other words, precarious housing can contribute to people becoming entangled in the criminal justice system.

"People are products of their environment, and if we can't solve those social issues, we're not going to solve the big picture in the end," said Clive Weighill, Saskatoon's chief of police and former president of the Canadian Association of Chiefs of Police. "Look at the United Way's 'Plan to End Homelessness': when you get people some proper housing and take care of them properly, you see how many fewer times they have interactions with the police, how many fewer trips to emergency, how many fewer ambulance rides. All of these things are very expensive. If you spend the money up front, you eliminate a lot of big costs."

There is substantial overlap between the social determinants of health and the social determinants of crime and victimization. That means that investments in things like addressing childhood trauma – along with housing, education, employment, and (as we will discuss next) mental health and substance use treatment – have a multiplicity of benefits, improving outcomes and reducing health care, social services, and criminal justice expenditures.

These investments in our communities help proactively improve safety and well-being. This is especially significant when we consider that, while Indigenous people and Black people are more likely to be victimized and involved in the criminal justice system, they are less likely to have post-secondary education, employment, housing, and liveable incomes. As we've seen, these outcomes are linked to systemic racism and the ongoing impacts of settler colonialism and anti-Black oppression.

Nationally, 46 per cent of Indigenous men have post-secondary qualifications compared to 64 per cent of non-Indigenous men; and 52 per cent of Indigenous women compared to 67 per cent of non-Indigenous women. A key reason for this is the chronic underfunding of Indigenous education, particularly on-reserve schooling, when compared to off-reserve schooling. This education deficit contributes to negative criminal justice outcomes.

"I strongly believe that providing opportunities and support for both survivors and offenders to access and complete higher education is crucial in reducing recidivism and for improving the lives of survivors and the community," said Skye, a survivor of intimate partner violence whom we heard from at the outset of this chapter. "This is something I would want to see more of."

While most Black youth (94 per cent) said they wanted to obtain a bachelor's degree or higher, only 60 per cent thought they could. Statistics Canada found that the unemployment rate for Black people is higher than for the rest of the population, "even after controlling for the effects of various socioeconomic factors, suggesting that other factors, not measured in the census, may be at work."

Multiple studies using fictitious résumés found those with racialized names were "significantly less likely to be interviewed than other candidates with the same levels of qualification and equivalent experience." In other words, racism in hiring, whether explicit or due to unconscious bias, is suppressing the economic opportunities of racialized people.

We know that education, employment, and housing are among the key social determinants of justice and that, by investing in these areas in Black communities and Indigenous Nations and through interventions at the individual level, we can expect to see real and lasting improvements in criminal justice outcomes.

"Heal communities, build communities. Communities create healthy individuals. Unhealthy communities generate unhealthy people," said Harold Johnson. "So, just heal the community, build the community up … anything, in any way that you can build the community up and just bring people together. Hold feasts, alcohol-free events, have conversations, bring people together, work together."

Robyn Maynard emphasizes the importance of confronting the criminalization of Black people, which requires dismantling institutions of Black oppression, including policing and corrections as well as settler colonial institutions. I'll discuss these in detail in chapters 15 and 17. She also points to the role of communities in "imagining Black futures." Maynard emphasizes that "Black communities have been multiple, plural and resistant" and asks:

"What would it look like to disinvest the incredible amount of public funds that are currently diverted towards police and prisons and invest, instead, in community-run, community-based institutions that serve people's very real need for security, education and dignity?"

CHAPTER THIRTEEN

Decriminalizing People: Public Health Approaches to Substances, Mental Health, Poverty, and Homelessness

"Shame on you!" shouted Zoë Dodd from the public gallery of the House of Commons.

Loud applause could be heard as Members of Parliament looked up at the commotion in the public gallery as security escorted Dodd out. A co-organizer with the Toronto Overdose Prevention Society, she had come to Ottawa on June 1, 2022, to watch as MPs voted on Bill C-216. The New Democratic Party (NDP) private member's bill sponsored by MP Gord Johns (Courtenay-Alberni, BC) would have repealed the criminal offence of simple possession of drugs, expunged certain drug-related criminal records, and required the minister of health to create a national strategy on substance use.

"I declare the motion defeated," said the Speaker, just moments before Dodd spoke out. The vote was 71 in favour of decriminalizing people who use drugs (NDP, Green Party, and Bloc Québécois MPs with a handful of Liberal MPs) and 248 opposed (Liberal and Conservative MPs). Their names are recorded for all to see.

While politicians voted down the proposal to decriminalize people who use drugs nation-wide, the federal government has taken some tentative steps in that direction. Just a day before, Carolyn Bennett, federal minister of mental health and addictions, announced that the federal government had approved a request by the Province of British Columbia for a three-year partial decriminalization of drug possession in the province. While this marks a step towards decriminalization of people who use drugs, it was seen by activists as a half-measure to draw attention away from the rejection of Bill C-216.

First, the exemption was limited to BC, despite the crisis's national scope: 73 per cent of unregulated drug deaths occur elsewhere in Canada. Second, the exemption only applies to people over eighteen years of age, meaning the threat of prosecution remains in place for those under eighteen. The youngest unregulated drug death recorded in BC to date is believed to be a twelve-year-old girl. Third, the exemption has a "sunset clause," meaning it only lasts for three years and can be revoked earlier if there's a change of mind or government (or both) at the federal level. This makes it vulnerable to shifting political winds. Finally, the "threshold" quantity of drugs that may be possessed for personal use without criminal sanction or confiscation was set at a cumulative 2.5 grams – much lower than what members of the Canadian Drug Policy Coalition (which includes groups of people who use drugs) say is reasonable for personal use. Minister Bennett revealed she'd listened to police who wanted a low threshold. Setting an overly low threshold creates incentives for the possession of more potent – and more dangerous – street drugs. In other words, the exemption could backfire. Despite these issues, other jurisdictions including Toronto have applied for a similar exemption.

There's no other area of criminal law where we see this buffet-style choice of whether something is criminalized or not, with various cities or provinces opting in or out of decriminalization. It underscores the politics at play in drug policy, with lives on the line. I'm glad Zoë Dodd called MPs out.

———

"I think we've lost a lot of focus on what is criminal justice or what is criminal behaviour and we criminalize all kinds of things all the time," said Howard Sapers, a criminologist with extensive experience, including as a former Parole Board of Canada regional vice-chair and correctional investigator of Canada. "And, I guess, in an effort to make the rest of us feel safer. But the criminal justice system is not the answer to poverty. It's not the answer to addiction. It's not the answer to mental illness. It doesn't help us right now to deal with the big questions of race and inclusion and disadvantage and privilege."

Sapers explained that we need "road blocks" to keep people from ending up with a criminal justice response, saying to people: "No, this is not the right place. You need to be in a hospital. You could be well supported in the community. Maybe all you really need is a safe place to live."

Many people I interviewed who have decades of experience working in and around the justice system agreed that we need to address the root causes of criminal justice involvement.

"Deal with the addiction, deal with the trauma, deal with the mental issues, deal with the racism and you'll minimize the number of people incarcerated," said André Poilièvre with STR8 UP.

"Why are we chasing all these Mickey Mouse warrants? Let's just get rid of them, and let's just work with people and giv[e] them an opportunity to succeed," said police chief Dale McFee.

"I think you have to prevent people from getting into the system. It is a system. Momentum of the system takes over," said a criminal defence lawyer.

We need a compassionate, evidence-based approach to helping people who use substances, have mental health disorders, or who are experiencing poverty and homelessness. As we have seen in chapters 2 and 3, the criminalization of these individuals has been cruel, costly, ineffective, and deadly. Instead, we need to address addiction, mental illness, poverty, and homelessness as the health and social issues that they are – and that means taking criminal justice responses out of the equation.

We need to look to the best available research about what helps people experiencing these often inter-related challenges because we know that policing, punishment, and prisons are fundamentally flawed tools that only serve to exacerbate the problem. I'm a criminal law professor – not a doctor or social worker – so I don't pretend to know what those solutions are. That's why I interviewed experts in these fields. We need to get police, lawyers, and judges who are bungling these societal challenges to take a big step back. They frequently do more harm than good.

Taking a public health approach means focusing on the "health, safety, and well-being of entire populations," drawing on medicine, epidemiology, sociology, psychology, criminology, education, and economics. It relies on a four-step process grounded in the scientific method. First, you start by identifying the problem and understanding its magnitude. Second, you look at factors that increase the risk of someone being a perpetrator or victim of violence (risk factors), and decrease that likelihood (protective factors). Third, you develop and then test strategies to determine their effectiveness. Finally, strategies proven to work are disseminated and supported for widespread adoption.

In other words, while criminalizing people who use drugs, have mental health disorders, and/or are experiencing poverty or homelessness is based on retribution, stigma, and fear, decriminalizing them and instead following a public health approach means adopting responses based on compassion, understanding, and evidence. I will discuss in chapters 16 and 17 how residual public safety risks in a new transformative justice approach would be addressed without reliance on problematic and flawed institutions that currently exist.

Decriminalizing simple possession of illicit drugs, providing rapid access to evidence-based treatments, and a regulated "safer supply" (drugs of known potency and contents for people with substance use disorders to use instead of toxic contaminated street drugs) are examples of taking a public health approach to substance use, rather than the criminal law approach of condemnation and punishment that we saw in chapter 2.

Opioid agonist treatments (e.g., methadone, buprenorphine, and slow-release oral morphine) help prevent withdrawal, lower cravings for opioids, and have been shown to reduce overdose deaths. There's also injectable opioid agonist treatment (iOAT) for people who have severe opioid use disorder involving injectable illicit drugs. When instead provided with pharmaceutical drugs of known contents and potency (e.g., diacetylmorphine or hydromorphone) in a supervised setting, research has found a range of positive outcomes, including improved physical and mental health, improved economic status, and better relationships with family members and communities. In other words, by not having to hustle for toxic street drugs – and suffer the deleterious effects of their consumption – these individuals were able to stabilize their lives.

"People can instead focus on housing, their self-care, food. And, ultimately, we have had people go to school and work," said Dr. Scott MacDonald at the Crosstown Clinic. Researchers also found that iOAT dramatically reduced the consumption of, and expenditure on, illicit drugs. Criminal defence lawyers told me they stopped seeing chronic clients after they started receiving such treatment. Yet the Crosstown Clinic had a waitlist in the hundreds when I last spoke to Dr. MacDonald.

Additionally, there have been growing calls to provide a more widely available regulated safer supply of drugs instead of leaving the drug supply up to organized crime to concoct. Pilot safer supply programs across Canada have found promising outcomes already, including reducing overdoses and the use of illicit street fentanyl. As they scale up, details of regulated safer supply approaches will need to be refined through further research so that we get it right and minimize unintended consequences.

"We want to make sure that people have access to a safe supply," said Dr. Shannon McDonald. "It's the difference between defining substance use disorder as a clinical problem as opposed to a behaviour problem. I don't have a problem with giving people the medication they need to be well."

"We've seen a lot of individuals who did really poorly on a street supply who, once given access to a safe supply can sustain housing, can hold a job, can see their family and do well. And then have conversations about wellness and not using. ... But there are so many things that we need to do to stabilize people before they can get there. And putting them at risk by throwing them at a system that's not supportive and not giving them the medication, it's not helpful."

Safer supply is an example of an intervention that should be monitored, refined, and expanded. Replacing toxic, contaminated street drugs with regulated drugs of known content and potency is an important piece of responding to the opioid crisis.

In my book *Overdose*, I summarized the key recommendations from my research on how to respond to the opioid crisis with a compassionate evidence-based approach. These recommendations were drafted in consultation with addictions experts, people who use drugs, and family members of people who have died during the opioid crisis. I list these key recommendations here as an example of addressing substance use issues from a public health – rather than a criminal justice – perspective. While some of them are being done through pilot projects or on a small scale, we need to go all the way forward. Notice how the criminal justice system is not part of what's needed. You will also see that it's not about harm reduction vs. recovery – a false dichotomy we hear in political debates about this issue – instead we need to do both, with evidence-based programs that work.

Recommendations to Address the Toxic Contaminated Drug Crisis:

1 Make naloxone (the temporary antidote to an opioid overdose) freely and widely available to individuals, and at public and private locations, and provide emergency first aid training in how to respond to an overdose;

2 Immediately expand, and remove all legal barriers to, supervised consumption sites, overdose prevention sites,
   witnessed-use rooms, and "no-questions asked" drug testing
   services in all affected communities;

3 Dramatically expand rapid access to evidence-based treatment
   as recommended in the national medical guidelines for treating opioid use disorder;

4 Provide legal, low-barrier, regulated access to opioids of
   known contents and potency ("safe supply") under medical
   direction and supervision to people with opioid use disorder
   who would otherwise use contaminated street drugs and be at
   greater risk of a fatal overdose;

5 Invest in research to develop new treatment options for opioid
   use disorder and a holistic response to responding to substance use disorders;

6 Increase support to Indigenous communities, front-line and
   peer-based organizations, and families of people with opioid
   use disorder so that they can enhance their response to the
   opioid crisis;

7 Stop criminalizing people who use drugs, including:
   a Expand "Good Samaritan" overdose laws to include im-
      munity from prosecution for any non-violent offence and
      related breaches of conditions and warrants, as well as in-
      crease awareness of this legal protection;
   b Decriminalize simple possession of illicit drugs;
   c Cease imposing "drug paraphernalia" prohibitions, which
      prevent the possession of naloxone kits and harm reduction
      supplies like clean syringes;
   d Stop criminal law conditions that prohibit people from us-
      ing illicit substances ("abstinence orders");

e End the imposition of geographic restrictions ("red zon-
   ing") of people who use drugs;

f Make substance use disorder a mitigating factor at
   sentencing;

g Expunge criminal records for possession of illicit
   substances;

h Provide people in prison with equal access to over-dose
   prevention services, harm reduction supplies, and evidence-based treatment options; and

i Prior to their release from custody, provide people with
   access to a medical practitioner who is trained in substance
   use disorders and who can provide them with the necessary
   information and medications to reduce their risk of suffering a fatal overdose.

———

Our response to mental health also needs to be dramatically improved and overhauled. There continues to be a vast gap between
how we as a society prevent and treat physical illness versus how
we address mental illness. Treating mental illness is key to min-
imizing harms. As forensic psychiatrist Dr. Sandy Simpson explained in chapter 3, when people with psychotic illnesses receive
treatment, they have "the same or lower rates of violence than the
general population."

The current failure of the system to treat complex mental health
challenges can manifest itself in so-called "stranger attacks" – unprovoked and seemingly inexplicable acts of violence. Rather than
more police, tougher sentences, and bigger jails, criminologists say
if we want to address this issue and achieve long-term reductions

in crime, we need to provide greater access to mental health resources and "invest significantly in addressing the systems-level issues that contribute to offending including systemic racism, poverty, inadequate health services, food insecurity, and housing unaffordability."

A national public health care system for mental health is desperately needed. Such investments alongside evidence-based, properly funded programs for harm reduction, substance use treatment, and recovery; mental health resources and interventions; trauma counselling; trauma-informed housing; and income support can better address these underlying issues than can the ever-growing litany of status quo criminal justice system responses.

"The major problem is the [criminal justice] system is getting bigger and expanding and contorting itself to look like it's making changes without actually making changes," said professor of criminology Jamie Livingston. "It's just sort of expanding its creep into areas where I see lots of problems. ... Specifically, I'm talking about mental health and substance use issues. So, you know, the scope creep of the criminal justice system into things like drug courts, mental health courts, police specific mental health response teams, forensic mental health, specialized prison mental health teams – you know, all of that are sort of ways that the system reforms itself. But by reforming itself, it expands, and keeps control and power of those issues."

Professor Livingston's observations build on those of Professors Joshua Sealy-Harrington and David Milward earlier – not only is "tinkering" and making "tweaks" ineffective at solving the social problems stemming from Canada's prevailing criminal justice responses, but it also serves to entrench a system that is fuelling these very problems.

Dr. Simpson explained, from his vantage point, the supports that need to be in place for people. "Mental health needs to get its act together; social housing needs to get its act together; income support needs to get its act together. So that police have other places to direct people to than courts, don't have to remand people in custody. Or when they are remanded in custody, the social support processes that are necessary for this group can be immediately there for them to stop from cycling through."

A new transformative justice vision would prioritize supports related to substance use, mental health, income, and housing – rather than denying access to these essential services due to someone's criminal justice involvement. Dr. Simpson illustrated the dysfunction of the current system by telling me about a recent patient who was criminally charged and denied bail, then released after two weeks. As a result, the patient was evicted from his housing, rendering him homeless upon release. He also lost his mental health support, since the Assertive Community Treatment (ACT) team responsible for his mental health needs refused to treat him anymore, saying, "No, he's off our list because he's on bail. We don't take people who are on bail." With these crucial supports gone, our society was rendered less safe, while spending more money on policing and jails. It's an all-too-common occurrence.

Instead, Dr. Simpson explained that our approach needs to be "informed about, and thoughtful about, the drivers of crime that relate to poverty, homelessness, substance misuse, and mental illness." Structured interventions that rapidly address these problems without involving the criminal justice system is the way forward, according to Dr. Simpson. "It's directing people into those services, not overseeing them by the court."

Howard Sapers also believes these services need to be expanded and provided outside of the criminal justice system so that our approach is more "smart and focused."

"Can you imagine anything really, well, more expensive and probably less useful than having somebody enter psychiatric support through the courts? Or psychiatric or health and addiction supports because they got arrested, because they spent time at the remand centre, because they went to jail? It doesn't make any sense to me," said Sapers. "What is the purpose of the criminal law? What are we trying to achieve here? How is society best served and protected?"

Criminalization of poor people, which is linked to their inability to afford legal counsel, is also a major impediment to their ability to improve their lot in life. In the last chapter, we talked about how we need to invest in the social determinants of justice, including housing, education, and employment opportunities. We need to stop putting up barriers to people accessing these necessities of life.

"Having a criminal record is just going to be hanging around the necks of some people forever," said Kimberly Mann, executive director of the Collaborative Justice Program. "You can't get good jobs or even housing. That can be impacted. I mean, what's more important than a job and a house? So, the stigma around that is terrible."

"The ability to get your record expunged in a timely manner, so that it doesn't become a life sentence to unemployment, has to be the last part of this puzzle," agreed Michael Bryant.

The potential positive impact is huge when, instead of punishing people, we support their mental health and well-being, provide harm reduction and treatment for their substance use, help them address their trauma, and meet their housing and employment needs. For many, I believe we can help them transform their stories and end their trips through the revolving door of the system where they're set up to fail again and again. Kimberly Mann gave me an example of the difference this can make in one person's life.

"I know someone who just went for a period of custody and he ended up – because he has a dual diagnosis of mental illness and addictions – he was sent to a hospital setting that's corrections, but it's in a hospital setting," said Mann. "And he attended courses that he had to take, he had a very good psychologist, psychiatrist there, he had a social worker, he had even a physiotherapist for some physical issues. And attended at least five different programs, healthy relationships, you know, good decision-making. He agreed to try a new medication where he was medication resistant prior to that."

Mann explained that her client made some meaningful relationships with other residents, was active outdoors, and worked out. The difference in him seen over five months in this more therapeutic setting – where his underlying issues were being addressed and he was able to connect with people and practice some self-care – was huge.

"And when he came out of there, probably five months or so in there, he's very healthy, he had a good attitude, he's on medication for the first time in years, his addiction is under control. And I think wow, did he ever luck out, right, having that experience instead of being at the Lindsay Superjail with everybody and so on. And then I was thinking, you know, that really should be everybody's experience."

"If we're trying to build healthy Canadians and they are going to be released to the community, why wouldn't we make sure that they're really good and healthy when they come out?" asked

Mann. "And that they have those resources as they come out and they can be handed off to resources in the community to continue that. It just seems like a no-brainer to me."

We also need to decriminalize Indigenous people and Black people. Authors like Robyn Maynard point out that any changes to the system are likely to fail without "concerted efforts towards seeing, naming and concertedly countering the demonization of Black life that permeates both state institutions and wider society." This includes an emphasis on Black leadership and guarding against efforts at transformative change being co-opted by the status quo and those with entrenched power. It means dismantling institutions that continue to oppress Black people including policing and prisons – which I will discuss in chapters 15 and 17 – as well as "simultaneously supporting Indigenous decolonization movements," which I will discuss in chapter 18 on Indigenous justice.

"With so many issues as criminal justice issues – that's going to require a fundamental rethink of how we respond to issues at earlier stages through prevention and through developing community-based supports, instead of waiting for them to become policing issues," said Professor Julius Haag. "I think there's a move for a larger and structural shift in our society, where we reduce our reliance on police by shifting resources away from an enforcement orientated approach to deal with issues at the root causes."

"I would probably start by heavily, heavily investing in things that are not criminal justice related. So, I think that's the starting point. And then you see what you're left with, and what you actually still need criminal justice for," said professor of law Adelina Iftene. "Start to envision how do we get people out of poverty, how do we address mental illness, how do we address addictions, how do we respond to the Truth and Reconciliation Report in a manner that doesn't include criminal justice."

Iftene pointed out that the criminal justice system is "just a tool" that "replies to a need." The problem is that "you're creating the need fuelling that institution. And it just feels a bit that we are in that kind of a wheel, where the system is itself creating its clientele and the system is just producing more work for itself. It's an industry. It becomes more and more like an industry."

In short, a new transformative justice vision requires a criminal justice revolution. It represents a shift from reactive crime control philosophies that have proven to be costly, ineffective, and deadly towards a proactive public health approach and targeted interventions that better respond to people who use substances, have mental health conditions, experience poverty and homelessness, and are Indigenous, Black, or people of colour.

CHAPTER FOURTEEN

Transforming Trauma: Holistic Support for People Who Were Harmed and Caused Harm

André Poilièvre is in his mid-eighties and lives in an old folks' home. His wrinkled hands show his age. But his eyes are bright when a smile flashes across his face. He's the last person you'd expect to stand toe-to-toe with people considered "high-risk" violent street gang members in Saskatchewan.

Poilièvre was coordinating chaplain at the Saskatoon Correctional Centre until he retired in 2002 – but he was no ordinary chaplain. Twenty-four years earlier, in 1988, Poilièvre – then a Catholic priest – had thrown out his clerical collar and started wearing street clothes. He moved up north and began working with Indigenous people. When he came back to Saskatchewan, he wanted to help incarcerated people. He insists on just being called André and has publicly called for the Catholic Church to release records of abusive priests as well as their enablers, and to compensate survivors of residential schools.

While a prison chaplain, André supported the Federation of Sovereign Indigenous Nations (FSIN) on its anti-gang strategy.

One day, he was approached by two young Indigenous men who were in gangs and wanted out.

"Well, I have no idea either what to do," André told them.

Nevertheless, he worked with them to exit the gang and turn their lives around – one had a partner who had been killed by a rival gang, while the other had two younger brothers whom he saw following in his footsteps. Before long, word spread on the street and in jail. Other young people started asking to talk to André.

Soon after, André retired from being a prison chaplain and co-founded STR8 UP to help others on their journey towards healing. They learned from leading gang-exit programs in the United States that had proven successful, but adapted these methods to the Canadian context, particularly for the predominantly Indigenous gang members who were seeking help.

"One of the conditions for joining STR8 UP is they have to come to us," said André. "We don't go recruiting. We don't go advertising. We don't go promoting. If we were to do that, our members would be threatened and, you know, hurt badly by active gang members. So, they have to come to us." André and STR8 UP members are respected by active gang members, including higher-ups, because they "won't rat out to the cops anything about gangs."

When someone comes to STR8 UP for support, it isn't enough to simply express an interest in getting on a better life path. The road isn't easy, and the requirements and commitments are heavy.

"If they come to us and say, 'We want to join STR8 UP' then I'd say, 'OK, here's what you got to do. Drop your colours. Write your autobiography. And then deal with your addiction.' So those are the three first conditions, and then there's three more: being honest, being humble, and you have to give us four years of your life."

"Dropping your colours" means leaving the gang. Leaving a street gang isn't like simply cancelling a dinner reservation over the phone. The process of dropping colours can be brutal – just as brutal as the process of joining the gang in the first place.

"So, you've got to get beaten in. If you want to get out, there are different ways of doing it. But the most common way for Indigenous street gangs is to get beaten out. It means getting beaten by four guys for a minute, and you can't defend yourself. If you do that, then you are allowed to go out," said André.

Being beaten in and beaten out is but a small reminder of what would happen to someone if they became a police informant – something there can be big money in doing – and that they could be killed for. A report commissioned by Public Safety Canada confirms these Indigenous gang norms.

In other instances, gangs may treat their members like indentured slaves, forcing them to earn or buy their way out. "I know we have one of our gang members, he had to give the gang $10,000 to get out. So, it varies with the gang, but with street gangs it's usually just getting beaten out."

Once someone wanting to join STR8 UP has dropped their colours, they still have to write their autobiography. But it's not the sort of autobiography that you might be picturing.

"You have to describe the root causes of why you became an addict and why you became a gang member – and you have to start at conception. Eventually, they'll have to go to generational, but in STR8 UP, it's: 'What happened when mom was pregnant with you? Did she do drugs? Was she sixteen, seventeen years old? And what was going on?' They need to know that, not to judge mom, but they have to be able to deal with that issue."

"Once they're born, then what happened? [The f]irst five years are extremely important. If you don't know, you've got to find out. You've got to find out. You've got to find out everything about yourself, not for me to know, but for them to become aware. And you have to do that all the way up to today. So, your autobiography, we don't want a book. We want three, four pages. And they can put it in two or three or four. And some of them are illiterate, so they tell us their story, and I'll write it out."

STR8 UP gets its members to identify and appreciate the "cause of causes" that lies at the root of their involvement in gangs – precisely the sort of trauma recovery work needed. But this is only the beginning. The autobiography they write on entering the program is just the opening chapter of their life. Similar to what Harold Johnson said, STR8 UP participants move forward to write "new and better stories."

"Once we have their story, now we say, 'Here's your issues. You were abandoned. You were rejected. Violence. Mom tried to abort you when she was pregnant with you. These are the things that you were given. You can be angry about that, but that's not going to help. You can deal with all the hate and the anger and the shame with alcohol and drugs and so forth; that's not going to help. What you have to do, you have to deal with it in a healthy manner.'"

After dropping their colours and writing their autobiography, individuals officially become members of STR8 UP and start addressing their addiction. Their autobiography forms the basis of understanding the myriad issues they need to heal from. There's spiritual, physical, mental, and emotional aspects to that healing.

"Being spiritual is not necessarily a belief," said André, "it's who you are." As he explained, it's our essence as a person, regardless of whether someone is atheist, agnostic, follows a certain religion or

Indigenous culture, beliefs, and practices. Many people don't know who they are, they've lost their sense of their true self – but "if you are going to heal, that's the door."

"[W]e say there are positive values, spiritual values. Being honest is one. But there are negative spiritual values; being dishonest," explained André. For each positive spiritual value, there is a corresponding negative one. "Being humble, being arrogant. Being faithful, being unfaithful. Being forgiving, being vindictive."

"And when my guys were gangbanging, their values were all negative. So now, if you want to change your life, you have to change what? Your values. You have to start by being honest and by being humble."

"Being honest and being humble means that you have to admit that you're an addict. You have to admit that you have all of these issues that you have to deal with. And being humble, you have to admit that you can't do this alone. You need support. You're the only guy who can do it, but you can't do it alone."

With a growing sense of who they are, combined with efforts to be honest and humble, STR8 UP members pursue a wide range of substance use treatment and recovery options – "whatever works for that person" – including counselling, in-patient treatment, recovery workbooks, Alcoholics Anonymous meetings, joining a faith community, and connecting with Indigenous teachings, Elders and ceremonies, including sweats.

"Eighty per cent of our people are First Nations, we really encourage them so they reconnect with their culture and they reconnect with Elders. They reconnect with whatever it is that is positive in their lives. They have to deal with their addiction, otherwise they can't deal with anything else. They can't deal with someone that's still shooting up drugs into their arm or getting drunk."

They work on their physical well-being ("what we do"), mental well-being ("what we think"), and emotional well-being ("how we feel"), committing four years of their life to being a member of STR8 UP.

Most men and women in STR8 UP are also parents. André described their goals as they progress along their healing journey: "First goal is to become a loving parent. The second goal is to become a faithful partner. And the third one is to become a responsible citizen. That's our goals. They all understand that."

"And so again, the conditions I just said: drop your colours, autobiography, addiction, honest, humble, four years of your life, to become a loving parent, a faithful partner, and a responsible citizen. That's STR8 UP."

In 2008, André was awarded the Order of Canada and Justice Canada featured STR8 UP members in its series on how we could do criminal justice differently. The non-profit organization has helped hundreds of gang members leave their gangs and it has over a hundred active members at various stages of their healing journey. Many former gang members are now peer mentors and involved in community outreach work. Independent evaluations of STR8 UP have been resoundingly strong but expressed concerns about a lack of permanent funding. André is quick to give credit to the team of people who work at STR8 UP, especially the members.

"It's about learning to live life without crime and to learn to accept where it's coming from," said Mandy, a member of STR8 UP. She was abused as a child by her mother, who is a residential school survivor. Starting at fourteen years of age, Mandy became involved in the criminal justice system as both a victim and offender because of "domestic violence, being involved in gangs, drinking and drugging, and living that kind of lifestyle." She was repeatedly in and out of prison. She eventually had six children, one of whom is deceased. One time, she was sent to jail for eighteen months for uttering threats because she wanted her children back from being in the custody of her mother. There were many other charges related to her gang involvement and substance use.

But a turning point came in jail one day after she forgot to go to the prison library to get some new books. "The guard was making fun of me," said Mandy. "She said, 'Oh, you missed book time.'"

The corrections officer had not come empty-handed. She brought some books for Mandy. Books that were different from what she usually read.

"She gave me these books, one was about child advocacy and about returning to the teachings. I was learning about the Aboriginal law before the Europeans came. I learned about that. And then I learned about STR8 UP."

STR8 UP has published two books. The first, *STR8UP and Gangs: The Untold Stories*, is written by thirteen ex-gang members and shares their stories. The second, *STR8UP: Stories of Courage*, is an extensive workbook for recovering gang members and people with addictions. It was one of these books that wound up in Mandy's hands as she sat in her cell.

"I don't know why she sent me those books. I read them. I couldn't stop reading them." Mandy reached out to André and joined STR8 UP.

"It helped me understand about myself, the history of myself, and my people," said Mandy. "How to get my children back and how to have a good relationship, how to get paid work and education. I'm a small business owner now. I got a couple of my kids in my care and they're slowly coming back to my life now. My mother and I get along now. It took a really long time, but I got my life together since then. I'm sober now."

Mandy's small business works to remediate issues with bed-bugs, cockroaches, and mould on reserve land (an ongoing legacy of settler colonialism), which has been called an "ongoing crisis" in many First Nations communities. She employs people with criminal records and gives them a chance to work. Then she gives them a reference for their next job application.

Other STR8 UP members told me how dealing with their childhood trauma and addictions in a healing, supportive group made all the difference in their lives – in contrast with decades wasted in the punitive criminal justice system.

"When I went to the prison, they didn't have really much help for people leaving the gang," said Danny, an Indigenous man we met at the beginning of chapter 5 whose parents were both Sixties Scoop survivors who struggled with substance use. Danny joined his older sibling's street gang at nine years of age after being abused in foster care. By age twenty-seven he had spent almost half of his life behind bars. While you have already heard that part of his story, it's not the end of it.

"In Saskatchewan, there's STR8 UP. They help you write your life story. You give four years of your life, and you jump out of your gang," said Danny. "So they help you with that and just more of those. That's what should be more in jails is more for us gang members and more addiction services, more of those type of programs and stuff like that. More programming for them and just more fun programming to do, to give prisoners and people a better understanding of their situations and how to get out of it and showing them a better life, I guess."

Danny says he also benefited from the time he spent attending *'Aghelh Nebun* (formerly Kenneth Creek Camp), a halfway house located in a wilderness area east of Prince George, BC. "You get with the Native culture and stuff like that. Sweats every week. So, I went to that camp in BC there," said Danny.

"Just going through my journey and dealing with addiction, and dealing with a lot of grief and loss of family and just the motivation. I'm just sick and tired of living that life, and wanting a life for my own of peace and happiness."

———

A new transformative justice vision is concerned with the well-being of both people who were harmed and people who caused harm. Rather than tearing down people by inflicting punishment on them, transformative justice is concerned with building up people through addressing underlying issues they face individually and broader societal issues.

Transformative justice adopts a trauma-informed perspective and provides trauma services to transform harm into healing, both for people who were harmed and people who caused harm. It seeks to support healing of trauma, rather than trigger or compound trauma. A holistic understanding of trauma recovery encompasses the person's physical, mental, emotional, spiritual, and social well-being. STR8 UP is an exciting, proven, real-life example of this approach in action.

Transformative justice reflects how crime and victimization are complex social phenomena requiring an interdisciplinary and multifaceted response – issues that the existing criminal justice system is fundamentally unable to address and actually exacerbates.

Once people who have been harmed and caused harm both have support, and safety is in place (as I'll discuss in chapter 15), then there may be a peacemaking and accountability process, as I will discuss in chapter 16. Both need healing.

When someone experiences harm, support needs to be made available to them unconditionally. There shouldn't be any requirement that they "cooperate" or "assist" in any investigation or proceedings involving the person who harmed them. It should be up to them whether to proceed with any such reporting of the incident to relevant authorities, absent direct risk of harm or death to someone else and then with disclosure only being as much as is strictly necessary to protect safety.

"No human being is ever beyond redemption," said Dr. Gabor Maté. "The possibility of renewal exists so long as life exists. How to support that possibility in others and in ourselves is the ultimate question."

"I myself run into criminal defence lawyers all the time. When I ask them 'have you ever had a client that you thought was evil or a bad person?' and I have many friends in criminal defence who say, 'No,'" said Michael Bryant. "I've met some really sick people, some really unwell people, psychotic people and so on. But evil? No. I'm sure they're out there, but I just haven't met the 'evil person' yet and we mix up evil with unwell, that these are people in pain. They're people in pain and that pain has got them into the criminal legal system. They deserve our help, not our condemnation. But, of course, we condemn them, we make them sicker and then we scratch our heads when it doesn't get better."

"The false premise is that these guys and gals that commit crime are responsible for it 100 per cent, and they've got to be accountable 100 per cent and they got to pay the price 100 per cent," said André Poilièvre. "Well in fact, that's false. When they commit a crime, there's a lot of issues, traumas that they've experienced, which with First Nations people and a lot of people is transgenerational, which means it might have started with their grandparents and then parents. The whole colonization and residential school system are part and parcel of the problem. Addiction is a way of dealing with the problem, but it's not the solution. So, many mental issues, traumas, we need to start from where they're at."

"What causes them to be a criminal and an addict? Don't start from there. Start from what caused that. So, you have to go to that issue, and the courts don't do that. They pretend to do it. And then they call our provincial system here correctional. It's not a correctional system at all. It's extremely punitive. And so, as long as you keep starting from the false premise, you won't be able to transform the justice system."

Dr. Maté's 2021 documentary *The Wisdom of Trauma* imagines "a trauma-informed society in which parents, teachers, physicians, policy-makers and legal personnel are not concerned with fixing behaviours, making diagnoses, suppressing symptoms and judging, but seek instead to understand the sources from which troubling behaviours and diseases spring in the wounded human soul."

As a key aspect of a new transformative justice vision, a trauma-informed approach:

- **Realizes** trauma has a widespread impact and understands potential paths for recovery;
- **Recognizes** the signs and symptoms of trauma in clients, families, staff, and others involved with the system;

- **Responds** by fully integrating knowledge about trauma into policies, procedures, and practices; and
- **Resists** retraumatization.

Services provided according to a trauma-informed approach "take into account an understanding of trauma in all aspects of service delivery and place priority on the individual's safety, choice, and control [to] create a treatment culture of nonviolence, learning, and collaboration." They are provided "in ways that recognize the need for physical and emotional safety, as well as choice and control in decisions affecting one's treatment." With a trauma-informed approach, the "safety and empowerment for the service user are central, and are embedded in policies, practices, and staff relational approaches. Service providers cultivate safety in every interaction and avoid confrontational approaches." The aim is to "create an environment where service users do not experience further traumatization or re-traumatization ... and where they can make decisions about their treatment needs at a pace that feels safe to them."

A new transformative justice vision would go beyond being trauma-informed to prioritize funding and access to trauma services for both people who were harmed and the people who caused them harm. This would "more directly address the need for healing from traumatic life experiences and facilitate trauma recovery through specialized counselling and other clinical interventions. They include specific therapies such as trauma-focused cognitive behavioral therapy and other approaches such as stress inoculation, exposure, skills development, sensorimotor psychotherapy, eye movement desensitization and reprocessing [EMDR], and healing and empowerment."

Many people experiencing developmental trauma never learned as children how to regulate their nervous systems because they were in a frequent survival state of fight, flight, freeze, or fawn. They did not develop a healthy attachment with parents or caregivers in order to co-regulate, manage difficult emotions, and navigate challenging situations. Trauma also impacted their brain development, as discussed in chapter 1. This presents a significant challenge in adolescence and adulthood: an ongoing inability to regulate their nervous system, which also makes the deeper work of healing from trauma impossible unless it is addressed.

Unfortunately, commonly used counselling approaches (as found in correctional settings) like cognitive behavioural therapy (CBT) or "talk therapy" "pay scant attention to the pre-programmed physical response [i.e., nervous system] patterns that have evolved and are evoked in response to situations experienced as personally threatening for the individual." In contrast, there are multiple somatic (body-centred) therapies, such as EMDR and sensorimotor psychotherapy, which help trauma survivors regulate their nervous systems as a first step in recovering from trauma. In institutional settings, sensorimotor psychotherapy also "offers a helpful framework for all staff to understand and intervene in client psychopathology and acting out behaviour when understood within the context of perceived threat." Staff can then respond in a trauma-informed way, rather than just focusing on the particular behaviour being exhibited.

If you're not regulated, you can't process trauma. Once the nervous system is no longer in such an activated state, trauma survivors can do the deeper work of confronting the traumatic experiences that they endured. Internal Family Systems (IFS) is an example of a therapy that can be helpful for treating anxiety, depression, and trauma in both survivors and people who have committed offences. Something common to all trauma recovery work is the need for self-compassion and understanding.

"When a person commits a crime, it's not 'what's wrong with you?' It's 'what happened to you?' That's a trauma-informed question: 'What happened to you?'" said Fritzi Horstman. "'Well, you know, my mother abandoned me when I was a little girl, my father committed suicide when I was ten.' Whatever the story is. But that's like, 'Holy shit, how did you survive?'"

"We resort to crime because we can't get our needs met, period. Be that a need as an addict, a need as a homeless person, a need as a jealous husband," said Horstman. "It's just a trauma response, and we have to see it that way. Once we're trauma-informed, we'll realize they're not bad people, they just did a bad thing."

Dr. Robert Maunder and Dr. Jonathan Hunter discussed how this approach can be implemented when interacting with individuals in health care settings. The same should apply in criminal justice interventions.

"Trauma-informed care emphasizes strengths over deficits, is attentive to the likelihood that those seeking care have experienced trauma, strives to avoid repeating the trauma, and is directed toward recovery," wrote Maunder and Hunter. "Highlight successful adaptation rather than symptoms. Some say, 'Don't ask *what's wrong with you? Ask what happened to you?'* This principle takes that idea a step further. Don't just ask what happened, also notice that [the person] has shown strength in adapting to what happened – even if the adaptations turned into problems over time."

"Invest in the therapy and the healing, the recovery, and dealing with the issues. Find out how come this person is doing what he's doing," said André Poilièvre. "Unless you know what the issue is, you're going to deal with all the guys the same way. And that's not going to work."

"If you could address that trauma, then you also cut off future offending," said Professor David Milward at the University of Victoria's Faculty of Law. "Unless we can find ways to address that trauma, whether it's through restorative justice, Indigenous healing, Indigenous legal orders, or some other way, you're not going to make much progress." In chapter 16, I will discuss restorative justice and, in chapter 18, I will explore Indigenous laws, healing, and wellness.

———

People who have been harmed (i.e., victims and survivors) need ready access to a range of holistic services (including physical health, mental health, emotional health, and spiritual supports) to help them recover. We should also remember that those who have been harmed today are at greater risk of harming others tomorrow, if their trauma isn't transformed. So there are many reasons to dramatically increase support for people who are harmed. With respect to victims of crime specifically, table 3 (below) identifies some of the fundamental needs they express.

Holistic, comprehensive victim services are crucial to properly responding to the needs expressed by people who have been harmed. This includes responding to the physical, emotional, mental, spiritual, and social impacts of the trauma they have experienced. It means providing publicly funded compensation for the harm they have suffered to help them recover. Notably, it is evident from these needs that victims desire a meaningful process where they have a voice and can have their views heard in relation to the

TABLE 3. *Overview of Basic Human Needs and Victims' Expressed Needs*

Basic Human Need	Needs Expressed by Victims
Physiological	Support: medical needs; rehabilitation Reparation: compensation/restitution (food, shelter, medication)
Safety and security	Protection; information
Belonging and acceptance	Emotional support; information (notification); reparation
Autonomy/self-realization	Information; recognition (consultation, voice); reparation (compensation)
Self-esteem/positive identity	Recognition; information; reparation
Effectiveness and control	Information; recognition (voice, consideration of views)
Comprehension of reality	Support; information; reparation
Justice	Reparation; recognition; information

person who caused them harm, which I will discuss in chapter 16. They also expressed a need for safety, a prerequisite to healing, which I will discuss in chapters 15 and 17.

In *Victim Law: The Law of Victims of Crime in Canada*, I explored the tentative patchwork of laws, policies, and programs that exist for victims of crime at the federal, provincial, and territorial levels. There remain substantial gaps in basic areas including victim services, compensation, protective measures, and meaningful opportunities for victims' participation in restorative justice programs and proceedings.

Skye, a survivor of intimate partner violence whom we met in chapter 8, shared their challenges with accessing victim services. All of this needs to be done differently.

"I'm getting three-quarters of a psychologist paid for by criminal victim services, but I don't really get to choose who is my psychologist. I don't get to choose who is caring for me. Based on my experience, I don't have a lot of faith in that," said Skye. "I'm going to see what happens and go anyway and hope for the best. And I had to fight tooth and nail for that. I had to go through a humiliating process to get that help. And I had to prove years after the fact that this happened, and I had to explain why I didn't ask for the help in the first place. They made me do that, and it was humiliating."

"A young woman's been raped many times, she's never dealt with that. A young man who's being bounced around from foster home to foster home has never dealt with that. He's lived with guilt and shame and anger and resentment and bitterness all of his life. That's where he's at. You start from there," said André Poilièvre. "Where are you at? Start from knowing where that young person is at. And you need to know that in detail so that you can assist, support that person."

"In what we were envisioning, there would be victim services automatically, victim support regardless of the severity of the crime and people would be reached out to, services offered, supported, provided information," said Kimberly Mann, executive director of the Collaborative Justice Program. "I think there should be offender services also, right, as soon as they're connected with the criminal justice system, they start to be connected with support services to address the root causes of a behaviour. Help them find housing if that's an issue, help them find addiction programs if that's an issue, you know, just get started working right away on all of those things that are going to help them have a healthier future and subsequently keep the community healthy."

Communities too need healing instead of more of the same. "We have 326 RCMP officers in Northern Saskatchewan for a population of 37,000," said Harold Johnson. "Whenever we ask for help, we get more police. What we need are more trauma counsellors."

CHAPTER FIFTEEN

Real Safety: Mobile 24/7 Non-police Responses

A woman is walking across an overpass, barefoot, alone, and wearing little clothing. Someone else is sleeping on a sidewalk and hasn't moved for five hours. A person is thinking of taking their own life. These are just a few examples of 911 and non-emergency police calls made in Eugene, Oregon.

In most Canadian cities, police would likely respond, especially if these calls were in rural and remote areas, or received on weekends, holidays, or late at night. Instead, it was Crisis Assistance Helping Out On the Streets (CAHOOTS) who was dispatched to respond.

CAHOOTS is a 24/7 non-police mobile crisis intervention team that is an initiative of the community-based White Bird Clinic in Eugene (population of 170,000). It has been providing a first response for people in crises related to mental health, homelessness, or substance use since 1989. In 2015, CAHOOTS expanded to neighbouring Springfield (population of 63,000).

"When a police officer goes and they look like me – gun, badge – it's a little bit demonstrative. And sometimes it has a tendency to escalate the situation," acknowledged Chief of Police Chris Skinner with the Eugene Police Department. "When somebody like CAHOOTS goes, where it's people that are just kind of dressed the same, they kind of look the same, they have a softer approach. It has a tendency to de-escalate those things."

"There are lots of these call types that are non-violent in nature. They're simply somebody crying out for help," said Benjamin Brubaker at White Bird Clinic, which runs CAHOOTS. "We need to change the way that our public safety systems work and see: how does public safety look through a different lens?"

When someone calls 911 or the non-emergency police line, dispatchers in the region are specially trained to use protocols with criteria that direct non-violent behavioural health calls to CAHOOTS. CAHOOTS teams carry a police radio, and calls are triaged so their most urgent calls (e.g., suicide risk) are addressed first.

This embedding within the emergency response system is important. In other words, police don't typically first arrive on scene and then call CAHOOTS or respond alongside CAHOOTS. Instead, the general model is that CAHOOTS teams are independently dispatched to their own calls.

If they feel the need, the CAHOOTS team can call for police backup, but that is incredibly rare. In 2019, CAHOOTS teams responded to around 24,000 calls. They only requested police to attend on scene 311 times, and only 8 per cent of those calls (25 calls, or roughly 0.1 per cent of all CAHOOTS dispatches) were for an immediate police emergency with lights and sirens. Backup calls were more likely for things like trespass that CAHOOTS was dispatched to address.

In practice, this means that on average 15–20 per cent of calls go to CAHOOTS as first responders. The Eugene Police say that 5–8 per cent of police calls are diverted to CAHOOTS, with the difference comprising things the police say they wouldn't typically respond to (e.g., a mother asking for help to take her and her son to a soup kitchen). In Eugene, the demand for CAHOOTS to respond to calls has almost doubled between 2014 and 2021.

CAHOOTS teams consist of two people: a crisis worker (who has substantial mental health training and several years of related experience) and a medic (a nurse, paramedic, or EMT). Before being placed on one of these teams, individuals must complete a 40-hour in-class program and spend 500–600 hours in the field. "Welfare checks," crisis counselling, suicide prevention, conflict resolution and mediation, supporting people suffering grief and loss, substance use issues, housing crises, first aid and non-emergency health care, transportation to other services, and referrals to other services are all aspects of what CAHOOTS covers. Teams also do outreach in the community and proactively help connect people with services.

One important aspect of their work is helping people who are disoriented, intoxicated, or showing signs of mental distress. None of the CAHOOTS teams carry weapons. Instead, they have medical equipment and harm reduction supplies, and use non-violent "trauma-informed de-escalation and harm reduction techniques" to resolve situations.

Importantly, CAHOOTS's services are voluntary for people to receive – they aren't coerced or forced. CAHOOTS teams are not dispatched for crimes, people who are potentially hostile, dangerous situations, or medical emergencies. However, the police also sometimes call CAHOOTS to assist on some of their calls to help with de-escalation, especially if there are mental health or sub-stance use issues involved. One of the aims of the program is that people can get help without becoming caught up in the criminal justice system.

"A team will respond, assess the situation and provide imme-diate stabilization in case of urgent medical need or psychological crisis, assessment, information, referral, advocacy, and, when war-ranted, transportation to the next step in treatment."

For example, rather than having police take an intoxicated per-son to a "drunk tank" (which we have seen in chapter 2 can lead to disruption of housing, loss of employment, and sometimes even death), CAHOOTS takes them to a 24/7 community-based "so-bering service" to safely be housed and monitored, without police involvement.

This non-police mobile crisis response is not only cost effective but generates net savings. While CAHOOTS has an annual budget of just US$2.1 million (funded by government funding and private donations), it is estimated to save the city of Eugene US$8.5 mil-lion in public safety expenditures annually. In contrast, the com-bined annual budgets for the Eugene and Springfield police are US$90 million. That means CAHOOTS is responding to up to a fifth of calls but with a budget that is a mere 2.3 per cent of the funding allocated to policing.

While a CAHOOTS crisis worker is paid just US$18 per hour (which amounts to US$37,440 if annualized), the starting base sal-ary for a Eugene police officer is US$65,832. As a result, despite its successes, the pay for CAHOOTS workers has been called inade-quate and there is high turnover.

In 2020, a US federal law created "988," a new three-digit na-tional phone number for suicide prevention and mental health crisis. There's also a push for more non-police mobile crisis response teams across North America. A small CAHOOTS-inspired pilot project in Denver, Colorado (population of 715,000), called Support Team Assistance Response (STARS), which only operated from 10 a.m. to 6 p.m. weekdays, has already shown "proof of concept" in diverting 3 per cent of police calls – none of which required police assistance and no arrests were made.

"STARS calls were focused in certain areas of the city, and most were calls for trespassing and welfare checks. Approximately 68% of people contacted were experiencing homelessness, and there were mental health concerns in 61% of cases – largely schizoaffective disorder, bipolar disorder, and major depressive disorder – with 33% of people having co-occurring conditions."

"There's a lot of energy around finding ways to do this based on the solutions that have been offered by models like CAHOOTS," said Professor Jamie Livingston, who is currently researching over one hundred non-police mobile mental health crisis response programs. For example, the City of Toronto started piloting the Toronto Community Crisis Service in 2022 in four areas of the city to offer a non-police response to people experiencing a mental health crisis and for "wellness checks." In its first six months it was already showing similar promising results to CAHOOTS. It all points to the need for a new approach.

"It's just so ludicrous that we've designed a system where the dominant way of responding to a mental health need is through the criminal justice system, when there's all sorts of other models that exist where that doesn't have to be the case, that are less traumatizing, that are better suited for people who are more often killed by the police, like people who are Indigenous and people who are Black, or people who have traumatic histories with the police," said Professor Livingston. "There's been a real upsweep in interest in reimagining mental health crisis response that doesn't involve the police."

A new transformative justice vision enhances safety for people with less police through a significant and fully resourced, 24/7, non-police mobile crisis response like CAHOOTS. In addition to responding reactively to 911 and non-police emergency calls, it would proactively do outreach and provide support as part of the public health and decriminalizing approach that I discussed in chapter 13. This would mean a corresponding reallocation of police funding and removal of police officers from these roles.

"If policing were the solution to crime, then more police should be associated with less crime. But the opposite is true. In 1991, there were slightly fewer police officers per capita in the United States than in 2017. Yet crime rates have declined without any major change in police numbers," according to Irvin Waller, emeritus professor of criminology at the University of Ottawa and author of *Science and Secrets of Ending Violent Crime.* "Clearly, the size of the police force does not correlate with violent crime rates in this important instance."

"England and Wales, for example, decreased the number of police by 22 percent through attrition and retirement without any direct impact on crime rates. So reacting to crime by spending more on policing is plain just not smart," added Waller. However, he notes that a certain minimum level of policing is needed and it should not be merely reactive. When there are no police (such as during police strikes in some jurisdictions) a short-term increase in property and violent crime is observed.

In a new transformative justice vision, police would no longer respond to a wide range of calls, but instead only respond to calls

involving criminal offences (which will be fewer due to the decriminalizing approach outlined in chapter 13) or where someone's safety or life is in jeopardy because of another person. I also
imagine non-police crisis teams being able to refer people to restorative justice (as in chapter 16) or, if they feel their lives or safety
or the lives or safety of others are threatened, to call for a police
response. However, as we have seen with CAHOOTS and STARS,
this is expected to be very rare. A new national three-digit non-
police crisis response number should also be created in Canada.

It comes as no surprise to learn that some police in Canada are not
supportive of a non-police model. They want to instead have a police
officer with a mental health worker. In other words, they still envision
having someone with handcuffs and firearms arriving at all calls.

"The first social worker that you send to that call and, god for-
bid us, somebody's killed or hurt badly, it's going back to the old
way. You know that, that's how all this stuff happens," said Edmonton's chief of police, Dale McFee. But Chief McFee's fears have not
been borne out in reality in over thirty years of non-police mobile
crisis response by CAHOOTS.

Of course, what Chief McFee described could happen, and it
would be tragic. But through proper training and use of criteria
for dispatching calls – along with being connected on the police
radio system to allow for immediate calls for backup – the risk of
such harm can indeed be managed. We have to also weigh the fact
that, as we have seen throughout part 1 of this book, police themselves are not safe for many people and have been involved in the
deaths of people on calls they respond to. Additionally, we need to
recognize the reality that health care work is already not a riskless
vocation. It is disheartening that 68 per cent of registered nurses
and support workers per year experience violence in their jobs.

Greater support is needed to protect them, but I bring this up to bring some context to Chief McFee's concerns that someone could be injured when responding to a non-police crisis call. Rather than fear driving policy, we need to look at what works.

"You know the police mandate fundamentally is enforcement orientated. You know, they're not social workers, they're not trained mediators, they're not trained conflict negotiators – I mean they get some training in these regards, but that's not fundamentally their mandate, right? So, we need to reduce our reliance on the criminal justice system as a response to so many social problems that have been downloaded on them from, you know, systematic defunding of other public sector agencies and other supports," said Professor Julius Haag.

Some parts of Canada had a short-term, unplanned experiment in de-tasking police during the COVID-19 pandemic. Professor Adelina Iftene explained that, in Nova Scotia, police were told not to bring people into custody unless it was a very serious crime, since there was limited space due to social distancing.

"What they ended up doing, they were calling all these organizations that we have that are finding housing for people that are criminalized," said Professor Iftene.

"So, first time ever that we're working with community groups is like, 'Oh, my god. I picked up this guy, was doing like a whole bunch of things, noise in the street and he's drunk. What do I do with him?' And instead of calling the police station or calling the prison, they would call these organizations because they knew that that was not an option. And when that option was removed, they all of a sudden found other solutions."

"And guess what? The crime rate did not increase. What did happen is that nobody died in a drunk tank as they used to die. We had two people dying in the drunk tank every year. Since COVID started, nobody died in the drunk tank because they haven't used it. It's mind blowing the things that have happened. So, they found solutions."

As with the CAHOOTS program, a new transformative justice vision would abolish police "drunk tanks" and instead provide community-based "sober services" where individuals with medical training would monitor and support people who were picked up for being publicly intoxicated and causing a disturbance. They would be provided with referrals for treatment and recovery instead of being criminalized and made subject to substance abstinence conditions, which, as we saw in chapter 2, do not work and only set people up to fail.

This new public health approach to these issues, rather than a criminal law approach, is also supported by expanding so-called "Good Samaritan" overdose laws, as I proposed in chapter 13, which legally protect people calling for help during an overdose event with immunity from prosecution for any non-violent offence and related breaches of conditions and warrants. Police should not be attending nonfatal overdose incidents at all – this directive should be respected by police and widely communicated in the community. The risk of police arriving on the scene of an overdose can deter reporting of these incidents by witnesses due to fear of prosecution, past negative encounters with police, outstanding conditions they may be under, and a general distrust of the authorities. Overdoses are medical events that need medical responses – they should not be treated as criminal incidents that need criminal responses. Fear of the police can literally be lethal.

———

A new transformative justice vision includes disadvantaged groups in community-level governance of public safety, including the authority of communities to de-task, disarm, replace, or re-task police services.

Not only can the movement towards non-police crisis responses help to more effectively and safely address mental health, substance use, and homelessness concerns, but it also has the potential to respond to grave concerns about the policing of Indigenous people, Black people, and people of colour. In chapter 18, I will further discuss Indigenous justice, including entirely removing settler police authority over Indigenous peoples.

In places like the Greater Toronto Area, where there are significant communities of people who are Black and people of colour, there is a need to give these groups a greater voice and role in governance of policing and policing practices, including over things like "street checks," use-of-force policies, strip search policies, patrols, policing oversight, transparency with data, training, hiring, and discipline, as well as policing tactics like "no knock" warrants (where police enter a residence unannounced – a practice that has been criticized for leading to deaths of Black people in particular).

"The basis of any effective strategy in the policing side of things has to be based on partnerships, on dialogue with community members, having community members as key stakeholders and determining the operational priorities and tactics of the police when they are used," said Professor Julius Haag.

"In the short to medium term, certainly reducing the scope and intensity of policing, increasing police accountability by having more commitment publicly in terms of transparency and conduct when it comes to police, having external bodies who are monitoring the police and having legal remedies in place to address

misconduct from the police that are not within the policing structure itself – because when it comes to our current police oversight
bodies, there is a real lack of confidence in these bodies to provide
effective oversight of the police."

Professor Haag also wants to see the massive imbalance in
funding between police departments and community-based organizations shifted to reflect the importance of the latter having a
greater role in community safety.

"The policing budget in Toronto being over a billion dollars a
year, but in my experience, community-based agencies that are on
the ground dealing with these issues on a day-to-day basis, often
operate on contingent or short-term funding. They operate on
two- or three-year funding mandates. They don't know when the
next project's grant is going to come. And there's very little stability
for them to do their work."

"I think the most effective street-level work [is done] without
government involvement. They're doing it without substantial operating funding, they're doing it through volunteers, they're doing
it through community-based supports."

"I would give that power back to the communities who are most
affected by the criminal justice policies because I think that's where
the answers are," agreed Professor Jamie Livingston.

"The set of violent offenders that exists there, you will need probably the police, and you would need them to respond properly to
that and to enforce the law, but certainly that wouldn't require the
amount of force and the amount of money that we currently have,"
said Professor Iftene. "I mean genuinely dealing with all the other options first before resorting to taking people to prison or in custody."

———

Victims of crime would also benefit from a reimagining of safety in our communities and how we achieve that safety in practical terms. Having non-police mobile crisis teams should also give people who have been harmed, or are at risk of being harmed, a non-police option. This could be especially valuable in situations involving someone looking to flee intimate partner violence.

This would represent a further expansion of the mandate of programs like CAHOOTS, requiring some additional training and the creation of referral arrangements with non-police victim services. Existing police-based victim services would transition to non-police victim services (presently there is a mix of the two, with non-police victim services having a long and successful track record).

It would be a powerful new way for victims to get the help and support they need if they are reticent to involve police for the multitude of reasons that we observed in chapters 8 and 9. The ability of such teams to give immediate physical, emotional, and psychological health support to victims, transport them to shelters or other victim services locations, and connect them with resources could be life changing for many survivors. Such a response would also have less potential to be traumatic and stigmatizing for survivors of sexual offences, intimate partner violence, and children witnessing these harms. A trauma-informed approach with non-police mobile crisis teams will also help prevent secondary victimization. Victims themselves can decide whether to contact a police or non-police response. They would have greater control and decision-making powers.

Under a new transformative justice vision, people who have been harmed or are at imminent risk of being harmed would be able to obtain a civil emergency protection order (EPO) when there is urgency and a serious risk to the safety, security, or property of a victim. These would be obtained in a similar way to emergency protection orders for domestic violence that are available in some provinces and territories – that is, available by phone from a justice of the peace on an *ex parte* basis (i.e., without notice to the person allegedly causing harm) and do not require police involvement (but could be made by a women's shelter staff member on the survivor's behalf, for example). These could be issued on the spot by the justice of the peace or within twenty-four hours.

An EPO could immediately give a victim legal protections including exclusive occupation of the residence (regardless of ownership or whose name is on the lease); directing a peace officer to remove the other party from the residence; directing a peace officer to accompany and supervise a specified person to remove personal belongings of the victim from the residence; restraining the other party from communicating with the victim or being within a certain distance from their residence, school, or work; surrendering firearms and weapons; temporary care and custody of children; and any other provision the justice of the peace considers necessary to immediately protect the victim.

To ensure fairness to the person against whom an EPO is ordered, it must be reviewed and confirmed by a judge within seventy-two hours. If the judge has doubts after this review, they can call for a hearing. The person against whom the order is issued can then, or at a later date, challenge the order to seek to have it varied or revoked. The person who sought the order can also ask to have it varied, revoked, or extended. So, there would be safeguards, but since these are civil orders and there are no criminal charges or criminal record involved, EPOs do not require the full panoply of rights that accused persons have under the *Charter*.

This strikes a better balance between the safety needs of victims and fairness to people subject to EPOs.

An EPO is typically issued for thirty to ninety days. It could be extended beyond this period if the grounds justifying its granting still apply. If there is no longer urgency, or there was no urgency to begin with, individuals can instead request a longer-term protection order (PO) where there are reasonable grounds to believe that there has been harm or risk to the safety, security, or property of a victim. These would be made with notice to the person against whom they are made so they could speak on those initial applications. Both the person applying for the order and the person against whom it would be made would be provided with legal counsel if they didn't have a lawyer.

Regardless of whether an EPO or PO is sought, neither would result in a criminal record. Both are granted where the civil standard of proof is met (that is, where a judge is convinced it is more likely than not that the criteria for an EPO or PO have been met, as compared to the higher criminal standard of proof beyond a reasonable doubt). It also does not necessitate police involvement, though a person who was harmed has the option to involve the police if they wish. Such EPOs and POs would help address issues raised in part 1 of this book, including a lack of meaningful protection for victims, secondary victimization, lack of access to justice, and the impact of criminal records.

If someone subject to an EPO or PO does not follow its stipulations, then the matter could be referred to a restorative justice process as set out in chapter 16. If the restorative justice process is unsuccessful – or if the infringement is very serious – the next step would be to resort to some of the additional measures discussed in chapter 17.

As more and more areas that have been dealt with by police are de-tasked from them, shifting to public health approaches and non-police responses, there will be a commensurate reallocation of police funding, reduction of officer numbers, and changes in related laws, regulations, and policies. The core of policing would be a narrower focus that is informed by trauma and overseen by the community. New and better non-police crisis responses would better meet the needs of a vast range of people caught up in the system presently.

Transformative justice puts a significant emphasis on non-state responses to violence. CAHOOTS is an example of an effective grassroots public safety initiative.

"I think that we've been too long socialized to believe that our government institutions hold the answers to our problems," said Professor Livingston, "when the answers are actually in the community."

CHAPTER SIXTEEN

Peacemaking and Accountability: Restorative Justice as the Primary Approach to Resolving Conflict

Dave looked in the mirror and could feel the rage welling up. The scars etched into the side of his face were a constant reminder of the night that Pierre struck him with a bottle at the bar, its broken glass leaving him permanently disfigured.

"There was much scarring and damage to his face when he first came to us to meet with us during the intake," said Kimberly Mann, executive director of Collaborative Justice Program: Restorative Justice Ottawa. "I mean he was very hostile, very angry – understandably, of course. He was filled with hate, he was just consumed with it."

Like Dave's physical injuries, his emotional wounds were raw and painful but more enduring. It's been said that "anger is an acid that can do more harm to the vessel in which it is stored than to anything on which it is poured."

Restorative justice is "a non-adversarial, non-retributive approach to justice that emphasizes healing in victims, meaningful accountability of offenders, and the involvement of citizens in creating healthier, safer communities." The Collaborative Justice Program is an example of an effective restorative justice program that deals with serious and violent offences. It began as a pilot program in 1999 and was later extended – but with scant funding, despite an evaluation commissioned by Public Safety Canada which found participating victims reported higher satisfaction, and offenders had lower rates of recidivism than those who went through the status quo criminal justice system.

The Collaborative Justice Program supported Dave and Pierre throughout the process, facilitating a back-and-forth sharing of information between them. Pierre showed great remorse for the harm he'd caused. He not only wrote multiple letters to Dave apologizing for what he'd done, he even wrote to Dave's parents and his sister apologizing for hurting someone they loved. Eventually, they met – something that doesn't always happen.

"It was very positive. I mean there was lots of tears shed, but some laughter also," said Mann. At one point during the circle, Dave was asked how he felt about the scars on his face.

"Well, this one used to really bother me," said Dave, moving his finger up to point at it. "No wait. It's … wait. I can't remember which side of my face it's on. Six months ago, I could've told you which side of my face it was on."

Dave still had the scar, but he had let go of it.

"I let go of my hate and anger," said Dave. "I got my spirit back."

Pierre had made amends in the way that Dave needed to heal the unseen wounds he'd been carrying. But Pierre was still facing criminal charges for the incident. It was a "wrong against the state," even though it was Dave's face that was cut open. Dave came to court as Pierre faced the charges.

"I don't want him to go to jail," Dave told the Crown prosecutor. "Jail's not going to help him, it's not going to help me. He's made it right with me, I don't need him to sit in jail."

You can already guess how the story ended. Pierre was sent to jail, albeit with a reduced sentence given his acceptance of responsibility. Yet he was exposed to the myriad harms, violence, new potential traumas, and failings of the corrections system that we saw in part 1 of this book. Rather than allow a cycle of violence to be put to rest through healing, our criminal justice system's response all but ensured it would continue.

Despite the decades-long success of the Collaborative Justice Program, it only has funding for three staff members. Yet it uses these humble resources to much better effect than the behemoth that is the criminal justice system. Dave and Pierre's story shows how the system is a juggernaut that rolls over efforts to do things differently, even when they have been proven to have better outcomes and cost less. In short, the seeds of restorative justice are given little chance to grow, being stifled and choked out by the system's thorny brambles.

———

"Our criminal justice system is supposedly restorative justice-based, but it's not. It's just not," said Skye. "We need to make more programs that kind of de-escalate this hatred towards offenders because it's really misplaced, and it is not helpful. And I feel we need to screen people who are in these jobs who are helping victims."

A new transformative justice vision creates opportunities to meaningfully address conflict in peaceful and restorative ways.

TABLE 4. *Aspects of Restorative Justice Practices*

- Focus on harms of wrongdoing more than the rules that have been broken;
- Show equal concern and commitment to victims and offenders, involving both in the process of justice;
- Work towards the restoration of victims; empowering them and responding to their needs as they see them;
- Support offenders while encouraging them to understand, accept, and carry out their obligations;
- Recognize that while obligations may be difficult for offenders, they should not be intended as harms and they must be achievable;
- Provide opportunities for dialogue, direct or indirect, between victims and offenders as appropriate;
- Involve and empower the affected community through the justice process, and increase its capacity to recognize and respond to community bases of crime;
- Encourage collaboration and reintegration rather than coercion and isolation;
- Give attention to the unintended consequences of our actions and programs; and
- Show respect to all parties, including victims, offenders, and justice colleagues.

Specifically, it would make restorative justice the primary way that interpersonal harms are addressed in most cases, based on established principles, including ensuring the safety of the person who was harmed and the voluntary participation of everyone involved.

Professor Howard Zehr, distinguished professor of Restorative Justice at Eastern Mennonite University's Center for Justice and Peacebuilding, is one of the founders of the restorative justice movement. Zehr explained three main drivers for why restorative justice emerged in the 1970s – each of them remains strikingly relevant today.

"One was the neglect of victims, and the traumatization or re-traumatization they often experienced in the justice process," said Zehr. "A second had to do with how we deal with offenders. We were convinced that offenders have deep denial processes, and that the legal system and the experience of prison tended to increase those denial mechanisms. We wanted a way to hold them accountable, in the sense of helping them to understand, to take some responsibility for what they were doing."

"And the third was the impact, and the involvement of, the community. We were concerned that justice not only did not reduce the tensions around the crime in the community, but often actually increased the conflicts and tensions around it. We felt that the community was often victimized and needed to have its needs addressed just like individual victims, but it also needed to be engaged in this process, and it needed to step up to the plate and accept its responsibilities."

Each of these three motivations for restorative justice were major themes in part 1 of this book. The sharp contrast between the status quo punitive legal system and restorative justice can be seen in the fundamental questions that they each ask in the aftermath of harm.

"In the legal system, we tend to ask, 'What laws were broken and who did it; what do they deserve?'" said Zehr. In restorative justice, the questions are instead: "Who has been harmed in this situation? What are their needs? Whose obligations are they?"

Restorative justice is generally recognized as having three overarching principles. First, restorative justice recognizes crime as "fundamentally a violation of people and interpersonal relationships." This means beginning with a recognition that people and communities have been affected, and the harm done to them must be addressed. Their role is central, while the state's role is minimal (i.e., supporting an investigation of what happened, facilitating the process, and ensuring people are safe). Notably, the state is not considered a primary victim in restorative justice.

"[U]nlike the criminal justice system where the victim is a witness to the crime against the state, in a restorative justice approach the harm to the victim is the starting point for recognition of the wrong and the search for a way to remedy it," wrote Professor Melanie Randall at Western University's Faculty of Law. "These empowerment elements include: psycho-education, provision of support, resources, options, opportunities to form a narrative of 'what happened,' and a view to how it affected the person in the various elements of their life."

The second key principle of restorative justice is that "violations create obligations and liabilities." In other words, the person who caused harm has a corresponding obligation to "make things right as much as possible." "Offenders are provided opportunities and encouragement to understand the harm they have caused to victims and the community and to develop plans for taking appropriate responsibility," explained Zehr.

The community also has obligations in restorative justice processes, being responsible for supporting people who have been harmed and those who caused them harm alike. A community is also responsible for "the welfare of its members and the social conditions and relationships which promote both crime and community peace." This differs from the status quo's hoisting 100 per cent of the blame onto people who commit offences, with zero acceptance of responsibility by society.

The third key principle of restorative justice is that it "seeks to heal and put right the wrongs" suffered, which involves engagement with those who have caused harm, suffered harm, and the broader community. Zehr explained that the research shows that "the more you involve victims and offenders in the outcomes, the more satisfied they are, and the more satisfactory the outcome."

Studies indicate victims report satisfaction in 75 per cent to 98 per cent of cases involving restorative justice. Again, this is at odds with the status quo (as we saw in chapters 8 and 9), where victims are often profoundly dissatisfied, marginalized, excluded, and further traumatized.

"There needs to be more of a role for victims. I think they need to be presented with more options of what can be done," said Skye, a survivor of intimate partner violence. "Testifying and then him being sent to prison, this is not so great either. What else is there? Could he go to a healing lodge? ... We need to be presented with more options and have a more active role as survivors of abuse or victims of any crime. Like, you need to have a role that helps you understand that the problem is getting better, or at least an effort is being made to making it better. And there needs to be more of a role that is conducive to healing in both parties."

Consensus between the people involved in the process prevails – not predetermined outcomes set by the state. The focus is on healing for everyone involved. Not on making a spectacle or example of the person who caused harm to deter others. Not on an uninvolved third party like a judge denouncing their conduct, but rather on having them accept responsibility for their own conduct. There's room for innovative, creative, and meaningful amends to be made – with people who have been harmed expressing both what they need and what terms and conditions of participation they want.

Of course, it may not always be in everyone's best interests – or even possible – for a victim and person who harmed them to collaborate in a restorative justice process. In these cases, a person who has been harmed or caused harm can participate in a "surrogate" victim/offender restorative justice dialogue, where they "meet with someone who committed a similar crime or who was similarly victimized, instead of meeting with the specific offender or victim in his or her case." Surrogates are used in restorative justice already. Meetings with surrogates "may also be helpful in preparing victims and offenders for an anticipated meeting at some point in the future." Surrogate victims would also be available where a victim could not be identified. Importantly, surrogate victims are not lawyers. They are not there to "make the case" against the person who caused harm but as fairly and reasonably as possible share the impact of the offence as understood by them, ideally with input from the actual victim, if they choose to do so.

Safety is another condition for restorative justice to be used. "The victim's concerns have to be accounted for and be made a priority during a restorative resolution as well," said Professor David Milward. "If you can't have that assurance that the person won't be a continuing danger to the victim and the victim's not going to feel safe – [that] there could be continuing danger – it may be an instance where you maybe shouldn't use restorative justice."

There is a significant body of research demonstrating "restorative justice programs are a more effective method of improving victim/offender satisfaction, increasing offender compliance with restitution, and decreasing the recidivism of offenders when compared to more traditional criminal justice responses."

A rich tradition of restorative justice approaches exists both globally and in Canada among Indigenous peoples and non-Indigenous peoples alike (particularly within faith-based communities). Healing and making peace are important values advanced through restorative justice along with mercy, reconciliation, and forgiveness. The relationality, compassion, and understanding fostered by restorative justice is inspiring. There are many details to work out to operationalize restorative justice on a broader scale – however, they are not insurmountable at all, and there's a vast body of literature to inform these decisions. At this point, we are focusing on the underlying philosophy and core principles of a new transformative justice approach.

Restorative justice is no gimmick. We can make it a reality as the central approach for the vast majority of harms in our society – both non-violent (which are the significant majority of offences currently) and even violent offences, as the Collaborative Justice Program in Ottawa has been doing for decades with success. There are courses, certificates, and professional training available for restorative justice practitioners widely available. In other words, we can have a high degree of confidence that restorative justice is up to the task of becoming the principal approach to addressing interpersonal harm in our society. Chapters 15 and 17 describe what a new transformative justice vision would do in cases where the safety of the victim or safety of the public cannot be fully addressed through a restorative justice process.

One critique of restorative justice that a new transformative justice vision directly addressed in chapter 14 is that it often provides inadequate support for victims. Studies have found that "[w]here offenders are provided with help to change their lives, but victims are not provided help to deal with their trauma, victims feel betrayed by the offender orientation of restorative justice." The new vision I've outlined instead begins with providing victims and perpetrators holistic support before restorative justice starts.

Kimberly Mann is excited about the prospect of having meaningful support for both those who were harmed and those who caused harm (i.e., victim services and offender services), before having them enter into a restorative justice process. The potential for even better restorative justice outcomes is significant as trauma begins to be addressed before meetings occur.

"[A]s a practitioner, I get a healthier offender who's being referred, I get a healthier victim who has already been receiving some support, and then I look after the communication between the parties. I mean, it seems to make sense."

———

"You know, I've been in and out of jail for ten years now. Since I was a teenager, I've been in provincial and federal institutions," said Derek, a twenty-five-year-old with a long history of substance use and a lengthy criminal record related to it. "This is the first time I've been held accountable."

Derek had broken into houses and cars, stealing things like hockey equipment and laptops to pay for street drugs. However, instead of being simply sent back to prison yet again, the half dozen victims who had been impacted agreed to participate in a restorative justice process with Derek.

"This case ended up in a circle with about five or six victims at one time," said Kimberly Mann. "It's addressing the harm that you've done, it's not being able to ignore, 'Oh yeah, they had insurance. They probably got new stuff. What's the big deal.' No, this is about hearing about how you hurt people, how when you took that laptop out of the guy's car, you took four years of his work and things like that, you know, that he didn't anticipate."

"Certainly, what we've heard when our program first started is that restorative justice is soft on crime. Anybody who's ever had to apologize to somebody, that's not easy. We had one offender say, 'You know, if I had known it was going to be this hard, I'd have taken the jail, you know,'" said Mann. "People feel badly, they have a need to apologize, especially if it was something that they did under the influence of alcohol or something."

"For victims, all of that can be quite healing," said Mann. "In the cases that we have where the accused is really, truly, truly remorseful and is willing to do anything, we found that the victims can be quite healed as a result."

The cost to taxpayers of just the time Derek spent in custody over ten years likely topped $1 million – not to mention the costs related to policing, prosecution, and the courts. None of the money spent had helped him or those he'd harmed. Restorative justice took less time, was a fraction of the cost, lacked the attendant harms of incarceration, and decreased the likelihood of Derek reoffending. Combine this with a public health approach to substances (chapter 13) and working to resolve underlying trauma (chapter 14), and you have a totally different approach to criminal justice with amazing potential for many people.

Despite a decade of being *punished* by the system, Derek said that he had never been *accountable* for how his conduct harmed others. Neither did his being incarcerated do anything to make amends for the harm he caused. But being in a circle surrounded by people he'd hurt, it finally came home to him.

"If any of us have had a conflict with somebody, that's what we need ... we want somebody to be accountable. We want to talk to them about it. We want an apology. We want them to make it right with us. We want to understand the context around what they were thinking. We want to be able to tell how it's impacted on us," said Kimberly Mann. "And so, it's what we should be doing when somebody has committed a criminal act."

Judge Barry Stuart, another early leader in the restorative justice movement, explained the way that restorative justice helps break denial structures that people who cause harm often have. "Only when an offender's pain caused by the oppression of the criminal justice system is confronted by the pain that victims experience from crime, can most offenders gain a proper perspective of their behaviour. Without this perspective, the motivation to success-fully pursue rehabilitation lacks an important and often essential ingredient." In other words, when we hurt people who have com-mitted crimes through harsh treatment and punishment, they may be rendered unable to have the capacity to understand the hurt they've caused others. This "compartmentalization" in thinking blocks meaningful accountability and restoration.

Making amends, including restitution, is also an important part of the process of healing for people who have been harmed, but also for those who caused them harm. It can restore a sense of dignity for everyone involved by redirecting internalized shame and allow people to move forward with their lives, as testified to first-hand by someone who had their conviction for a break and enter dealt with through a circle process.

"You know, at first I didn't even think about paying back any-thing, eh. Not the first time I've done a B&E and been to jail. But when the circle came up with that idea, at first I still didn't think much of it," said Darren, a twenty-one-year-old Indigenous man from Yukon. "But after I did it – felt good about it – you know, good about doing it – and good for me. Now, with them [the victims] accepting my apology, like, who could have ever believed that I'd get forgiven by them, eh? I feel like it's a new start with them – and for myself. My family was proud I worked to pay them back – so was I."

Being accountable for harming others and participating in a process with them to make it right as much as possible can contribute to transformation in the lives of people who have been harmed and caused harm. As Fritzi Horstman with Compassion Prison Project told me: "Accountability cancels shame." Even lawyers admit restorative justice may be a better way.

"I'm a big proponent of restorative justice – of people talking to each other, not talking at each other. 'Why did you do this? What happened?' Sitting down across from the person you hurt, looking in their eyes, not dodging their questions is a very transformative event," said a criminal defence lawyer.

"I was defending a young man charged with impaired driving causing death. The deceased was a passenger who was his best friend. The father of the deceased and the driver had restorative justice. The father went from literally wanting to kill the driver to becoming that person's best friend, to the extent he went to the parole hearing and asked for his release. He realized he saw his son in this man, and he basically adopted him as his own son. He's just a regular person. The father's son was the last person alive in his family: he had lost his wife to cancer, lost his daughter, this was the last member of his family who was killed by this impaired driver. When I saw this happen, it was really amazing."

———

While restorative justice would be the gateway to conflict resolution and the primary approach for addressing harm, there will inevitably be some situations where restorative justice is either unworkable or, after attempts, unsuccessful. For example, when either the person who was harmed or the person who caused harm refuses to participate, there is fundamental disagreement about whether the person actually caused harm or the extent of harm alleged, the person who caused harm is unable to accept responsibility, or a resolution is not achieved and the person who was harmed wants further steps to be taken.

In any of these instances, there would be a lack of meaningful accountability for the harm alleged, so further action could be necessary. Instead, a fact-finding and accountability process would be needed that is fair to the person against whom allegations have been made; this process also must not result in secondary victimization of the person who was allegedly harmed. The goals are resolving the conflict, bringing healing for everyone involved, and ensuring accountability of the person who caused harm towards those they hurt. There are many different forms this could take, but their success would be contingent on broader changes in the operation of the criminal justice system.

For example, one idea I could imagine when restorative justice has been unsuccessful would be for a conflict resolution committee, comprised of a team of professionals (e.g., a mental health and substance use professional, a social worker, and a victim services worker), to meet and make an assessment recommending which of three paths a person who allegedly caused harm would take. The goal would be to have the person who allegedly caused harm dealt with through the least serious means necessary to ensure healing and accountability for them, and healing and safety for the person they allegedly harmed and the community.

At the meeting of the conflict resolution committee, the person who was allegedly harmed would be able to share what happened and what they would like done about it. Affected community members could do the same. They wouldn't be subject to any form of cross-examination or the like. These views would then be shared with the person who allegedly caused harm, and they would have an opportunity to respond to the committee and share their views. This would be a less formal process where the conflict resolution committee would be encouraged to explore a mediated outcome in a community-type setting.

After hearing from everyone, the conflict resolution committee would proceed on one of three pathways for the person who allegedly caused harm: (1) a voluntary treatment and support plan developed without further monitoring by the committee; (2) voluntary acceptance of responsibility and an accountability and rehabilitation plan that is monitored by the committee; or (3) referral to police for investigation with charges approved by a prosecutor and tried in specialized courts with trauma-informed practice, where the accused is represented by legal counsel, where victims have substantive rights of participation, and where there are three possible verdicts (not guilty, likely guilty, or guilty beyond a reasonable doubt).

Pathway #1 would be a straightforward voluntary treatment and support plan for the person who caused harm. It would be documented to provide a degree of formality to it. There would be no criminal charges laid, no criminal record, and no conditions to be followed that are subject to threat of further state action. While support would already have been offered to both the person who allegedly caused harm and the person who was harmed (as outlined in chapter 14), for people who allegedly caused harm that weren't previously interested in that support, the committee's involvement could have some added encouragement and weight through this process to prompt them to begin their healing journey and take steps towards accountability for their conduct. The person who was allegedly harmed would continue to be supported throughout this process through holistic victim services as described in chapter 14.

Pathway #2 is a step up in that it involves the person voluntarily accepting responsibility for their alleged conduct and agreeing to participate in creating an accountability and rehabilitation plan. They would be supported in implementing the plan. If they do not follow that plan, they would be reassessed by the conflict resolution committee to determine if the plan should be changed, or the person given another chance, or if they should be escalated to be dealt with under the third option. Again, with Pathway #2, there are no criminal charges or criminal record, but (unlike Pathway #1) there is monitoring of following the plan to see if further interventions are needed. The primary outcome if the plan is not being followed would be first to assess the reasons why and see if the plan should be adapted or if further support is required. If the conflict resolution committee finds that the plan is being intentionally not followed, despite efforts to support the person to follow it, and those reasons are not attributable to a mental health or substance use disorder or disadvantage, then they can move the matter to the final pathway. Importantly, when it comes to substance use issues, the conflict resolution committee would have expertise to understand that relapses are an expected part of the recovery process and not at all necessarily indicative of fault, instead requiring understanding and further support.

The most serious option is Pathway #3, used only when neither of the other two options are adequate (i.e., where Pathways #1 or #2 are inappropriate or unsuccessful; there are fundamentally contested facts of whether harm was done or the extent of it, the committee considers there to be a significant risk to the victim's safety or public safety, or the conduct of the person shocked the conscience of the community). Importantly, nothing that the person who allegedly caused harm said – during any early efforts to resolve the matter through any prior restorative justice processes or before the conflict resolution committee – could be used against them at this stage.

Pathway #3 consists of a referral of the matter to police for investigation for potential criminal prosecution in specialized courts with judges and lawyers trained in trauma-informed practice. Under this option, police can recommend charges, which must then be reviewed by a prosecutor before the charges are laid (i.e., "charge approval"). If charges are laid, both accused persons and victims would also have the right, if they choose, to be represented by a lawyer (publicly funded, if necessary). Victims could choose to participate in proceedings, along similar lines of forums like the International Criminal Court and some civilian jurisdictions, by making submissions, introducing evidence, and cross-examining witnesses. Rules of procedure and evidence would be significantly simplified. The victim could choose whether to participate or testify as a witness or not – it would be entirely at their discretion. The victim would be entitled to have any of the testimonial aids that they wanted (e.g., testifying behind a screen, by closed-circuit television from another location, with a support person, with a publication ban, not having the accused personally cross-examine them, etc.). The verdict would be either not guilty, likely guilty (civil standard of a balance of probabilities), or guilty beyond a reasonable doubt (criminal standard of proof beyond a reasonable doubt).

An accused who is not guilty would have nothing further occur. An accused found "likely guilty" would not receive a criminal record but could be subject to a civil protection order if the victim desires (see chapter 15), required to complete community service, or ordered to pay restitution to the victim (if they have the means to pay).

An accused person found guilty beyond a reasonable doubt could be subject to any of the same consequences as someone found "likely guilty" and, if there's a risk of safety to the victim or public, to supervision in the community. If there is a significant risk of harm to the victim or public that cannot be managed under community supervision, the person who caused harm would be separated from society for the minimal time that is necessary in a healing and rehabilitation centre – traditional prisons and jails being abolished (as I'll discuss in the next chapter). Separation from society could also be needed if the harm to the victim and community was so egregious that it shocked the conscience of society – a very high standard.

I emphasize that this is just one idea of many that we could imagine to better reflect the values of this new approach guided by compassion, understanding, healing, peacemaking, and accountability. Values that the status quo is lacking entirely.

CHAPTER SEVENTEEN

Rehabilitation and Healing: Abolition of Traditional Prisons and Jails

Gardening, strumming a guitar, going to a yoga class, playing volleyball, making ceramics, baking a birthday cake, playing a game of cards, having a visit from distant family, learning how to fix a car, journaling, going for a stroll among the silver birch and placid pine trees.

Eyes on fire from pepper spray, bruised wrists from handcuffs put on too tight, vomiting from withdrawal, being stabbed, being mocked and ridiculed by guards while naked in an open area shower, drinking methadone someone else vomited up to get a buzz, witnessing someone being beaten into a bloody pulp.

The first set of events describes the experience of people in custody in Norway's Halden maximum-security prison. The second is what I personally heard time and again from those who have spent time in Canada's prisons and jails. And, unsurprisingly, the divergence in the outcomes of these two approaches is just as stark.

"The basic question that we ask ourselves in Norway: 'what kind of neighbour do we really want?' Because they could move into my neighbourhood, and they could move into your neighbourhood. That should have an influence [on] how we work inside prisons," said Jan Strømnes, deputy governor of Halden Prison. "The most important thing is how we treat people."

Halden opened in 2010 and has been called the "most innovative" and "most humane" prison in the world. To be sure, Halden has a secure perimeter, including a twenty-five-foot unpolished concrete wall rising from the ground with security cameras. But the award-winning architecture of the place is designed to blend in with foliage and trees so it feels less like a prison when you're inside it.

In the 1980s and early 1990s, the recidivism rate for Norwegian prisons was around 60–70 per cent. Their focus was on security and punishment. Conditions were hard, as is typical of traditional prisons and jails. There were riots, and two prison guards were killed. It was a wake-up call. Norwegian authorities admitted that their system wasn't working, and it was time for a new path. They abandoned being "tough on crime" in favour of a more humane approach. A fundamental shift was made to focus on rehabilitation and healing.

"We make sure an inmate serves his sentence, but we also help that person become a better person," said Are Høidal, governor of Halden Prison. "We are role models, coaches, and mentors. And since our big reforms, recidivism in Norway has fallen to only 20 per cent after two years and about 25 per cent after five years." This means that significantly fewer people are reoffending when compared with the discredited, costly, and ineffective "tough on crime" approach. What's behind the success of Halden?

Halden recognizes that people who are separated from society will eventually return to the community. This includes people who have committed serious violent crimes. So, it is both in their best interests and the best interests of society that they get the support they need. Halden's approach is both pragmatic and humanitarian.

In Norway, depriving someone of their liberty is already considered a form of punishment, so people aren't deprived of other rights while in custody. Other than the restrictions placed on their mobility through their confinement, they have the same rights as other people living in Norway. And Halden is committed to the principle that people shouldn't "serve their sentence under stricter circumstances than necessary for the security in the community."

Four key principles are at work in Halden: normality, humanity, dynamic security, and an emphasis on reintegration. The principle of normality means that living conditions mirror life on the outside as much as possible, with prisoners able to cook their own food, shop at the commissary store, and wash and wear their own regular clothes. As mentioned, the architecture and physical environment is also designed to put people at ease. Other than the outer perimeter, the look and feel inside is that of a trendy hostel. This is very intentional, with the idea being that a more tranquil environment will minimize the sense of being imprisoned, reduce aggression, improve relationships, and provide a place more conducive to healing.

In a typical day at Halden, residents wake up at 7:00 a.m., with everyone released from their cells at 7:30 a.m. for breakfast. Tasks for the day are reviewed and distributed. Starting at 8:15 a.m., residents participate in educational activities or work throughout the day. Residents and officers even eat meals together.

Halden's activities are structured with an emphasis on learning that will lead to meaningful employment. Residents take skill-based programs and certification for a range of vocations, including carpentry, auto mechanics, woodworking, restaurant and food processing, metalworking, welding, graphic design, and electronics. There are also language courses (English and Norwegian), information technology, music, and support to complete high school and prepare for further education. Halden residents even run their own restaurant and have published their own cookbook.

A study found that, among people who were unemployed prior to going to Halden Prison, after release there was a 40 per cent increase in employment rates (over a five-year period).

The second principle, humanity, is about being treated with kindness, dignity, and respect. Interactions with staff are based around these concepts. Treating residents in this way serves as the basis for everyone's safety, doing the work of healing and rehabilitation for entry back into society. It also helps give residents a sense of hope.

"To me, the most dangerous man on the planet is a man that doesn't have hope," said Fritzi Horstman.

Traditional maximum-security prisons and jails like those in Canada rely heavily on physical security measures like multiple locked doors, metal bars, and use of force including restraint equipment, physical handling/control, chemical or inflammatory agents (e.g., pepper spray), batons, intermediate weapons, displaying or using firearms, and intervention by Emergency Response Teams. In contrast, the "dynamic security" of Norwegian prisons (their third defining principle) is about having positive interpersonal relationships between officers and residents.

Every resident at Halden has their own primary "contact officer" who is only responsible for two to three people. They're much more like personal social workers than guards. "Guards and prisoners are together in activities all the time," said Are Høidal, governor of Halden Prison. "They eat together, play volleyball together, do leisure activities together and that allows us to really interact with prisoners, to talk to them and to motivate them."

Officers at Halden are also trained completely differently for this role than in traditional prisons and jails. In Canada, corrections officers only require a high school diploma, First Aid, and a CPR course. They receive four weeks training by e-learning, spend two to four weeks doing assignments, and twelve to thirteen weeks of in-person training with a heavy emphasis on use of force, focusing on "law and policy, use of firearms, chemical and inflammatory agents, fire safety, self-defence and arrest and control techniques, use of batons as a defensive technique, suicide prevention, [and] the Engagement and Intervention Model." Once this is complete, they are given a start date. The contrast with Norway's approach couldn't be greater.

"Creating good relationships with inmates is an important part of being a contact officer. Good conversations are our best weapon," said Maria Frøvik, a contact officer at Halden. "Although there have been tense situations, I've never been afraid. I am confident in our security procedures. If I were to experience a situation so threatening that I had to trigger the alarm, my colleagues would be with me within seconds. And I am certain that many of the inmates would also help me. This is because we are always building trust and relationships between employees and inmates, which is also an important element of our security procedures."

Norwegian contact officers like Frøvik are required to have post-secondary education from a university or college. Officers undergo a rigorous two-year training program covering law, psychology, criminology, communication techniques, conflict resolution, safety, ethics, human rights, professionalism, values, cultural understanding, mental health, and understanding the effects of isolation. They also learn self-defence and extraction techniques, but that is a small part of their overall lengthy training.

Norwegian prison guards are expected to be respectful, help to give residents hope, and keep people busy doing productive things. There's an understanding that people are more likely to reoffend if sentences are lengthy, conditions are harsh, strict discipline is used, or there's frequent sanctions like cancellation of phone calls or visitors. Violence and use of force is rare. Officers don't carry batons or wear Kevlar vests. The relationships that get formed in this environment can make a big difference.

"There was an inmate who I had formed a strong connection with who had cut himself through self-harming, and who wanted to talk to me afterwards," said contact officer Frøvik. "[I] made a difference to him by giving him hope. This was an experience that made me understand that this is not just a job, but that I am also an important supporter for people in difficult situations." This caring response stands in stark contrast to what Dr. Ivan Zinger revealed in chapter 3 about an Indigenous woman in a Canadian prison who was self-harming. She was instead isolated in a room alone and then pepper-sprayed when she continued to hurt herself.

It's been said that while most prisons try to keep you in, Halden is designed to get you out. This means that contact officers not only play games with residents but help them to develop and implement their own personal rehabilitation plans. Contact officers get to know them well. They help them complete applications, encourage them, assist them with networking, and connect them with supports and resources in the community.

Residents are able to participate, both on their own and in groups, in a wide range of programs at Halden to help them address the underlying issues that contributed to their harming others. This includes programs dealing with relationships and cohabitating, parenting while in prison, general parental guidance, substance abuse, coping with stress, anger management, breaking out of a criminal lifestyle, managing personal finances, conflict resolution, sports leadership, choosing your path, and other topics. Thirty different instructors participate in program delivery.

Norway's prisons are generally small capacity, typically with only 100 people. Halden is the second largest, with a capacity of 250. This has some big advantages, including keeping residents closer to their families, allowing them to maintain and support important social connections. By contrast, some Canadian jails have a capacity of over 1,000.

Separating someone from society is the last resort in Norway. Other responses to criminal convictions include low-security facilities (including halfway houses), a sentence served in an organization other than correctional, an electronic bracelet monitoring sentence, a community sentence, drug programs with court control, and probation.

———

"I think we'll look upon the way we treat prisoners one day the way we look upon a previous generation and how they invented the idea that a woman was a witch and treated her as such and burned her," said Michael Bryant with the Canadian Civil Liberties Association.

"We have to change the whole approach," said James Bloomfield, Prairies regional president for the Union of Canadian Correctional

Officers and a federal correctional officer with the Correctional Service of Canada. "We can keep doing what we're doing, but we're not doing anything different in the basics. Like when you sit and write it down, that's the same damn thing we've been doing for one hundred years. It's just less archaic in the way we're doing it right now. It doesn't make any difference and our results aren't changing. Nothing is changing."

"Just as the size of the police force does not correlate with rates of violent crime, incarceration also does not correlate with violent crime reduction," according to Professor Emeritus Irvin Waller. "If incarceration were the major contributor to safer communities, the United States, which incarcerates 20 per cent of everyone in the world behind bars, would be the world's safest affluent country. It is not."

"I used to believe that we can change the current system, but I've been working for too long with Correctional Service Canada to believe the best possible anymore," said Professor Adelina Iftene. "[T]here have been more than a few times when I thought you just need to put this into the ground and start from ground zero.'"

There was even support for taking a different approach to corrections among victims of crime I interviewed, including Skye, a survivor of domestic violence.

"I certainly don't like the idea of prison at all. In an ideal world it wouldn't exist," said Skye. "I don't think it's feasible to just remove them, however there is room for drastic improvements. There are many countries that are doing it really well. There are very low rates of recidivism. They actually rehabilitate their prisoners and they treat them with respect and give them responsibility and they encourage learning. ... We need to develop a better system that doesn't screw people up so much."

A new transformative justice vision would abolish traditional prisons and jails. It would significantly expand community-based alternatives to incarceration that support rehabilitation and healing. And it would only separate people from society as a last resort if there is a significant risk of harm to the victim or public that cannot be managed under community supervision, or the harm done was so egregious that it shocks the conscience of society (i.e., if reasonably informed members of the public would consider a non-custodial sentence to be grossly unjust). Separation from society would be in secure rehabilitation and healing centres, similar to Halden in Norway. As I discuss in the next chapter, Indigenous peoples would have self-determination over justice – including corrections – for their Nations' citizens.

Throughout my interviews with criminal justice practitioners and people with lived experience who have spent decades in Canada's prisons and jails, there were resounding calls to radically change our approach towards incarceration. Again and again, people pointed me to Norway's approach as something Canada should use as a starting point to be further improved upon and tailored to the Canadian context.

"Well, I did mention the Scandinavian countries," said Dr. Ivan Zinger, Correctional Investigator of Canada. The key aspects he highlighted were a "much higher trained, educated workforce," "they see use of force as a failure," "they focus on de-escalation," and "their perimeter fences are very strong, but inside their penitentiary there is a lot less harshness. They try [to] normalize the environments better."

"I think those are the kinds of models that we should be looking at," said Dr. Zinger. "Corrections is not law enforcement and that's where the orientation – certainly during the Harper years – is, a law enforcement model, as opposed to a truly correctional rehabilitative model that Canada needs."

Howard Sapers, a criminologist who was former regional vice-chair of the Parole Board of Canada, recommended that places of detention be "very porous to the community. It'd have to be as normalized an environment as possible. People would have rooms, not cells. There would be opportunities to spend time with family or to maintain contact with community." He too highlighted key aspects of the Norwegian approach, including its architecture, recreation, programming, health care, and treatment opportunities.

Even most "prison abolitionists" concede that there will still be a need for a small number of people to be separated from society for safety reasons. But in this new transformative justice vision, even in these cases, the conditions would be much more humane and geared towards their rehabilitation.

People with lived experience in Canada's prisons and jail spoke powerfully to me about how they would like to see things change. I could hear their despair, frustration, anger, and hopelessness. But, with those emotions, I could grasp their wisdom regarding what needs to be done differently. Here's a glimpse of what I heard from several different folks:

"Honestly, the CSC, like they really gotta fucking really look at their fucking rules and regulations. Honestly, their whole system is just a big mess. I don't know. This is just from my personal experience, right?"

"Jail is not the answer. … [L]ike you release them and they go back on the street. They have no homes. You can't release people with no supports. You just can't do that. I mean it's common sense."

"They could do a lot of things different, really. I don't know. They need to be more helpful. … [Y]ou should be able to go out to work. It's something. Imagine, people have families at home. And now, we're in jail, and we can't provide for our family. So, it's a hard thing there."

"Well, you're just throwing good money on top of fuckin' bad money, right? The Canadian government, I mean I don't know what the budget is for CSC or criminal justice in general, but I've got to say it's probably a good penny. It's some serious money. So, what, would you keep throwing something in a fuckin' hole hoping to see a return on what you're putting in? You're not getting anything from it."

"When you come out of custody, the access to services is so limited. You don't know who to connect to, you don't know where to connect. The wait lists are insane. You have a criminal record, so that makes things harder. We need a place, a hub, an anything that can help our people coming out of custody [and that] they can go to. Get their ID, get help with housing, get connected to an addiction counsellor, somewhere that is central and accessible."

"I think the staff needs to have some trauma-informed care, some addictions training. And at the end of the day, remembering that we're human beings and just giving those extra supports is going to make all the difference. And it costs a whole [lot] less for someone to see a counsellor than for them to sit in jail, so give them that trauma therapy or whatever it is. So, if the government's concern is finances then maybe they should weigh the options of helping someone as opposed to punishing them."

The other people who have spent the most time in Canada's places of confinement – corrections officers – look with awe at what is being done in some progressive European countries.

"I'm not saying theirs is right or wrong, I'm just saying I look at that model and they've gone from an approach that is very old school. A similar base approach like the rest of the world – lock them up and move them when you have to – to such a process where it is all about trust and being open all day and not being locked up all day," said James Bloomfield.

While there was widespread support among the people whom I interviewed for a Nordic, specifically Norwegian, approach to separating people from society when strictly necessary, I also heard some constructive criticism about how this could be made even better.

"Everybody's hailing the Nordic system as being like so amazing and so great. They do certainly do a better job than us, but they also rely on very extensive periods of isolation and solitary confinement," said Professor Iftene. "The person is made extremely comfortable in their room, but it's still in one room by themselves. So, I'm not sold. I haven't seen a system [to adopt]. Certainly, there are systems that are less reliant on incarceration, including the Nordic systems. So those are certainly positives, but in terms of actually seeing an institutional model and looking at it and saying, 'Wow, you're doing such a great job' – I don't think I've seen one."

Professor Iftene's words of caution mean that, while Norway's approach is a good source of inspiration, it is not an end point, but rather a helpful waypoint along the road. Additionally, Canada's settler colonial context has far-reaching implications for reimagining criminal justice, as discussed in the next chapter. Whenever someone is separated from society, we have all failed in some way. It underscores that the other key features of a new transformative justice approach are so crucial, particularly its proactive and preventive aspects, like supporting early childhood development and investing in social determinants of justice.

———

Another aspect of a new transformative justice vision is reducing reliance on separating people from society altogether – or "de-carceration." "When you look at the *Criminal Code*, you'd be hard-pressed to find an offence for which jail isn't a possibility," said Professor David Milward. "So, there's questions about the breadth to which incarceration is being used as a recourse."

As I noted in chapter 7, literally every offence in the *Criminal Code* – and tens of thousands of other federal and provincial offences – carries the prospect of imprisonment, even for minor offences. Imprisonment is threatened at nearly every turn.

In addition to decriminalizing people who use drugs and experience poverty or homelessness in favour of a public health approach (as discussed in chapter 13), we need to drastically reduce – and even eliminate – the availability of imprisonment for non-violent offences, in favour of other outcomes, such as those described in the last chapter (i.e., resolving them through peace-making and non-custodial forms of accountability). All of these, along with the other aspects of a new transformative justice vision, would significantly reduce the number of people in custody. And those who remain a significant risk to victims or the public, or whose conduct is so heinous as to shock the conscience of society, would be separated in humane conditions in institutional settings similar to Halden that focus on rehabilitation and healing.

There's also a need for enhanced community-based alternatives to incarceration for people who have risks that can be managed while they remain in the community. However, in implementing these measures, we need to ensure we do not further broaden the scope of surveillance on people. To begin with, no one should be in custody on account of them not having a place to live, a person to vouch for them as a surety, or money for bail. A new transformative justice system would instead provide appropriate monitored housing with regular check-ins, up-to-and-including electronic monitoring, but only if strictly necessary. And the focus of these efforts would be on rehabilitation. As less restrictive safety measures are made available we must guard against them being used to expand state control over people.

A new transformative justice vision would significantly expand and improve community-based alternatives to incarceration that would support rehabilitation and healing. This could include a number of options to address potential residual risks to public safety, such as supervision in adequately funded and resourced halfway houses with meaningful programming, a sentence administered by a community-based organization, and electronic bracelet monitoring (but only where strictly necessary).

I asked André Poilièvre, co-founder of STR8 UP (which we learned about in chapter 14), what he'd do if he could reimagine criminal justice. "It would look like STR8 UP with a therapeutic centre attached to it, with a physical program for guys to be physically fit. So, there'd be an educational component, there'd be a physical component. There'd be opportunities for guys to share their emotions. And there'd be a spiritual component. So that's what it would look like. It would attempt to assist the guys to learn how they do things, how they think, how they feel, and who they are. That would be my world. Nothing to do with, you know, with like solitary," said André.

"You know, putting guys in solitary and remand and all that stuff, that doesn't help. None of that stuff helps. Treat them like citizens."

CHAPTER EIGHTEEN

Indigenous Justice

"You need to give a shit." Those were the last words that I remember Harold Johnson say publicly before he died.

I'd invited Harold to give a lecture to the entire first year class at UBC law. They needed to hear about his experience as an Indigenous Crown prosecutor and criminal defence lawyer. His lament about how despite his hope of changing the system, it changed him. His righteous anger over the devastation and harm the system is causing Indigenous people. But most of all, they needed to hear what he thought should be done about it.

I had no idea at the time, but Harold already had advanced lung cancer. He passed away three months later on February 9, 2022 – but not before taking the opportunity to once again plead his case for Indigenous justice.

"To Indigenous peoples across Canada, I remind you, you do not need permission to create your own justice systems," said Harold, pointing out that Indigenous peoples already have the resources,

Elders, Knowledge Keepers, lawyers, judges, court workers, and police to "work for the people instead of against the people."

Replacing deterrence with redemption is the way forward, according to Harold. For those who cause harm and are "unwilling to accept responsibility for their actions, to apologize and work at making things right," there would still be removal from society – but that would be far fewer people. He's under no illusion about the uphill battle that such a change will take.

"But it's not going to happen overnight, we're not going to get rid of the colonial system and replace it immediately," Harold told me. He explained that, as Indigenous communities begin to revitalize their own legal systems, they can gradually start taking cases that they are comfortable taking on. "Over time, they will become more and more comfortable handling more and more complex cases until our system eclipses the colonial system. That's how I'm imagining going forward." Harold is not alone.

In 1999, the Report of the Aboriginal Justice Inquiry of Manitoba concluded that "[s]imply providing additional court services in Aboriginal communities or otherwise improving what is inherently a flawed approach to justice is not, in our view, the answer." Instead, the commission recommend "the establishment of Aboriginal justice systems in all Aboriginal communities, operated and controlled by Aboriginal people," including a fully functional legal system complete with policing, justice services, courts, and support services.

"It's time for Indigenous people to take the driver's seat," said Renzo Caron, provincial director of Indigenous justice centres at the BC First Nations Justice Council, and a member of the Sagamok Anishnawbek First Nation.

"I want to see a completely sovereign and self-determining Indigenous justice system where we're in control. We write the laws.

We have the courts. We have the police – what we would call like warrior societies – that uphold the laws, and we run our own justice system, not based on the principles of punishment and deterrence but like based on our own principles," said André Bear, a Nêhîyaw (Plains-Cree) writer and advocate of inherent and treaty rights.

A new transformative justice vision recognizes and supports the revitalization of Indigenous laws and legal orders and affirms the inherent right of Indigenous peoples to self-government and self-determination in criminal justice matters. That includes the right to decide on their own laws, their own dispute resolution forums, their own peacekeeping, and their own remedies for harm, all in their own languages. It would also include fully implementing the 94 calls to action of the Truth and Reconciliation Commission and the 231 calls for justice of the National Inquiry into Missing and Murdered Indigenous Women and Girls.

"You should just basically try something more bold and giving the driver's seat to Indigenous communities to do it themselves would probably foster that result," said Dr. Ivan Zinger. "And even if there are some mishaps, it can't be worse than what is going on right now."

Canada is recognized as having "three founding peoples": Indigenous, French, and British. While French civil law applies in Quebec and English common law applies in the rest of Canada, Indigenous laws have been suppressed. A new transformative justice vision would right this wrong so that the first founding peoples of Canada would have their laws gain the recognition they deserve. A "plurinational state" is the concept towards which Canada should strive as it moves forward in a nation-to-nation relationship with Indigenous peoples as they have an inherent right to self-government and self-determination.

Some Indigenous peoples in other settler societies already have a long history of operating their own legal systems, including with criminal law jurisdiction. Notably, the American tribal court system, including the Northwest Intertribal Court System in Washington state, serves Indigenous populations of between two hundred to five hundred people (similar in size to many First Nations in Canada) with small reservations.

"In the United States, while tribal courts were initially designed to assimilate Indigenous peoples, tribes are slowly subverting these plans and are making courts vehicles for self-determination," wrote Professor John Borrows, Loveland Chair in Indigenous Law at the University of Toronto, Faculty of Law. "Congress has recognized their importance for maintaining law and order for many years. In fact, Congress recently passed the *Tribal Law and Order Act* to strengthen Tribal Courts and thereby more effectively confront public safety challenges facing reservation communities." These tribal courts "are strong evidence that separate Aboriginal justice systems are possible and practical" wrote the Aboriginal Justice Inquiry of Manitoba.

In 2021, the US Supreme Court recognized in *United States v. Cooley* that Indigenous tribal police officers have the authority to detain non-Indigenous individuals where it is necessary to "address 'conduct [that] threatens or has some direct effect on … the health or welfare of the tribe.'" This further demonstrates the feasibility of empowering Indigenous peoples in the criminal sphere. But there is a need for greater coordination and collaboration between Indigenous and non-Indigenous police forces in the US.

In Canada, we have already seen real-world examples of Indigenous peacekeeping in policing and Indigenous-led healing lodges in corrections in chapter 7. These efforts should be substantially funded, not just at levels comparable to the equivalent non-Indigenous institutions, but with a higher level of investment due to the greater needs arising from the ongoing impacts of colonialism, need for capacity building and expansion, and to reflect the rural, remote, and/or dispersed urban populations that they would serve.

Unfortunately, Canada is off to a lethargic, tentative start in supporting Indigenous justice. In January 2023, Minister of Justice and Attorney General of Canada David Lametti announced $1.5 million for the Métis Nation as part of $11 million in total funding for developing Indigenous justice strategies. The total amount is so small that it is akin to a rounding error in the federal budget and represents a mere 0.04 per cent of the budget of the settler criminal justice system. The amount allocated to the Métis Nation is less than the lifetime criminal justice expenditures for just one high-risk offender.

Is this the start of transformative change? Or another example of the system making the bare minimum adaptations to whitewash it enough to keep on going? Given the track record of chronic underfunding of Indigenous-led policing and corrections that we observed in chapter 7, this seems like more of the same from the federal government. And the funding could dry up quickly if there's a change in government. Yet that isn't dissuading Indigenous leaders from moving ahead.

"It's re-assuming jurisdiction over the criminal justice system for the Métis Nation," said Cassidy Caron, president of the Métis National Council. She emphasized that the revitalization of Métis legal systems means an emphasis on restorative justice and rehabilitation, rather than punishment. "We'll be moving forward on it regardless of what government is in place."

While the historical, moral, and practical imperatives necessitate change, there will be many issues to resolve in this era of the resurgence of Indigenous justice. As Professor David Milward at the University of Victoria, Faculty of Law, a member of the Beardy's & Okemasis First Nation in Saskatchewan, points out: "the fact of the matter is that everybody is interconnected to some degree or another. So, you can't ... just create silos out of Indigenous communities. But, at the same time, I do think there are some real potential roles for Indigenous legal orders to emerge and to actually provide some more constructive approaches to these issues."

For some Indigenous Nations, revitalizing their criminal justice system has had to take a back seat to other, more acute community crises. "Criminal justice is a difficult thing to take on, and it is often – from a perspective of a community – it's one of the last things," said Jonathan Rudin, program director at Aboriginal Legal Services. "You know, you don't have clean drinking water, you don't have a lot of access to education. Is justice your number one thing? Maybe not, and maybe as much as you don't like the current system, you don't really have the resources to address someone who is either a nuisance or more a danger to people."

Another major theme that emerged in my research was that the revitalization of Indigenous justice is not a romanticized going back in time to the pre-contact era. All laws change and adapt to our ever-changing world.

"We need to create something new – just take what we can from the past and take what we can to revitalize," said André Bear. "Use our language, our values, and all of that, but take the best from the future too. Take what's working in Denmark, in Norway, and Sweden and all of these places who are doing the justice system right and try to create something new."

I am sure that some will object to the idea of Indigenous peoples exercising criminal law and criminal justice jurisdiction, based on the idea that Canada should have one system for everyone and that, if we have different systems based on nationality, then that is discriminatory and wrong. My first reply would be we already have different systems in practice now: the research and lived experience shared in chapters 4, 5, and 7 demonstrates that Indigenous peoples are subject to a functionally different justice system due to systemic racism, and it has had devastating effects. Second, as I have demonstrated above and in chapter 7, Indigenous peoples are distinct in that they are Nations within Canada. It is incumbent that they be recognized as such. Finally, the French civil law system has been operating smoothly alongside the English common law system for centuries. It is time that Indigenous peoples are able to have this same opportunity.

———

Indigenous laws speak to how harm and wrongdoing can be addressed and reveal how these diverse approaches contrast sharply with the settler criminal justice system. Before looking at some examples of this, a word of caution:

"When working with Indigenous legal traditions one must take care not to oversimplify their character," wrote Professor John Borrows. "Indigenous legal traditions can be just as varied and diverse as Canada's other legal traditions, although they are often expressed in their own unique ways." What appears below should accordingly be seen as the smallest glimpse into the different worldviews reflected in just a few of the laws of some Indigenous peoples.

"In our community, it's called *Skén:nen Aonsón:ton*," said Chief Peacekeeper Zacharie, meaning: "'To Become Peaceful Again.' It is the process within the Kahnawà:ke Justice System that is used to resolve and rectify criminal and civil conflict in a peaceful, non-adversarial way."

The *Kahnawà:ke Justice Act*, which is based on inherent rights, institutes several judicial forums within the Territory to "maintain peace, order and justice." Skén:nen Aonsón:ton Alternative Dispute Resolution is a process that marks the "entry point for the Kahnawà:ke Justice System" to address all "situations of conflict." It can take the form of restorative justice, mediation, peacemaking circles, or other approaches. Legal counsel is generally excluded. The *Kahnawà:ke Justice Act* also institutes an Administrative Tribunal and the Court of Kahnawà:ke, which is "the court of original general jurisdiction within the Territory in all civil, criminal and penal matters." There is also a Kahnawà:ke Court of Appeal. Proceedings can be in Kanien'kéha or English, with translation provided in criminal or penal matters.

The Kahnawà:ke Justice Commission is mandated "to integrate traditional Kanien'kehá:ka principles into the Kahnawà:ke Justice System; assure fair and just resolution of conflict through the creation or modification of justice services; plan and implement prevention of conflict, violence and crime by developing relevant programs and to educate the public on justice initiatives and administer and order the justice system of Kahnawà:ke." Laws and decisions of these judicial forums are enforced by the Kahnawà:ke Peacekeepers, who are governed by the *Kahnawá:ke Peacekeepers Law*.

"We have developed a new court system, but our community is in the process of negotiating with the province to have our own recognized system so we can hear all offences that happen in this territory," said Chief Peacekeeper Zacharie. "And anybody in the territory would be required to attend Court here."

"I think we want to handle everything that we could in Kahnawà:ke," said Kahnawà:ke's Commissioner of Justice Kevin Fleisher. He spoke about how as more criminal justice jurisdiction is taken up, that greater resources will be needed to build the capacity necessary in the community, including people to work in it, facilities, and services for victims. Community input into new laws and initiatives plays a major role in the revitalization of Kahnawà:ke justice. Commissioner Fleisher also spoke about the need for recognition or reciprocal agreements with non-Indigenous justice systems. "I see it as ground-breaking. And there's a challenge with it, let's see if we can do this thing, create this whole new justice system. So, I always take it in terms of we're creating something new and maybe in some ways creating a little bit of local history with it."

Some examples of varied approaches to addressing harm can also be seen in Mi'kmaq, Cree, Métis, and Inuit law. "In the Mi'kmaq legal tradition, *abeksikdawaebegik* (reconciliation) not only entails forgiveness, but also requires that the offender take *abeksikdewapan* (responsibility). In the Cree tradition, healing of the offender is of primary importance. However, when a *wetiko* (dangerous person) refused healing and remained a risk to the larger community, then the offender was avoided or separated from the community."

In *The Wetiko Legal Principles: Cree and Anishinabek Responses to Violence and Victimization*, Professor Hadley Friedland at the University of Alberta, Faculty of Law, built on Professor Borrows's work to bring a trauma-informed approach to describing how

Indigenous legal principles may apply to intimate partner violence and child victimization, including the following key stages:
(1) "wait, observe, and collect information"; (2) "Counsel with
friends and neighbours when it is apparent something is wrong";
(3) "If the person does not respond to help and becomes an
imminent threat to individuals or the community, remove them
so that they do not harm others"; (4) "Help those who rely on
that person by restoring what might be taken from them by the
treatment"; and (5) "Have both the collective and the individual
participate in the restoration." Professor Friedland emphasized
that "despite the ongoing presence of the Canadian legal system, some people *do* practise *wetiko* law today, and more people
could practice it, at least without running into Canadian legal
barriers."

For Métis people, while shaming, dishonour to family, humiliation, and chiding may be consequences of misbehaviour, Elders
may require restitution to be provided to the person who was
wronged. Exile was reserved for serious offences, such as murder,
assault, and sexual assault – with the person able to return later
with community approval. A person who committed theft may
have their horse equipment and clothing cut up, but remorse and
their heartfelt apology would see them restored – "the men would
replace the equipment and clothing from their own supplies." This
approach points to the principle of healing in Métis law: "The disruption to community relationships must be repaired and harmony must be restored. It is in the interest of all to cultivate and
preserve peace."

In *Inuit Qaujimajatuqangit* (a term encompassing "values,
knowledge, behaviour, perceptions and expectations"), there are
many guiding principles in addressing violence, including:

- *Inuuqatigiitsiarniq*: respecting others, relationships, and caring for people.
- *Tunnganarniq*: fostering good spirit by being open, welcoming, and inclusive.
- *Pijitsirniq*: serving and providing for families and communities.

In *Inuit Qaujimajatuqangit*, we again see a sharp contrast with settler law. While the former emphasizes relationality, openness, and community, the latter treats people who cause harm as an island unto themselves, encourages them to be silent and deny wrongdoing, and ignores the role of families and communities in the process.

The important work of revitalizing Indigenous laws is underway. For example, in British Columbia, the 2020 BC First Nations Justice Strategy (developed by the BC First Nations Justice Council and Province of BC) is following a two-track approach: first, reforming the justice system "to be safer and more responsive to Indigenous peoples" and, second, "restoration of First Nations Justice systems, legal traditions and structures."

Indigenous laws are being taught in courses at some Canadian law schools, and there is even a joint four-year degree program at the University of Victoria where graduates receive a Juris Doctor (JD) in Canadian Common Law and a Juris Indigenarum Doctor (JID) in Indigenous Legal Orders. In core courses like criminal law, Canadian law is taught alongside Indigenous laws (such as Cree law in Professor David Milward's course), topic by topic. The University of Victoria's joint JD/JID program mirrors McGill's "transsystemic" approach, where the common law is taught alongside civil law, and students graduate with both a JD in common law and Bachelor of Civil Law.

And at the community level, Indigenous peoples are reinvigorating laws, customs, and traditions that have been disrupted and suppressed for hundreds of years. While it will take substantial work, investment, and support, Indigenous justice is an exciting and central part of a new transformative justice vision.

———

In 2013, the BC First Nations Health Authority (FNHA) became the first Indigenous health authority in Canada, charged with delivering health services to First Nations people in place of federal or provincial governments. I bring it up here for two main reasons.

First, the FNHA is a concrete example of the taking up of Indigenous self-governance in an important jurisdictional area that was previously occupied by federal and provincial governments. I asked Dr. Shannon McDonald, acting chief medical officer at the FNHA, what she thought should be done about the criminal justice system. She is Métis/Anishinabe with deep roots in the Red River Valley of Manitoba.

"Definitely need[s] an overhaul. But nothing's hopeless. I mean the First Nation's Health Authority didn't exist until 2013," said Dr. McDonald.

Second, the FNHA takes a holistic approach to wellness that is trauma-informed and invests in social determinants of health. These priorities, of course, are mirrored in the early chapters of part 2 of this book as part of a new transformative justice vision.

Land-based healing is an example of an Indigenous approach being used to address many issues that are currently caught up in the criminal justice response. It's a way for people who have been harmed or caused harm to experience renewal and transformation.

Land-based treatment and healing involves a variety of approaches for Indigenous people to spend time on the land, returning or reconnecting to the land alongside supports to help them "relearn, revitalize, and reclaim" traditional Indigenous wellness practices. Examples include culture and language camps, traditional food harvesting and medicine gathering, cultural activities, programs with Elders, teaching traditional birthing and parenting customs, and revitalizing Indigenous ceremonies and celebrations on the land.

"One of the things that we talk about quite often with the Elders is land-based healing," said Dr. McDonald. "I think there is a real opportunity to combine mental health treatment, substance use treatment, and supporting people whose behaviour has caused them to interact with the justice system to take them to the land, to work with community, to participate in shared activities, to take responsibility not only for their actions but their life going forward. I think there are real potentials for that."

"We tried self-medicating with alcohol and other substances. They didn't work. They brought more suffering and trauma," said Harold Johnson. "Then we tried land-based healing. We knew from memory and from the words of our Elders and the few remaining Knowledge Keepers that the land was healing, that it rejuvenated us."

Johnson explains that, while Western-based therapies for substance use disorders have success rates of between 2 and 8 per cent, the Camp Hope land-based initiative by Jarred Nelson and Joyce Knight at Montreal Lake, Saskatchewan, had success rates approaching 70 per cent. It incorporated Western knowledge around trauma, including a trauma counsellor, combined with land-based healing practices.

"The reason for the success of Camp Hope was that the clients were reconnected with the land. They discovered who they were. They were Indians. They discovered where they belonged. They belonged here. This was their home, their birthright. When people know who they are and where they belong, their essence increases. Land-based healing is a resurrection," said Harold. "We've proven it works. Take people back out onto the land, allow them to reconnect, work them through the trauma wrought by colonization and they will respond."

There is a growing array of Indigenous land-based healing and recovery initiatives throughout Canada. However, they often lack adequate funding and the capacity to support people reintegrating back into their communities.

"We do have Jackson Lake Healing Camp, and that's run by Kwanlin Dün [First Nation], and it's very good," said Elder Soltani. "It brings healing. It brings peace. It keeps us grounded."

"Jackson Lake gives them a good start and they come home – they're so proud of the drum they made. They're so proud of, you know, the beading that they did. They're so proud of the berries that they dried. They're so proud of a painting they did. They're so proud of the carving that they did," explained Elder Soltani. "But what happens when they come back to Whitehorse after twenty-eight days out on the land? Bingo – their friends see them, and they're back off doing exactly what they were doing within an hour which was why they had to leave and go to the healing camp. There is no place for them to go to continue what they have learned out there. ... There is zero aftercare." This gets back to the need for healing in communities and greater resources and support for Indigenous Nations.

"I'm hearing a lot more people creating land-based healing justice programming," said Métis-Cree lawyer Myrna McCallum.

"And I really think that's what particularly Indigenous people need because prisons don't address healing. Prisons are not interested in helping return your spirit back to you, or helping you find [a] place back in community."

———

Earlier, I shared that one of the foundational principles of restorative justice is that when harm is done, it must cease, and there is a corresponding obligation to "make things right as much as possible."

Canada has caused, and continues to cause, great harm to Indigenous people. This is a reality we must grapple with. Part of making it right (as much as that is possible) is to make substantial investments and ensure the necessary legal and policy reforms to support the recognition, revitalization, and resurgence of Indigenous laws. This process of actual decolonization will take time – after all, it took hundreds of years to get us to this tragic point with epidemic rates of victimization and incarceration. But it is the only way to move forward. The process must be driven by Indigenous peoples, on their timelines and in their ways.

"As much as possible stand out of the way. Recognize that you're doing harm," said Harold Johnson. "But more importantly, when Aboriginal people are ready to take over, stand out of the way. Don't defend your turf."

CHAPTER NINETEEN

"New and Better Stories"

Evenings under the canopy of the majestic stars. Mornings warming by the crackling fire, listening to bubbling streams. The warmth of his horse carrying him along as its enormous lungs breathed the crisp, clean mountain air, slowly in and out. The prayers. The poems. The peace. All of it was gone. The vision quest was over – or so he thought.

Being in RCMP custody was a triggering experience for my father-in-law Greg because of what he had experienced as a child during his prior institutionalization, combined with his FASD. His life in detention contrasted sharply with his life during the vision quest, writing poetry, and praying in the wilderness.

"When I was incarcerated for about five or six hours in there, I couldn't stop pacing. Not crying or sobbing, but on the verge of it," said Greg. "In retrospect, I guess they were watching me the whole time – that I was under a tremendous amount of torture."

"They came in after I thought I couldn't take it anymore and said, 'Listen, there's too many charges here to follow-up on.' I had about half a dozen 'failure to appears' and whatnot. They said, 'Your son is on the way to pick you up.'"

"I think they kinda understood that I was out there trying to find my way out of a crack addiction. They'd never seen anything like that in their life. I think they really believed that it was working, and that the wrong thing would be to put me in jail – just let him keep doing what he's doing."

As the police officers waved him off, one of them said, "Put me in your book, Greg."

Although the police ultimately let him go, the experience of being pursued, tracked down, arrested, and locked up was too much for Greg to handle. Not to mention Spirit and Cougar, his horses, were still in the custody of animal services. That night, Greg checked into a motel, made a familiar phone call, and relapsed.

The next morning, he went to get his horses back. He would return to the mountains. The vision quest wasn't over yet. Perhaps it was just beginning. His poetry continued.

The periodic breaks in the mists offer glimpses of spectacular mountainous terrains as I reflected on the beautiful trip back on Terrace Trail. With Cougar at his very best, I didn't really notice when it was that we slipped into ONENESS, kinda where you and your horses, the cadence of their hooves beating, the unequalled mountain air, nature's sounds and sights, and the trail hypnotize you into harmonic timeless bliss.

"One of the most important parts of the vision quest and how it affects one is called instinct," said Greg. "The definition of instinct is when you have to make an important decision without enough information. And today's world, we have computers, Google. We have all kinds of information and very seldom do we make any decision without having the proper information."

"Most of us have a highly developed instinct," said Greg. "We don't use it anymore."

Greg would begin to trust his instincts. He found that, when he did, it made travel much easier. No longer would he go down the wrong road, then have to turn back, only to end the day right back where he started. Instead, he developed an innate sense of where to go – and paths to avoid. It was a parable of sorts that he would take with him after the vision quest was over.

"I found when I got back, I could avoid the wrong road so much easier. So-and-so would call and say, 'Come on over,' and I'd say, 'Yeah, I'll be right over.' Then think about it for a sec and realize that I would be going four hours down the wrong road, four hours back, and worse off than when I started. It played an important part in my recovery, that instinct."

Like many Indigenous people, being separated from his mother at age three and dislocated from his community left him with little to go on about their traditional ways. Yet he innately knew he needed to be on the land. And he had gleaned what he could from the documentary he'd seen just before he left. This turned out to be the knowledge that he needed. I asked Greg how he knew when it was time to end his vision quest.

"There's three things: one, you'll know when it's over. Two, you'll know what animal – Indian animal – you have. And number three, you'll have a vision."

One day, as Greg ascended a steep mountain pass with Cougar and Spirit, he found a flat place to make camp. It rained for four days straight. His few belongings were soaked through, and a dull aching cold set in. He used a tarp to collect rainwater, which he would drink as he watched bolts of lightning arc through the valley below, thunder cracking and reverberating off the granite.

Then he saw something else.

"What I first saw in my vision was all these Indian men packing up to go to war, and the wives crying that they'll never see them again. All getting on their horses and leaving their families behind. And then there's this big Indian Chief. He pointed at me and pointed for me to get in the lineup. That was that."

"Quite a vision."

Thunder accompanied this morning's prayers. Tears of thanks to my brave and wise Indian Forefathers who with great courage gave their lives in huge numbers, against an unbeatable foe never known before, to protect this land. If I could have just a sliver of their strength I prayed. Thunder echoes in the valleys below. "Yes, we still live here" they say.

Days later, he would learn his vision quest animal.

"It was snowing, cold. I couldn't get the fires going in the morning," said Greg. Then all of a sudden it hit him. He knew what his vision quest animal was. "I'm an eagle! I'm an eagle! It was like getting an 'A.' I always thought I was deer, running. Yeah, time to go home."

After seventy-nine days, Greg was ready to return from his vision quest, eager to share what he'd experienced.

"I always had a huge desire to share this story," he said. "It's been fifteen years now that I've been completely sober from my addiction that I suffered going in."

"It's a miracle," said Greg. "The spirituality. The nature. That vision quest was a wonderful way to alter my subconscious. I can't think of any other way to do it."

So when touched this way, you have a heightened awareness to the
beauty that surrounds. It's mystical how nature's blend of soft cloud
and hardened rock, so eloquent, far surpasses an artist's touch.
The magic as the heavens open above, thru clouds, the sun shows its
sudden might by lighting up the picture around to a brilliance that
glistens in its glow. I loved that moment – where we were all one.

I shudder at the thought of what could have happened to my
father-in-law if those RCMP officers had gone by the book. If they
had, he may never have recovered. He wouldn't have been there to
ride on horseback alongside his beautiful daughter – my wife – on
our wedding day in the foothills of those same Rocky Mountains,
then walk her down the aisle under the wide-open skies as thunder
clapped in the distance the moment we said, "I do." And my children may have never known their grandfather or heard him tell his
incredible story.

———

I am so grateful to everyone who trusted me with their stories and
shared from their hearts their experiences with the criminal justice system. I hope that these seeds – planted in this book – will
bear fruit by helping others understand how deeply and fundamentally flawed our society's efforts are in addressing harm, hopelessness, and trauma. I also hope that, like my father-in-law Greg
and the late Harold Johnson, we can together create "new and better stories."

I'm encouraged and excited that there already exist proven
ways to address conflict and harm, substance use and mental
health issues, poverty and homelessness, and systemic racism and

colonialism without the same old cruel, costly, ineffective, and often deadly trifecta of policing, punishment, and prisons.

Instead of ignoring childhood trauma and its ongoing impacts, we can imagine a world where we proactively act to prevent and mitigate childhood trauma, and invest in the social determinants of justice, to foster healthy kids and communities. A world where a trauma-informed approach is taken by everyone involved when harm occurs.

Instead of an adversarial system where victims of crime are mere pieces of evidence to be used and cast aside, we can imagine a world where there are holistic healing opportunities available after harm occurs for everyone involved as well as meaningful opportunities for participation in restorative justice and accountability. Where there is actual protection and safety. Where harm is understood as being a wrong against the person who was hurt.

Instead of Indigenous people being subjected to increasingly catastrophic outcomes of victimization and criminalization, we can imagine a world where Indigenous justice is revitalized, ending centuries of colonial settler oppression through criminal law. Where Indigenous peacekeepers, on-the-land healing, healing lodges, and a diverse array of laws, customs, and traditions support the healing of people, families, communities, and Nations.

Instead of Black people being underprotected and overpoliced, we can imagine a world where there is community-level governance over police services and meaningful investments in social determinants of justice to begin the process of redressing the ongoing legacies of slavery, segregation, and systemic racism. Where allegations of police profiling, misconduct, brutality, and killings lead to action and accountability.

Instead of criminalizing people who use drugs, we can imagine a world where substance use is addressed as a social and health issue using a compassionate, evidence-based approach. Where there is harm reduction to keep people alive, a safer supply to replace toxic contaminated street drugs, and rapid access to evidence-based treatment and recovery opportunities. Where we see people who use drugs differently – worthy of dignity and support, not judgment and punishment.

Instead of armed police officers doing mental health "wellness" checks with fatal outcomes, non-police mobile crisis teams would respond to meet people where they're at. Instead of criminalizing poverty and homelessness, we can imagine a world where there are Housing First policies, and investments in education, employment opportunities, and income support.

Instead of spending more and more on "fighting" crime without actually enhancing public safety, we can imagine a world where we have safer communities through specialized non-police mobile crisis responses to meaningfully support people with substance use disorders, mental health challenges, and those who are experiencing poverty and homelessness. Where police are excluded from situations that are worsened by handcuffs, tasers, and guns. Where trauma counsellors, peer-support workers, nurses, and social workers can respond 24/7. Where there is a rebalancing of funds to these professionals who can respond in a less traumatizing, more humane, and ultimately safer way for everyone.

Instead of a punitive, retributivist philosophy that favours punishment, denunciation, and deterrence, we can imagine a world where a relational philosophy, with a focus on healing, guides the response to harm and protects people's safety.

Instead of cruel, costly, and ineffective prisons and jails, we can imagine a world where the emphasis is on healing and rehabilitation. Where there exists a range of community-based alternatives to protect people. Where people are only separated from society when they pose a significant risk to others' safety or their conduct has shocked the conscience of the community – not to exact retribution or as part of a quixotic quest to deter. Where rehabilitation and healing centres are places where people leave better than when they entered, ready to live new lives as children, siblings, partners, parents, co-workers, and neighbours. Where underlying issues and unresolved traumas are addressed, education is upgraded, meaningful skills are learned, and jobs are readily available on return. Where staff are there to encourage, support, and mentor folks along the way.

This is a new transformative justice vision for Canada. It is real, it is inspiring, and it is achievable in our lifetimes if we start now. The evidence for these new approaches is strong and well-tested. These are not just "neat ideas." I have already shared examples of real programs, currently in action, that reflect this new vision. They have been operating for decades and have achieved better outcomes, typically at a fraction of the cost. They show us that this vision is not only possible, but that it can work in practice: from the Nurse-Family Partnership and Roots of Empathy initiatives in British Columbia; to safer supply programs and Housing First; to STR8 UP in Saskatchewan; to CAHOOTS in Oregon; to restorative justice with the Collaborative Justice Program in Ontario; to Halden Prison in Norway; to Indigenous-led healing lodges, the Kahnawà:ke Peacekeepers, and an entire renewal of Indigenous laws and institutions in Kahnawà:ke; to the taking up of Indigenous jurisdiction by the BC First Nations Health Authority and its holistic approach to well-being.

———

What are the potential obstacles to a new transformative justice vision for Canada? I will briefly address five: money, politics, power, racism, and stigma.

First, money. How much is this going to cost? This is the easiest objection to put to rest. We can have a high level of confidence that the net cost of this new vision would be materially less than the status quo. No one keeps track of how much the status quo costs. A keen law student did research for me calculating public expenditures on criminal justice as well exceeding $25.5 billion per year in Canada. The lifetime criminal justice expense for just one high-risk offender is conservatively estimated at $1.7 million. The estimated cost of a single police stop related to substance use is $794.92, and I spoke with many people who told me they'd experienced countless police interventions, which only made things worse and never provided any actual help with their substance use disorder.

It is well accepted that timely preventive action avoids unnecessary costs. An ounce of prevention is truly worth a pound of cure. At its core, the status quo is reactive. This new vision is proactive and holistic. For example, it is estimated that every dollar spent on substance use treatment saves the health care and criminal justice systems up to $12. As we've seen earlier in this book, many of the programs that I mentioned a moment ago generate positive net returns – meaning they actually yield savings exceeding their operating costs (e.g., CAHOOTS generates an estimated US$8.5 million return on a US$2.1 million annual expenditure). If these seem too good to be true, consider that the money we currently spend is essentially being thrown away due to the system's faulty assumptions about crime and human nature. In fact, it's worse than that, as these misdirected funds lead to further social harms, which require further funds to address. The status quo is responding to symptoms rather than causes, particularly trauma – the "cause of causes" – and it is doing so incredibly poorly.

"One example of cost-benefit analysis is a study that examined seven delinquency, violence, and substance abuse prevention programs in the state of Pennsylvania. The programs were found to produce a return on investment of between $1 and $25 per dollar invested," according to a Public Safety Canada report. "Collectively, these programs not only paid for themselves but represented a potential return of $300 million to the state treasury due to reduced corrections costs, lower social services costs, savings in mental health and drug treatment, and increased employment and tax revenue."

"Governments in Canada spend billions of dollars each year in responding to the symptoms of the intergenerational trauma of residential schools. Much of this money is spent on crisis interventions related to child welfare, family violence, ill health, and crime," according to the Truth and Reconciliation Commission of Canada. "Despite genuine reform efforts, the dramatic over-representation of Aboriginal children in foster care, and among the sick, the injured, and the imprisoned, continues to grow. Only a real commitment to reconciliation will reverse the trend and lay the foundation for a truly just and equitable nation."

The second obstacle to a new vision for criminal justice is politics. Time and again, I heard from people during interviews for this book that the primary thing holding back meaningful change is that politicians either gain votes by being "tough on crime" or they fear losing them by being branded "soft on crime." What's behind this base instinct for increased policing and ever stricter punishment?

"The punitive model doesn't work, and I'd say the punitive model is a response, a trauma response. So, when someone hits you, you want to hit them back," explained Fritzi Horstman. We're responding to a perceived risk to ourselves out of fear and are trying to protect ourselves by lashing out at others – a "fight" response. Sensational media coverage of crime and social media amplification fuels that fear, making us *feel* unsafe in our communities – after all, there's an old saying "if it bleeds, it leads" in the news headlines. Safety is an essential human need, but "tough on crime" has only made things worse as we've seen throughout this book.

In fact, I'd like to officially replace the term "tough on crime" with "stupid on crime." It doesn't work. It makes us less safe, while costing a ton of taxpayers' money. More public education, critical journalism, and citizen activism is needed to shift public opinion on these issues so that politicians are compelled to catch up – or lose their jobs. And if politicians are too slow to act on compassionate, evidence-based criminal justice policies, then we may find some recourse on certain issues through the courts via *Charter* litigation. Based on the research I've personally seen and shared in this book, a raft of laws, policies, and government actions on criminal justice likely infringe *Charter* rights. But the courts are also, in many ways, part of the system, entrenched in its dogma. So fundamental change will need to come from elected officials. How do we do that?

Conservative politicians in Canada and Republican politicians in the United States have made "tough on crime" policies their stock-in-trade for decades. In political lingo, it is "red meat" for voters – a sure bet to rile people up to vote, sign up for a membership, donate, and volunteer. This crass, cynical game is destroying lives, and it has to stop. There are strong arguments against "tough on crime" policies that can be made to conservative constituencies. For fiscal conservatives, I go to the economic arguments above. "Tough on crime" is costly and ineffective – it is really "tough on taxpayers." A waste of taxpayer dollars. We should instead be "smart on crime" and follow the evidence of what works. For libertarians, the ever-expanding role of the state in policing and corrections should spark a concern about government overreach, including interference with things like personal choices around substance use.

Social conservatives predominantly identify as Christians. While some Christians are conservative-minded, many are progressive, liberal, and even socialist. Almost two-thirds of Canadians identify as Christians. So talking about the interface between faith and criminal justice politics is necessary.

While I always thought of myself as a Christian (a "professing Christian"), I only really began following Jesus and started turning my life over to him in recent years. This change of my heart and outlook has been transformative in challenging my previously held views on criminal justice. So, I'd like to briefly unpack a few key reasons why I think more Christians should be supportive of a new vision for criminal justice. This is also a topic I've shared about on the John Howard Society blog, if anyone is interested in reading more about it.

In Jesus' life and teachings, I see a major emphasis on mercy, forgiveness, reconciliation, compassion, and humility. I hear Jesus saying, "Blessed are the merciful, for they will be shown mercy." Calling on people to forgive each other: "forgive us our trespasses, as we forgive those who trespass against us." Pleading with us to reconcile our interpersonal conflicts informally: "Settle matters quickly with your adversary who is taking you to court. Do it while you are still together on the way." I also see Jesus forgiving the woman caught in adultery – a capital offence at one time in Jewish law. When everyone else wanted to stone her, Jesus said, "Let any one of you who is without sin be the first to throw a stone at her" – and, one by one, they left. I see him calling us to help those who have been victimized and wounded, as in the parable of the Good Samaritan who was beaten and robbed. I hear him saying: "I was in prison and you came to visit me." And I see Jesus as someone who was wrongfully convicted and executed by an occupying power.

Most of all, I see myself as no better and no worse before God than someone who is a convicted criminal, even someone guilty of heinous crimes. The Bible says we have all fallen short, yet we are all deeply loved by God and can receive his free gift of forgiveness through faith in Jesus Christ. I'd challenge any professing Christian to let God search their hearts and test their minds to see if they really believe that too, and if their actions align with those professed beliefs – or if their hearts are hard and unmerciful. No one is beyond redemption. For me, these currents move strongly down the river of mercy, peacemaking, and compassion for broken people.

I know I'm not alone in taking this perspective. John Howard, Elizabeth Fry, and William Booth were all Christian prison reformers. More recently, in *Rethinking Incarceration: Advocating for Justice That Restores*, African American Christian author Dominique DuBois Gilliard makes the theological and policy case against the war on drugs, mass incarceration, and other "tough on crime" policies. Gilliard concludes: "We serve a God whose final word is not retribution but restoration, who desires liberation, reconciliation, and reintegration for those behind bars."

The third obstacle to a new vision for criminal justice is power. A key question to ask when systems that are flawed prove stubbornly resistant to change, and even seek to rebrand or reinvent themselves just enough to stay afloat, is "who benefits from the status quo?" Often, answering this question can help identify those who will oppose changes that go against their self-interest. Certain power-holders have a vested interest in the current state of affairs, even absent any conscious malice on their part. Their stake in the status quo is massive, and they have been indoctrinated into it. So, who benefits from the status quo criminal justice system?

There are hundreds of thousands of people who benefit directly from the status quo, including tens of thousands of police officers, thousands of criminal lawyers, judges, corrections and probation officers, and other criminal justice practitioners. Not to mention criminal law professors (including myself), criminologists, and other professionals whose employment and income are predicated on the system.

And then there are the tens of millions of people who benefit from a system that keeps their neighbourhoods clear of people who are "not like them" because they are experiencing homelessness and poverty, use substances, are in mental health distress, or are racialized. Out of sight, out of mind. Rather than address underlying inequalities, racism, and social determinants of justice, it seems easy to move people to the "other side of the tracks" or warehouse them in cages. But we have seen throughout this book that is a cruel, ineffective, expensive, and often deadly approach.

Some police officers and corrections officers would need help in transitioning to other lines of work – vocations that don't traumatize these officers and impact their families to such a degree. For example, most corrections officers under the status quo certainly couldn't be expected to adapt to a new approach based on rehabilitation and healing. It is a bridge too far. I heard time and again that no amount of policies or directives make a big enough difference in corrections. Instead, it is necessary to disband federal, provincial, and territorial corrections departments and staff. Start fresh with new people, not tainted by the status quo. This is controversial, but necessary. Organizational "culture," as it is often called, runs deep and is rarely amenable to reform. Many of these status quo staff and employees, particularly corrections officers, will need their own support to recover from these jobs where they too experienced trauma, and they should be provided that help. They will need to receive educational opportunities and retraining to take up new jobs in other fields. We will all be better for it, including them.

The fourth obstacle to a new vision for criminal justice is racism and privilege. It is very clear that racism against Indigenous people, Black people, and people of colour (IBPOC) is insidious and widespread in public institutions, including criminal justice, health care, employment, and so on. This includes both overt, intentional racism and the systemic racism and unconscious bias that can be inadvertently propagated by even well-meaning people who think of themselves as progressive. I don't have big solutions on this front, but if you're white, I suggest reading *White Fragility* by Robin DiAngelo, *Peace and Good Order* by Harold Johnson, and other books by IBPOC authors in topics you're interested in. You may be surprised what you learn. That's what has helped me to see clearer my own unconscious biases and ways that racism infects everything. I too still have much more to learn.

The fifth obstacle to a new vision for criminal justice is stigma. The judgment, condemnation, and fear that we as a society – and we as individuals – have towards people not like us. Stigma towards people convicted of criminal offences, people who use drugs, people with mental illness, and people experiencing poverty and homelessness. Stigma makes our hearts hard and closes our minds. We need soft hearts and open minds. Eyes to see, and ears to hear the pain, brokenness, trauma, and suffering of others. To approach people with a spirit of humility and compassion, rather than one of pride and condemnation.

———

In many ways, we as a society are like my father-in-law Greg when he first embarked on his vision quest. He had lost his way. None of his previous efforts had worked. Doing more of the same hadn't helped. "I didn't know myself at all. I had lost myself. I had no identity," he told me. But in the wilderness, he found who he really was as he waited and listened.

We too are lost as a society. I hope that on this journey together we can find a better way – one that follows new paths as well as old ones, long overgrown but still there to follow if we're willing to slow down and take the time to look for them.

Acknowledgments

My first word of thanks is to everyone who shared their stories and expertise with me for this book. I learned so much from you and am deeply indebted. Daniel Quinlan and the team at the University of Toronto Press were incredible – I appreciated his enthusiasm, editorial support, and willingness to go way beyond my expectations to make this book a reality.

I am grateful for financial support for this research from the Law Foundation of British Columbia and the UBC Hampton Fund, and research assistance from Thor Paulson, Ryman Yeung, and Lara Mercier-Jung. Michael McLaughlin and the team at Transcript Heroes were a pleasure to work with and integral. I also want to acknowledge Professors Robert T. Muller, Robert Maunder, John Borrows, Ben Goold, Graham Reynolds, Robert Clifford, and Debra Parkes as well as Claudia Ho Lem for providing me with invaluable feedback at various stages of this project.

I want to thank Dean Ngai Pindell along with colleagues and staff at the UBC Peter A. Allard School of Law for their encouragement and support, especially Aki Nishida, Paige MacKenzie, Daniel Johnstone, Fiona Chan, Monzur Siddique, and Debbie Cua. Finally, I want to thank Jesus Christ, my wife (whose own incredible resilience and healing journey taught me so much, and who was my most ardent critical reader and encourager – all at the same time), my kids, my parents, my mother- and father-in-law, Dan G. and the other guys, Jenny Watt, and our family pets for being my circle of support as I shared both my sorrow and excitement with you over this book. Thank you all.

Methodology

The primary research for this book consisted of seventy-one interviews: thirty-five with criminal justice practitioners and professionals (minimal risk, semi-structured, attributed with consent), and thirty-six with people with lived experience of the criminal justice system (medium risk, unstructured, in-depth, unattributed). Wherever a quote is provided in this book that is not specifically cited in the endnotes, it is from this original, primary-source, qualitative, empirical research material. Quotes have been minimally edited to remove verbal fillers and for grammar to ensure comprehensibility.

All interviews were conducted with the prior written informed consent of participants and followed protocols based on approvals by the UBC Behavioural Research Ethics Board (Certificate Nos. H18-02865 and H22-00110). These interviews took place by Zoom or telephone between April 2021 and June 2022, with one final interview in December 2022. They were digitally recorded with the consent of participants and professionally transcribed, except for one person who asked that notes be taken instead by the interviewer. All interviews were conducted by the principal investigator, Professor Benjamin Perrin, and interview data was analysed using thematic analysis, supported by Nvivo 12 software.

Other materials were consulted for purposes such as fact-checking interviews, including media reports and other public records where possible. Secondary research for this book included scholarly literature in a wide range of fields (e.g., law, criminology, public health, psychology, economics, and sociology), governmental and non-governmental reports, podcasts, audiovisual media, and documentaries. Specific secondary sources relied on appear in the endnotes.

Content Notes

This book includes potentially triggering content that may be difficult for some readers. The following is a chapter-by-chapter description of such content for your safety.

Please consult the Counselling and Mental Health Resources if you need support.

Some people find it helpful to be made aware in advance of potentially triggering content, so we are providing that information here. This book deals with potentially triggering material, including descriptions of physical, sexual, and psychological violence, neglect, emotional abuse, racial profiling, police brutality, colonialism, racism particularly against Indigenous people and Black people, substance use, mental health disorder, suicide, overdose deaths, and poverty. There are some additional specific aspects in each chapter that are summarized below.

Chapter One

This chapter includes a description of the arrest of an Indigenous man by police. Sexual assault and intimate partner violence are referred to in general terms. It also includes descriptions of a suicide attempt by an incarcerated Indigenous woman held in solitary confinement; a woman's experience with childhood sexual abuse, domestic violence, and multiple suicide attempts; an Indigenous man's childhood neglect and gang involvement; and a man's graphic descriptions of violent domestic abuse perpetrated by his father against his mother. There is a detailed discussion of trauma, particularly early childhood trauma.

Chapter Two

This chapter includes in-depth descriptions of substance use and resulting harms. A woman describes her substance use, self-harm, and negative interactions with law enforcement and institutionalized addiction treatment from when she was a teenager. There are graphic descriptions of substance use and concealment in prisons. A formerly incarcerated person describes witnessing an overdose. Overdose deaths and prison violence are discussed.

Chapter Three

This chapter includes a graphic description of a man's suicide attempt and self-harm; a description of the events leading to a twenty-six-year-old Indigenous woman's death during a police "wellness check"; the fatal shooting of a sixty-two-year-old Muslim man by police; a thirty-six-year-old man describes abuse, mistreatment, and other negative impacts of incarceration, leading to homelessness and drug use; graphic description of the in-custody death of a thirty-year-old man with schizophrenia; and the suicide of a twenty-seven-year-old Indigenous man. There is also a discussion of police use of force and tactics.

Chapter Four

This chapter includes descriptions of the intergenerational trauma caused by the cultural genocide of Indigenous peoples in Canada. An Indigenous woman describes being a victim of sexual violence and racist bullying, committing a violent act against her bully, being physically abused by her father, using substances, and four instances of being the victim of an assault. Another Indigenous woman describes her experience with police brutality when she was pulled over by the police and includes graphic descriptions of injuries. A third Indigenous woman describes her son's involvement in a gang and his death while being pursued by law enforcement.

Chapter Five

This chapter includes an Indigenous man's descriptions of his gang involvement and incarceration. It also includes an Indigenous woman's description of being subject to physical violence perpetrated by corrections officers and sexual harassment from other people while incarcerated.

Chapter Six

This chapter includes multiple references to police brutality and prejudice committed against Black people; a graphic description of a Black university student who is assaulted by two police officers; and a forty-one-year-old Black man's death during a confrontation with police.

Chapter Seven

This chapter includes descriptions of the intergenerational trauma caused by the genocide of Indigenous peoples in Canada, as well as examples of overt and systemic racism by the Canadian government against Indigenous people.

Chapter Eight

This chapter includes descriptions of domestic abuse by a former partner, victim-blaming by the authorities; suicide; multiple sexual assaults of a woman's daughter by her ex-partner; and a woman's sexual assault by a family member. There is also a discussion of the institutionalized discrediting of sexual assault victims during legal proceedings and Missing and Murdered Indigenous Women and Girls.

Chapter Nine

This chapter includes descriptions of a police intervention in a situation of ongoing domestic abuse suffered by a woman at the hands of her ex-partner. The ex-partner is given a lenient sentence in exchange for cooperating with the authorities, causing emotional harm to the woman. Numerous acts of violence are referred to and described.

Chapter Ten

This chapter includes general references to systemic racism, violence, substance use, and trauma.

Chapter Eleven

This chapter includes a general reference to a suicide attempt.

Chapter Twelve

This chapter includes references to a woman's experience of domestic abuse and victim-blaming by legal personnel.

Chapter Thirteen

The chapter includes general descriptions of substance use.

Chapter Fourteen

The chapter includes descriptions of gang violence.

Chapter Fifteen

The chapter includes non-specific references to poverty, substance use, and emergency interventions.

Chapter Sixteen

This chapter includes the graphic description of an assault that left a man permanently disfigured and descriptions of acts of theft.

Chapter Seventeen

This chapter includes graphic descriptions of prison violence, abuse, and neglect.

Chapter Eighteen

This chapter includes discussions of the ongoing colonial oppression of Indigenous peoples.

Chapter Nineteen

This chapter includes a description of an Indigenous man relapsing with substances after police intervention.

Mental Health and Counselling Resources for Readers

If you or someone you know is in immediate danger, please call 911 (or the emergency number in your jurisdiction) or go to your nearest hospital.

It's important to get help if you or someone you know is going through a crisis or thinking about suicide. Help is available. Learn about the resources available to you.

You should access support if you want to talk and you

- are not feeling yourself
- are experiencing a crisis
- have emotional pain
- have thoughts of suicide
- know someone who needs help

Canada Suicide Prevention Service

If you or someone you know is thinking about suicide, call Talk Suicide Canada at 1-833-456-4566 (24/7): https://talksuicide.ca.

For residents of Quebec, call 1-866-APPELLE (1-866-277-3553).

Visit Talk Suicide Canada to find the distress centres and crisis organizations nearest you: https://talksuicide.ca/community -resources.

Kids Help Phone

Call 1-800-668-6868 (toll-free) or text CONNECT to 686868.

Available twenty-four hours a day to Canadians aged five to twenty-nine who want confidential and anonymous care from trained responders.

To access support through Facebook Messenger, see the Kids Help Phone website: https://kidshelpphone.ca/.

Victim Services

The Victim Services Directory (VSD) has been created by the Policy Centre for Victim Issues of the Department of Justice Canada to help service providers, victims, and individuals locate services for victims of crime across Canada: https://www.justice.gc.ca/eng /cj-jp/victims-victimes/vsd-rsv/index.html.

Resources for People

Here is a list of links for federal and provincial governmental and non-governmental organizations that provide services and support to offenders: https://johnhoward.ca/resources/links/.

Additional Resources for Indigenous People

Hope for Wellness Helpline

Call 1-855-242-3310 (toll-free) or connect to the online Hope for Wellness chat: https://www.hopeforwellness.ca.

Available to all Indigenous people across Canada who need immediate crisis intervention. Experienced and culturally sensitive helpline counsellors can help if you want to talk or are distressed.

Telephone and online counselling are available in English and French. On request, telephone counselling is also available in Cree, Ojibway, and Inuktitut.

Indian Residential School Crisis Line

A national service for anyone experiencing pain or distress as a result of their residential school experience. Call toll-free at 1-866-925-4419.

KUU-US Crisis Line Society

Provides crisis services for Indigenous people across BC. Adults/ Elders line: 250-723-4050; Youth line: 250-723-2040. Or call toll-free at 1-800-588-8717. Learn more at https://www.kuu-uscrisisline.com.

Métis Crisis Line

A service of the Métis Nation of British Columbia. Call 1-833-MétisBC (1-833-638-4722).

First Nations Virtual Doctor of the Day

Provides virtual health care and referral support for people who do not have a doctor or are unable to get an appointment. It is for all First Nations people living in BC and their family members, including family members who are not Indigenous. Doctors are available by video or phone from 8:30 a.m. to 4:30 p.m. every day. Call 1-855-344-3800 to book an appointment. Learn more at https://fnha.ca/virtualdoctor.

Virtual Substance Use and Psychiatry Service

The Virtual Substance Use and Psychiatry Service of the BC First Nations Health Authority (FNHA) provides virtual specialist support in addictions medicine and psychiatry. The FNHA and other organizations provide culturally safe and trauma-informed cultural, emotional, and mental health services to Indigenous people in BC. Learn more at https://www.fnha.ca/what-we-do /ehealth/virtual-substance-use-and-psychiatry-service.

This service requires a referral from a health and wellness provider who can support the individual on their journey. If you do not have a provider who can refer you to the program, First Nations Virtual Doctor of the Day can provide referral support.

Indian Residential School Survivors Society (IRSSS)

A partner with the BC First Nations Health Authority (FNHA) in providing access to counselling, cultural, and emotional support services to former students of residential and day schools, and their families, regardless of status. Call toll-free at 1-800-721-0066 or visit https://www.irsss.ca.

Tsow-Tun Le Lum Society

Provides confidential outreach services such as counselling, cultural supports, and personal wellness programs. Call toll-free at 1-888-403-3123 or visit https://www.tsowtunlelum.org/.

Indian Residential Schools Resolution Health Support Program

Provides access to cultural supports and mental health counselling for former students of Indian Residential Schools. The program is available to anyone who attended a school listed in the 2006 Indian Residential School Settlement Agreement, and their family members. Call the FNHA Indian Residential Schools Information Line toll-free at 1-877-477-0775.

Mental Health and Wellness Counselling in BC

You may be eligible for Health Benefits coverage. Many providers are registered to bill Health Benefits directly for services so clients do not have to pay out of pocket. Before booking an appointment with a counsellor, call 1-855-550-5454 or visit https://fnha.ca/benefits to check if they are registered and if the service is eligible for coverage.

Missing and Murdered Indigenous Women and Girls Health Support Services

A national program administered in BC by First Nations Health Benefits. Services are available to survivors, family members, and others who have been affected. Call Health Benefits toll-free at 1-855-550-5454 for more information.

Suicide Prevention Toolkit

Help, Hope and Healing: A Planning Toolkit for First Nations and Aboriginal Communities to Prevent and Respond to Suicide is available at https://www.fnha.ca/WellnessSite/WellnessDocuments/FNHA-Hope-Help-and-Healing.pdf.

We acknowledge the Government of Canada's "Mental Health Support" website and other resources in putting this resource guide together.

Notes

Epigraph

vi *indictment* ... "Indictment" in *Oxford Learner's Dictionary* (2022), online: <https://www.oxfordlearnersdictionaries.com>.

1. "It Looked like Madness"

1 *Its quarry was my father-in-law, Greg* ... Interview with author on 17 May 2022.

5 *"Stop holding conferences ..."* Harold Johnson, *Peace and Good Order: The Case for Indigenous Justice in Canada* (McClelland & Stewart, 2019) at 146 [Johnson, "Peace and Good Order"].

6 *Courtney, a thirty-nine-year-old Indigenous woman from Yukon* ... Interview with "Courtney," 30 March 2022 (to protect her privacy, a pseudonym has been used).

8 *The Myth of Normal* ... Gabor Maté & Daniel Maté, *The Myth of Normal: Trauma, Illness & Healing in a Toxic Culture* (Knopf Canada, 2022).

9 *"experiences that overwhelm ..."* BC Provincial Mental Health and Substance Use Planning Council, *Trauma-Informed Practice Guide* (May 2013) at 6 [TIP Guide].

9 *"feelings of powerlessness ..."* Nicole C McKenna & Kristy Holtfreter, "Trauma-Informed Courts: A Review and Integration of Justice Perspectives and Gender Responsiveness" (2020) 30:4 Journal of Aggression, Maltreatment & Trauma 450 at 451.

9 *There are six major types* ... See TIP Guide at 6.

9 *Developmental trauma can lead to unique diagnoses ...* Arielle Schwartz, *The Complex PTSD Workbook: A Mind-Body Approach to Regaining Emotional Control & Becoming Whole* (Althea Press, 2016); Pete Walker, *Complex PTSD: From Surviving to Thriving* (Azure Coyote Book, 2013).

9 *"The basic architecture of the brain ..."* Harvard University Center on the Developing Child, "The Science of Early Childhood Development", online (pdf): <https://harvardcenter.wpenginepowered.com/wp-content/uploads/2007/03/InBrief-The-Science-of-Early-Childhood-Development2.pdf> [emphasis added].

9 *"can have especially negative consequences ..."* TIP Guide at 7.

9 *Trauma in the first five years ...* BC Ministry of Children and Family Development, *Healing Families, Helping Systems: A Trauma-Informed Practice Guide for Working with Children, Youth and Families* (January 2017) at 7 [Healing Families].

10 *intergenerational trauma is the result of ...* ibid at 4.

10 *There are a range of factors contributing ...* Substance Abuse and Mental Health Services Administration, *Concept of Trauma and Guidance for a Trauma-Informed Approach* (July 2014) at 8 [SAMHSA Guidance]; Louise Ellison & Vanessa E Munro, "Taking Trauma Seriously: Critical Reflections on the Criminal Justice Process" (2016) 21:3 International Journal of Evidence & Proof 183 at 185; Healing Families at 6.

10 *Jessica, an Indigenous woman ...* Interview with "Jessica," 27 April 2022 (to protect her privacy, a pseudonym has been used).

12 *lasting changes in brain structure and functioning ...* J Douglas Bremner, "Traumatic Stress: Effects on the Brain" (2006) 8:4 Dialogues in Clinical Neuroscience 445.

12 *"memory, learning, navigation ..."* Johns Hopkins Medicine, "Brain Anatomy and How the Brain Works", online: <https://www.hopkinsmedicine.org/health/conditions-and-diseases/anatomy-of-the-brain>.

12 *"associated with the brain's reward ..."* ibid.

12 *"regulation of complex cognitive ..."* "Prefrontal Cortex" in *Merriam Webster Medical Dictionary*, online: <https://www.merriam-webster.com/dictionary/prefrontal%20cortex>.

12 *often in a state of hyperarousal ...* SAMHSA Guidance at 8; TIP Guide at 7.

12 *engaging our automatic fight-flight-freeze ...* See MJ Friedman, "The Human Stress Response" in NC Bernardy & MJ Friedman, eds, *A Practical Guide to PTSD Treatment: Pharmacological and Psychotherapeutic Approaches* (American Psychological Association, 2015) at 9–19; JJ Donahue, "Fight-Flight-Freeze System" in V Zeigler-Hill & TK Shackelford, eds, *Encyclopedia of Personality and Individual Differences* (Springer, 2020).

12 *amplified in people who have experienced trauma ...* Kristen L Thompson, Susan M Hannan & Lynsey R Miron, "Fight, Flight, and Freeze: Threat Sensitivity and Emotion Dysregulation in Survivors of Chronic Childhood Maltreatment" (2014) 69 Personality and Individual Differences 28. One study found that younger children whose sexual abuse was shorter than other participants may exhibit an absence of automatic response: Carmit Katz, Noga Tsur, Anat Talmon & Racheli Nicolet, "Beyond Fight, Flight, and Freeze: Towards a New Conceptualization of

Peritraumatic Responses to Child Sexual Abuse Based on Retrospective Accounts of Adult Survivors" (2021) 112 Child Abuse & Neglect 104905.

12 *"secreting large amounts …"* Bessel van der Kolk, *The Body Keeps the Score: Brain, Mind, and Body in the Healing of Trauma* (Penguin, 2015) at 30.

13 *"Fawn," a fourth trauma response …* See "The Fawn Response: How Trauma Can Lead to People-Pleasing" (9 January 2022), online: *PsychCentral* <https://psychcentral.com/health/fawn-response>; Z Zingela, L Stroud, J Cronje et al, "The Psychological and Subjective Experience of Catatonia: A Qualitative Study" (2022) 10 BMC Psychology 173.

13 *a courtroom that doesn't understand trauma …* See Thor Paulson, Benjamin Perrin, Robert G Maunder & Robert T Muller, "Toward a Trauma-Informed Approach to Evidence Law: Witness Credibility and Reliability" Canadian Bar Review (forthcoming).

15 *The ACEs survey …* Robert Maunder & Jonathan Hunter, *Damaged: Childhood Trauma, Adult Illness, and the Need for a Health Care Revolution* (University of Toronto Press, 2021) at 16 [Maunder & Hunter, "Damaged"].

16 *Other supplementary ACEs …* ibid.

16 *about 60 per cent of people …* ibid at 15.

16 *ACEs increase the risk of prolonged …* Centers for Disease Control and Prevention, "Fast Facts: Preventing Adverse Childhood Experiences" (6 April 2022), online: <https://www.cdc.gov/violenceprevention/aces/fastfact.html>.

16 *"Given the cascade of negatives …"* Maunder & Hunter, "Damaged" at 4.

16 *"radically different life-course …"* See MA Bellis et al, "Measuring Mortality and the Burden of Adult Disease Associated with Adverse Childhood Experiences in England: A National Survey" (2015) 37:3 Journal of Public Health (Oxford, England) 445. See Centers for Disease Control and Prevention, "Fast Facts: Preventing Adverse Childhood Experiences" (6 April 2022), online: <https://www.cdc.gov/violenceprevention/aces/fastfact.html>.

16 *"First Nations, Inuit, and Métis children …"* Maunder & Hunter, "Damaged" at 194.

17 *Residential school survivors are estimated …* Kat Chief Moon-Riley et al, "The Biological Impacts of Indigenous Residential School Attendance on the Next Generation" (2019) 7:100343 SSM Population Health 1 at 2.

17 *"[o]ne of the most enduring …"* ibid at 1–2.

18 *"[T]he victimization rates for incarcerated …"* Sandra M Bucerius, Temitope B Oriola & Daniel J Jones, "Policing with a Public Health Lens – Moving towards an Understanding of Crime as a Public Health Issue" (2021) The Police Journal 1 at 4 [emphasis in original].

18 *The Trauma-Informed Lawyer podcast …* Myrna McCallum, "The Trauma-Informed Lawyer", online: <https://thetraumainformedlawyer.simplecast.com>.

18 *majority of incarcerated people were victimized …* Maunder & Hunter, "Damaged" at 101.

19 *"a key risk factor for …"* Michael T Baglivio et al, "The Relationship between Adverse Childhood Experiences (ACE) and Juvenile Offending Trajectories in a Juvenile Offender Sample" (2015) 43:3 Journal of Criminal Justice 229 at 229; see also Katie A Ports et al, "Adverse Childhood Experiences and Sexual Victimization in Adulthood" (2015) 51 Child Abuse & Neglect 313; BH Fox et

al, "Trauma Changes Everything: Examining the Relationship between Adverse Childhood Experiences and Serious, Violent and Chronic Juvenile Offenders" (2015) 46 Child Abuse & Neglect 163.

19 *"children and adolescents exposed ..."* Ports, 2015.

19 *eight times more likely ... ibid.*

19 *"later criminality by approximately 50%"* ... Baglivio, 2015 at 229. See also A Caspi et al, "Role of Genotype in the Cycle of Violence in Maltreated Children" (2002) 297:5582 Science 851.

19 *"ACEs not only increase ..."* Michael T Baglivio et al, "The Prevalence of Adverse Childhood Experiences (ACE) in the Lives of Juvenile Offenders" (2014) 3:2 Journal of Juvenile Justice 1.

19 *challenges with school or work ...* See, e.g., James Bonta & DA Andrews, *Risk-Need-Responsivity Model for Offender Assessment and Rehabilitation 2007–06* (Ottawa: Public Safety Canada, 2007) at 6.

20 *"central belief of trauma-informed ..."* TIP Guide at 51.

20 *"neuroplasticity" is the remarkable ...* See, e.g., Joyce Shaffer, "Neuroplasticity and Clinical Practice: Building Brain Power for Health" (2016) 7 Frontiers in Psychology 1118.

20 *"positive psychological growth ..."* Healing Families at 5.

20 *"the development of resiliency ..."* Charles R Figley et al, "The Study of Trauma: A Historical Overview" in SN Gold, ed, *APA Handbook of Trauma Psychology: Vol 1, Foundations in Knowledge* (American Psychological Association, 2017) 1 at 7. For more information about post-traumatic growth, see Lawrence G Calhoun & Richard G Tedeschi, eds, *Handbook of Posttraumatic Growth* (Psychology Press, 2014).

21 *"Healing childhood trauma involves ..."* Schwartz at 11.

2. "Set Up to Fail"

25 *"I grew up in a very ..."* Interview with "Kaila," 26 April 2022 (to protect her privacy, a pseudonym has been used).

26 *While it may seem counter-intuitive ...* National Alliance on Mental Illness, "Self-Harm", online: <https://www.nami.org/About-Mental-Illness/Common-with-Mental-Illness/Self-harm>.

26 *Adaptive coping strategies are constructive approaches ...* Renee J Thompson et al, "Maladaptive Coping, Adaptive Coping, and Depressive Symptoms: Variations across Age and Depressive State" (2010) 48:6 Behaviour Research and Therapy 459 at 461.

26 *maladaptive coping strategies may provide ...* McKenna & Holtfreter at 451.

27 *"high levels of psychological distress ..."* Thompson at 459.

27 *greater risk of abusing substances ...* McKenna & Holtfreter at 451.

27 *People who experienced five of the ten ...* SR Dube, VJ Felitti, M Dong, DP Chapman, WH Giles & RF Anda, "Childhood Abuse, Neglect and Household Dysfunction and the Risk of Illicit Drug Use: The Adverse Childhood Experience Study" (2003) 111:3 Pediatrics 564–72.

27 *Firewater ...* Harold R Johnson, *Firewater: How Alcohol Is Killing My People (and Yours)* (University of Regina Press, 2016) [Johnson, "Firewater"].

28 *"the exclusion of fire water ..."* Annual Report of the Department of the Interior for the Year Ended 30th June 1876 (Ottawa, 1877), online: <http://central .bac-lac.gc.ca/.item/?id=1876-IAAR-RAAI&op=pdf&app=indianaffairs>.

28 *"no intoxicating liquor shall ..."* Treaty No. 6, 1876.

29 *harassing the Chinese-Canadian population* ... Benjamin Perrin, *Overdose: Heartbreak and Hope in Canada's Opioid Crisis* (Penguin Random House, 2020) at 49ff [Perrin, "Overdose"]. All excerpts from *Overdose: Heartbreak and Hope in Canada's Opioid Crisis* by Benjamin Perrin, © Benjamin Perrin. Reprinted by permission of Viking Canada, a division of Penguin Random House Canada Limited. All rights reserved. Any third party use of this material, outside of this publication, is prohibited. Interested parties must apply directly to Penguin Random House Canada Limited for permission.

29 *"early drug use, peer influence ..."* ibid at 39.

29 *The American Psychiatric Association* ... See, e.g., American Psychiatric Association, *Diagnostic and Statistical Manual of Mental Disorders*, 5th ed (American Psychiatric Publishing, 2013) at 541–6 ["DSM-5"].

31 *Between January 2016 and* ... Government of Canada, "Opioid- and Stimulant-Related Harms in Canada" (March 2023), online: <https://health -infobase.canada.ca/substance-related-harms/opioids-stimulants/> [Government of Canada, "Opioid- and Stimulant-Related Harms in Canada"].

31 *the leading cause of unnatural death* ... British Columbia Coroners Service, *BC Coroners Service Death Review Panel: A Review of Illicit Drug Toxicity Deaths: Report to the Chief Coroner of British Columbia* (Victoria, BC, 2022) at 11.

31 *Indigenous women also have* ... British Columbia Coroners Service, *BC Coroners Service Death Review Panel: A Review of Illicit Drug Overdoses: Report to the Chief Coroner of British Columbia* (Victoria, BC, 2018) at 12, 14, 18–19 ["BC Death Panel Review, 2018"].

31 *80 per cent of overdose deaths* ... British Columbia Coroners Service, "Illicit Drug Toxicity Type of Drug Data – Data to August 31, 2022" (28 September 2022), online: <https://www2.gov.bc.ca/assets/gov/birth-adoption-death-marriage- and-divorce/deaths/coroners-service/statistical/illicit-drug-type.pdf>; see also Government of Canada, "Opioid- and Stimulant-Related Harms in Canada".

32 *at home with basic college* ... Perrin, "Overdose" at 57.

32 *Fentanyl is thirty to fifty times* ... ibid at 17.

32 *Carfentanyl is one hundred times* ... ibid at 18.

32 *self-medicating unresolved trauma* ... Dube et al.

32 *"Heroin is a drug that makes ..."* Interview with "Jimmy," 6 May 2022 (to protect his privacy, a pseudonym has been used).

36 *Two hours is the optimal* ... Perrin, "Overdose" at 183.

37 *"cause of causes" – their physical* ... Maunder & Hunter, "Damaged" at 4.

37 *"Canadians with a mental ..."* Jillian Boyce, Cristine Rotenberg & Maisie Karam, *Mental Health and Contact with Police in Canada, 2012* (Ottawa: Statistics Canada, 2015) at 14–15.

38 *A CBC investigation found* ... Kristin Annable, "Dozens of People Arrested for Intoxication Have Died in Police Holding Cells. These Are Their Stories", *CBC News* (14 December 2021).

39 *"root cause" of the crime* ... See, e.g., Provincial Court of British Columbia, "Drug Treatment Court of Vancouver", online: <https://www.provincialcourt. bc.ca/about-the-court/specialized-courts/DrugTreatmentCourt>.

40 *violating conditions, rather than* ... Office of the Correctional Investigator, "Aboriginal Offenders: A Critical Situation" (16 September 2013), online: <https://www.oci-bec.gc.ca/cnt/rpt/oth-aut/oth-aut20121022info-eng.aspx>.

43 *"Upon admission to federal custody ..."* Fraser McVie, *Drugs in Federal Corrections – The Issues and Challenges* (Correctional Service of Canada, 2015).

43 *up to 93 per cent of people* ... Don Head, "Alcohol and Drugs: A Perspective from Corrections in the Province of Saskatchewan" (2001) 13:3 FORUM on Corrections Research 10 at 10.

43 *3.4 per cent have a substance use disorder* ... Boyce et al at 3.

43 *Analysts at the Correctional Service of Canada* ... Serge Brochu et al, "Drugs, Alcohol, and Criminal Behaviour: A Profile of Inmates in Canadian Federal Institutions" (2001) 13:3 FORUM on Corrections Research 20 at 22–3.

44 *"The amount of blood ..."* Interview with "Martin," 9 May 2022 (to protect his privacy, a pseudonym has been used).

45 *"If you had anything ..."* Interview with "Nate," 2 May 2022 (to protect his privacy, a pseudonym has been used).

46 *the reuse and sharing of syringes* ... Nicola Bulled & Merrill Singer, "Syringe-Mediated Syndemics" (2011) 15:7 AIDS & Behavior 1539 at 1539.

47 *"Post-release, their prospects ..."* Claire Bodkin, Matthew Bonn & Sheila Wildeman, "Fuelling a Crisis: Lack of Treatment for Opioid Use in Canada's Prisons and Jails", *Dal News* (9 March 2020).

47 *Two-thirds of all illicit* ... BC Death Panel Review, 2018 at 19.

47 *one in five people...* ibid.

47 *In Alberta, 50 per cent* ... The Breakdown, "Kenney came out strong today against BC's decision to decriminalize individual amounts of hard drugs. And he seemed to do so by implying that at least half of the victims of overdoses are criminals anyways?" (31 May 2022 at 12:13), online: *Twitter* <https://twitter.com/TheBreakdownAB/status/1531715531434123266?s=20&t=u9u-zrFhoXgeizs8YDzr1Q> (video of Alberta Premier Jason Kenney).

47 *multiple peer-reviewed studies* ... Fiona G Kouyoumdjian, "Mortality Over 12 Years of Follow-up in People Admitted to Provincial Custody in Ontario: A Retrospective Cohort Study" (2016) 4:2 CMAJ Open E153; Stuart A Kinner, Simon Forsyth & Gail Williams, "Systematic Review of Record Linkage Studies of Mortality in Ex-prisoners: Why (Good) Methods Matter" (2013) 108:1 Addiction 38; Ingrid A Binswanger et al, "Mortality after Prison Release: Opioid Overdose and Other Causes of Death, Risk Factors, and Time Trends from 1999 to 2009" (2013) 159:9 Annals Internal Medicine 592; Parvaz Madadi et al, "Characteristics of Opioid-Users Whose Death Was Related to Opioid-Toxicity: A Population-Based Study in Ontario, Canada" (2013) 8:4:e60600 PLOS ONE 1.

48 *"People die because they ..."* Interview with "Duncan," 11 April 2022 (to protect his privacy, a pseudonym has been used).

48 *use alone* ... BC Death Panel Review, 2018.

3. "From Protectors to Villains"

49 *"I had a good childhood ..."* Interview with "Will," 12 April 2022 (to protect his privacy, a pseudonym has been used).

51 *including feeling numb ...* McKenna & Holtfreter at 451; Ellison & Munro at 185, 188; TIP Guide at 7.

51 *"reexperiencing a previous ..."* United States, Substance Abuse and Mental Health Services Administration, *Trauma-Informed Care in Behavioral Health Services* (SAMHSA, 2014) at 68.

51 *"reminder of the traumatic ..." ibid.*

51 *Trauma increases the risk ...* McKenna & Holtfreter at 451.

51 *trauma is a broader concept than ...* PTSD is a diagnosis that is assessed according to the American Psychiatric Association diagnostic criteria: see DSM-5 at 309.81 (F43.10). It defines trauma as "exposure to actual or threatened death, serious injury, or sexual violence." The DSM-5 definition recognizes the potential for vicarious trauma and trauma arising from either one or multiple events. To qualify as PTSD, *inter alia*, the exposure to trauma must be accompanied by symptoms from each of four symptom clusters (intrusive recollections, avoidance of stimuli associated with the traumatic event(s), negative alterations in cognitions and mood; and, hyperarousal symptoms) that persist for at least four weeks. The DSM-5 definition of trauma and requirement that certain symptoms persist for a particular length of time artificially narrows the concept of trauma, which risks concealing from the trauma-informed researcher and practitioner the true scope of the issue of trauma. See Ellison & Munro at 186. In this book, the definition of trauma that I am using extends beyond PTSD and comes from leading trauma-informed guidelines in Canada and the US, namely the TIP Guide and SAMHSA Guidance. See chapter 1.

51 *depression, dissociation and ...* Constance J Dalenberg et al, "Defining Trauma" in SN Gold, ed, *APA Handbook of Trauma Psychology: Vol 1, Foundations in Knowledge* (American Psychological Association, 2017), 15 at 22. See also Derek Summerfield, "The Invention of Post-Traumatic Stress Disorder and the Social Usefulness of a Psychiatric Category" (2001) 322:7278 British Medical Journal 95.

51 *impact on the neurochemistry ...* SAMHSA Guidance at 8; Dalenberg et al at 22.

52 *cognitive processes, including memory ...* For an in-depth explanation of trauma's impact on memory, see M Rose Barlow et al, "Trauma and Memory" in SN Gold, ed, *APA Handbook of Trauma Psychology: Vol 1, Foundations in Knowledge* (American Psychological Association, 2017) at 307; SAMHSA Guidance at 8.

52 *"leads to narrative incoherence ..."* Maunder & Hunter, "Damaged" at 63.

52 *"uncontained communication that ..." ibid* at 65.

52 *chronic pain, gynaecological difficulties ...* TIP Guide at 7; Helping Families at 6.

52 *difficult to trust others ...* SAMHSA Guidance at 8.

52 *interferes with parenting ...* Maunder & Hunter, "Damaged" at 101.

52 *"increased appreciation of life ..."* US Department of Veterans Affairs, National Centre for PTSD, "Spirituality and Trauma: Professionals Working Together", online: <https://www.ptsd.va.gov/professional/treat/care/spirituality_trauma.asp>.

53 *"loss of faith, diminished ..." ibid*; Gene G Ano & Erin B Vasconcelles, "Religious Coping and Psychological Adjustment to Stress: A Meta-Analysis" (2005) 61:4 Journal of Clinical Psychology 461.

53 *"When the healthcare system fails ..."* John Howard Society of Ontario, *Unlocking Change: Decriminalizing Mental Health Issues in Ontario* (John Howard Society of Ontario, 2015) at 19.

53 *"Do you need police ..."* "How 9-1-1 Works", online: *E-Comm* <https://www.ecomm911.ca/911-dispatch/how-9-1-1-works/>.

54 *Over two-thirds (68 per cent) ...* Inayat Singh, "2020 Already a Particularly Deadly Year for People Killed in Police Encounters, CBC Research Shows", *CBC News* (23 July 2020); see also BC Coroners Service, *Opportunities for Different Outcomes – Police: A Crucial Component of BC's Mental Health System: A BC Coroners Service Death Review Panel Report Examining Deaths among Persons with Recent Police Encounters* (Victoria, BC, 2019).

54 *investigation by the Globe and Mail ...* Nancy Macdonald, "Police Oversight Bodies Hindered by Silence of Accused Officers, Globe Analysis Finds", *Globe and Mail* (27 February 2023).

54 *In Toronto, 20,000 calls ...* John Howard Society of Ontario, *Broken Record: The Continued Criminalization of Mental Health Issues* (John Howard Society of Canada, 2021) at 9 [JHSO, "Broken Record"].

54 *more likely to be arrested ... ibid.*

55 *Chantel Moore, a twenty-six-year-old ...* Quotes and information on Moore's case are from Kevin Bissett, "Chantel Moore Shot by N.B. Police Officer in Chest, Abdomen and Leg, Inquest Hears", *CTV News Atlantic* (18 May 2022).

55 *Regis Korchinski-Paquet, a twenty-nine-year-old ...* "Hundreds of Protesters Mark 1 Year Since Death of Regis Korchinski-Paquet during Police Call", *CBC News* (24 May 2021).

55 *Ejaz Ahmed Choudry, a sixty-two-year-old ...* Quotes and information on Choudry's case are from Shanifa Nasser, "No Charges in Death of Ejaz Choudry, 62-Year-Old Shot and Killed by Police While in Crisis", *CBC News* (6 April 2021).

57 *may escalate rather than de-escalate ...* Richard G Dudley, Jr, *Childhood Trauma and Its Effects: Implications for Police* (US Department of Justice, National Institute of Justice, 2015) at 10. See also US, Bill HR 2992, *TBI and PTSD Law Enforcement Training Act*, 117th Cong, 2021; Bill Pascrell, "Pascrell, Bacon, Demings, Rutherford Reintroduce Bipartisan Legislation to Improve Trauma Training for Law Enforcement" (4 May 2021), online: *Bill Pascrell, 9th District of New Jersey* <https://pascrell.house.gov/news/documentsingle.aspx?DocumentID=4746>.

57 *inclined to "fight" to ...* Dudley at 11.

58 *fight-flight-freeze response ...* Karin Roelofs, "Neuro-Endocrine Control Mechanisms in Social Motivational Actions, Relevance for Social Psychopathologies" (2018) 28 European Neuropsychopharmacology S58 at S58.

58 *"National Use of Force Framework ..."* See Toronto Police Service, "Race and Identity Based Data Collective Strategy" (June 2022) at 30, online: <https://www.scribd.com/document/578462243/Toronto-police-report-on-systemic-racism

-in-officer-use-of-force-and-strip-searches#download&from_embed> [Toronto Police Service]; Kurtis Doering, "Arresting Officer in Toronto Van Attack Said to Exemplify Use of Force Training", *CityNews* (24 April 2018).

59 *CAMH publicly called for ...* Shanifa Nasser, "Canada's Largest Mental Health Hospital Calls for Removal of Police from Front Lines for People in Crisis", *CBC News* (23 June 2020).

60 *Joshua Nixon, a twenty-three-year-old ...* Information and quotes related to Nixon's case from Molly Hayes, "Ontario Police Watchdog Clears Stratford Officers for Violent 2015 Arrest of Indigenous Man with Autism", *Globe and Mail* (6 February 2021).

61 *Nate, a thirty-six-year-old ...* Interview with "Nate," 2 May 2022 (to protect his privacy, a pseudonym has been used).

62 *"an almost guaranteed outcome ..."* Sylvia Novac, Joe Hermer, Emily Paradis & Amber Kellen, "A Revolving Door? Homeless People and the Justice System in Toronto" in J David Hulchanski, Philippa Campsie, Shirley Chau, Stephen Hwang & Emily Paradis, eds, *Finding Home: Policy Options for Addressing Homelessness in Canada* (Cities Centre, University of Toronto, 2009).

63 *people with mental health issues are disproportionately incarcerated ...* Public Safety Canada, *Risk and Mental Disordered Offenders* (Public Safety Canada, 2013).

63 *exacerbates pre-existing mental ...* Naomi F Sugie & Kristin Turney, "Beyond Incarceration: Criminal Justice Contact and Mental Health" (2017) 82:4 American Sociology Review 719 at 719.

63 *overwhelming majority of people who are incarcerated ...* Claire Bodkin et al, "History of Childhood Abuse in Populations Incarcerated in Canada: A Systematic Review and Meta-Analysis" (2019) 109:3 American Journal of Public Health e1 at e1.

63 *prison environment can be profoundly triggering ...* Niki A Miller & Lisa M Najavits, "Creating Trauma-Informed Correctional Care: A Balance of Goals and Environment" (2012) 3:17246 European Journal of Psychotraumatology 1 at 1; Alicia Piper & David Berle, "The Association between Trauma Experienced during Incarceration and PTSD Outcomes: A Systematic Review and Meta-Analysis" (2019) 30:5 Journal of Forensic Psychiatry & Psychology 854 at 868.

64 *The prison environment itself ...* M Katherine Maeve, "Speaking Unavoidable Truths: Understanding Early Childhood Sexual and Physical Violence among Women in Prison" (2000) 21:5 Issues in Mental Health Nursing 473 at 480; Sugie & Turney at 719.

64 *being imprisoned can replicate ...* Jan Heney & Connie M Kristiansen, "An Analysis of the Impact of Prison on Women Survivors of Childhood Sexual Abuse" (1998) 20:4 Women & Therapy 29 at 29; Maeve at 480.

64 *reliving their past childhood traumas ...* Maeve at 480.

64 *"by perpetuating feelings ..."* Louise Bill, "The Victimization ... and ... Revictimization of Female Offenders" (1998) 60:7 Corrections Today 106 at 107.

64 *"helplessness and terror ..."* Judith Herman, *Trauma and Recovery: The Aftermath of Violence – From Domestic Abuse to Political Terror* (Basic Books, 1992) at 33.

64 *prison environment can lead to ...* Mika'il DeVeaux, "The Trauma of the Incarceration Experience" (2013) 48:1 Harvard Civil Rights–Civil Liberties Law Review 257 at 258–61.

64 *an unconscious, automated psychological ...* Roelofs at S58.

64 *behaviours are interpreted as noncompliance ...* Dudley at 10.

65 *is to ignore the role ...* See Vittoria Ardino, "Offending Behaviour: The Role of Trauma and PTSD" (2012) 3:18968 European Journal of Psychotraumatology 1 at 1.

65 *"window of tolerance" for ...* John R Purcell et al, "A Review of Risky Decision-Making in Psychosis-Spectrum Disorders" (2022) 91:102112 Clinical Psychology Review 1 at 12; Maeve at 477–8; Amy FT Arnsten, "Stress Signalling Pathways That Impair Prefrontal Cortex Structure and Function" (2009) 10:6 Natural Reviews Neuroscience 410 at 410–12; FM Corrigan, JJ Fisher & DJ Nutt, "Autonomic Dysregulation and the Window of Tolerance Model of the Effects of Complex Emotional Trauma" (2011) 25:1 Journal of Psychopharmacology 17 at 17–19.

66 *restraint equipment, physical handling ...* Correctional Service Canada, *Use of Force* (Commissioner's Directive), No 567-1 (Correctional Service Canada, 2016), Annex A [CSC, "Use of Force"].

66 *"Frustrating, violent, or impulsive ..."* JHSO, "Broken Record" at 15. See Mimosa Luigi et al, "Shedding Light on 'the Hole': A Systematic Review and Meta-Analysis on Adverse Psychological Effects and Mortality following Solitary Confinement in Correctional Settings" (2020) 11:840 Frontiers in Psychiatry 1.

66 *Four in ten (41 per cent) ...* Ivan Zinger, *Annual Report 2020–2021* (Office of the Correctional Investigator, 2021) at 14 [Zinger, "Annual Report 2020–21"].

66 *pepper spray is overused ... ibid* at 11, 53.

67 *"used two separate bursts ..." ibid* at 2.

67 *who constitute a majority of incarcerated women ...* Bodkin at e1.

67 *"Overcrowding and double-bunking ..."* Zinger, "Annual Report 2020–21" at 30.

68 *eight times more likely to die ...* Thomas Gabor, *Deaths in Custody – Final Report* (Office of the Correctional Investigator of Canada, 28 February 2007).

68 *"[a]pproximately half of all deaths ..."* Adam D Vaughan, Denise M Zabkiewicz & Simon N Verdun-Jones, "In Custody Deaths of Men Related to Mental Illness and Substance Use: A Cross-Sectional Analysis of Administrative Records in Ontario, Canada" (2017) 48 Journal of Forensic & Legal Medicine 1.

68 *Soleiman Faqiri, a thirty-year-old ...* Amira Elghawaby, "Canada's Prisons Are Failing the Mentally Ill", *Toronto Star* (8 January 2020); Robyn Crawford, "Ontario Man Whose Brother Died in Jail Holds Public Forum in Vancouver", *Global News* (24 February 2019).

69 *"The coroner's report was ..."* Elghawaby. The Office of the Chief Coroner of Ontario declined to provide me with a copy of the coroner's report in relation to this incident, citing privacy laws.

69 *"even after the province's ..."* Shanifa Nasser, "They Wanted Justice for Their Mentally Ill Loved One Who Died in Jail. Now Those Hopes Are Crushed", *CBC News* (23 August 2022).

69 *"[p]ersons who self-injure ..."* Mandy Wesley, *Marginalized: The Aboriginal Women's Experience in Federal Corrections* (Public Safety Canada, 2012).

70 *Tu'Inukuafe has spoken out in the media ...* Thia James, "Questions Remain More than a Year after Curtis McKenzie's Death at Sask. Penitentiary", *Saskatoon StarPhoenix* (24 March 2021).

70 *"[I]t's simply immoral ..." ibid.*

71 *average life expectancy for prisoners ...* Adelina Iftene, "Life and Death in Canadian Penitentiaries" (2020) 66 Canadian Family Physician 759 at 759. See also Ivan Zinger, *Office of the Correctional Investigator Annual Report 2017–2018* (Office of the Correctional Investigator, 2018) at 28; Statistics Canada, *Life Expectancy and Other Elements of the Complete Life Table, Three-Year Estimates, Canada, All Provinces except Prince Edward Island*, Table 13-10-0114-01 (Statistics Canada, 2022); Statistics Canada, *Life Expectancy and Other Elements of the Abridged Life Table, Three-Year Estimates, Prince Edward Island and the Territories*, Table 13-10-0140-01 (Statistics Canada, 2022).

71 *"Correctional institutions are not ..."* Office of the Auditor General of Ontario, *Annual Report 2019: Reports on Correctional Services and Court Operations*, vol 3 (Office of the Auditor General of Ontario, 2019) at 18.

72 *"most have had difficulty ..."* Ivan Zinger, *Annual Report 2019–2020* (Office of the Correctional Investigator, 2021) at 68.

72 *Grade 7–8 is the average ...* Roger Boe, *A Two-Year Release Follow-Up of Federal Offenders Who Participated in the Adult Basic Education (ABE) Program* (Correctional Service of Canada, February 1998).

72 *"Convicted persons with steady ..."* Tim Quigley, "Some Issues in Sentencing of Aboriginal Offenders" in Richard Gosse, James Youngblood Henderson & Roger Carter, eds, *Continuing Poundmaker and Riel's Quest: Presentations Made at a Conference on Aboriginal Peoples and Justice* (Purich Publishing, 1994) 269 at 275–6 cited in *R v Ipeelee*, [2012] 1 SCR 433 at para 67.

73 *"After an average of 14 ..."* Kelly M Babchishin, Leslie-Anne Keown & Kimberly P Mularczyk, *Economic Outcomes of Canadian Federal Offenders* (Public Safety Canada, 2021) at 2.

73 *National Advisory Council on Poverty ...* Employment and Social Development Canada, *Opportunity for All: Canada's First Poverty Reduction Strategy* (Employment and Social Development Canada, 2018); Employment and Social Development Canada, *Understanding Systems: The 2021 Report of the National Advisory Council on Poverty* (Employment and Social Development Canada, 2021).

74 *"assisting the rehabilitation of ..."* Corrections and Conditional Release Act, s 3(b).

75 *overall crime rates have declined ...* Greg Moreau, *Police-Reported Crime Statistics in Canada, 2021* (Statistics Canada, 2022) at Chart 1; MarcoTrends, "Canada Crime Rate & Statistics 1990–2023", online: <https://www.macrotrends.net/countries/CAN/canada/crime-rate-statistics>.

75 *proportion of people in custody in Canada ...* Jamil Malakieh, *Adult and Youth Correctional Statistics in Canada, 2018/2019* (Statistics Canada, 2020) at 4.

75 *any other G7 country ...* "World Pre-trial/Remand Imprisonment" in Roy Walmsley, World Prison Brief, 4th ed (ICPR, undated).

75 *Two-thirds of people (67 per cent) ...* Statistics Canada, "Table 35-10-0154-01 – Average Counts of Adults in Provincial and Territorial Correctional Programs."

75 *72 per cent of those in ... ibid* at 4, 9.

75 *a meta-analysis of fifty studies* ... Paul Gendreau, Claire Goggin & Francis T Cullen, *The Effects of Prison Sentences on Recidivism* (Public Works and Government Services Canada, 1999).

75 *($318 per day per* ... Malakieh at 6.

4. "Justice Is Not Blind"

76 *"I'm an Indigenous treaty ..."* Interview with "Angeline," 6 April 2022 (to protect their privacy, a pseudonym has been used).

76 *this caused Indigenous children to experience* ... See Truth and Reconciliation Commission of Canada, *Honouring the Truth, Reconciling for the Future: Summary of the Final Report on the Truth and Reconciliation Commission of Canada*, vol 1 (Truth and Reconciliation Commission of Canada, 2015) at 68–9, 137–8 [TRC Summary].

76 *"Cultural genocide" is how* ... Review Committee on Indian and Métis Adoptions and Placements, *No Quiet Place: Final Report to the Honourable Muriel Smith, Minister of Community Services* (Manitoba Community Services, 1985) at 328–9.

78 *While 16.6 per cent of the* ... Statistics Canada, *Census Profile, 2016 Census, Saskatchewan [Province] and Canada [Country]*, (Table), Catalogue No 98-316-X2016001 (Statistics Canada, 2017); Julia Peterson, "Saskatchewan First Nation Gets Control of Children in Care", *Globe and Mail* (6 July 2021).

78 *16.5 per cent of children* ... Sonia Hélie et al, "Placement Stability, Cumulative Time in Care, and Permanency: Using Administrative Data from CPS to Track Placement Trajectories" (2017) 14:11 International Journal of Environmental Research & Public Health 1405.

79 *"the over-representation of ..."* Department of Justice Canada, *Overview of Department of Justice Canada Policy and Program Initiatives to Reduce Violence and Increase Safety for Indigenous Women, Girls and 2SLGBTQQIA People* (22 October 2018) at 17.

82 *Attempting to spit on* ... See, e.g., *R v GP*, 2020 ONSC 3240 at para 10; *R v Bear*, 2003 SKPC 117 at para 17.

84 *Reconciliation and Indigenous Justice* ... David Milward, *Reconciliation and Indigenous Justice: A Search for Ways Forward* (Fernwood Publishing, 2022).

85 *"deliberate, often covert campaign ..."* National Inquiry into Missing and Murdered Indigenous Women and Girls, *Reclaiming Power and Place: The Final Report of the National Inquiry into Missing and Murdered Indigenous Women and Girls*, vol 1a (2019) at 5.

86 *Lana is a thirty-nine-year-old* ... Interview with "Lana," 6 April 2022 (to protect her privacy, a pseudonym has been used).

89 *One-in-five Indigenous* ... Adam Cotter, "Perceptions of and Experiences with Police and the Justice System among the Black and Indigenous Populations in Canada" (Statistics Canada, 16 February 2022) [Cotter, "Perceptions"].

89 *"the ability of police ..."* ibid.

89 *(45 per cent), compared with 36 per cent* ... ibid.

90 *"Black people were 1.9 times ..."* Jennifer Pagliaro, "9 Key Findings from the Landmark Toronto Police Report on 'Systemic' Anti-Black Discrimination", *Toronto Star* (15 June 2022); see Toronto Police Service at 56.

90 *"Anyone in the justice system ..."* The Aboriginal Justice Implementation Commission, *Report of the Aboriginal Justice Inquiry of Manitoba*, vol 1, ch 1 (1999) [AJIC, "Report"].

91 *"For every year of incarceration ..."* See, e.g., Evelyn J Patterson, "The Dose–Response of Time Served in Prison on Mortality: New York State, 1989–2003" (2013) 103 American Journal of Public Health 523.

91 *"We lived in the reserve," began ...* Interview with "Tracy," 4 April 2022 (to protect her privacy, a pseudonym has been used for her and her son "Dylan").

92 *"[I]n many cases Aboriginal ..."* Jana Grekul & Patti LaBoucane-Benson, *An Investigation into the Formation and Recruitment Processes of Aboriginal Gangs in Western Canada* (Public Safety Canada, 2006) at 2.

94 *"An Indigenous person in Canada ..."* Ryan Flanagan, "Why Are Indigenous People in Canada So Much More Likely to Be Shot and Killed by Police?", *CTV News* (19 June 2020).

96 *50 per cent of admissions to ...* Scott Clark, *Overrepresentation of Indigenous People in the Canadian Criminal Justice System: Causes and Responses* (Department of Justice Canada, 2019) at 11.

96 *In 2019/20, the proportion ...* Calculations based on data from Statistics Canada, "Table 35-10-0007-01 – Youth Admissions to Correctional Services, by Indigenous Identity and Sex".

5. "Thrown in with the Wolves"

98 *"No, I never really ..."* Interview with "Danny," 31 March 2022 (to protect his privacy, a pseudonym has been used).

101 *Table 1 – Over-representation of ...* Corrections data for 2019–20 from Statistics Canada, "Table 35-10-0016-01 – Adult Custody Admissions to Correctional Services by Indigenous Identity" ("Total custodial admissions are totals of sentenced (including intermittent sentences), remand and other custodial status admissions"); population data from Statistics Canada, "Aboriginal Identity Population by Both Sexes, Total – Age, 2016 Counts, Canada, Provinces and Territories, 2016 Census – 25% Sample Data" in *Aboriginal Peoples Highlight Tables, 2016 Census* (Statistics Canada, 2017).

101 *Indigenous people comprised 17.6 per cent ...* Office of the Correctional Investigator, *Annual Report 2021–2022* (30 June 2022) [OCI, "Annual Report 2021–22"].

101 *"the rate of Indigenous male ..."* Clark at 9.

102 *routinely classified as higher risk ...* Office of the Correctional Investigator, "Aboriginal Offenders: A Critical Situation" (16 September 2013), online: <https://www.oci-bec.gc.ca/cnt/rpt/oth-aut/oth-aut20121022info-eng.aspx>.

104 *"Since I was twelve until ..."* Interview with "Courtney," 30 March 2022 (to protect her privacy, a pseudonym has been used).

104 *a co-ed institution ...* See, e.g., Council of Elizabeth Fry Societies of Ontario, "Facilities for the Incarceration of Women in Ontario", online: <https://www.cefso.ca/institutions.html>.

107 *"all available sanctions, other ..."* Criminal Code, RSC, 1985, c C-46, s 718.2(e) [*Criminal Code*].

107 *"a crisis" ...* R v Gladue, [1999] 1 SCR 688 at para 58 [*Gladue*].

107 *"(A) The unique systemic ..."* ibid at para 66.

108 *In 2012, thirteen years ... R v Ipeelee*, [2012] 1 SCR 433.

108 *ballooned to nearly 22 per cent ...* Office of the Correctional Investigator, "Indigenous People in Federal Custody Surpasses 30% – Correctional Investigator Issues Statement and Challenge" (21 January 2020).

108 *"not had a discernible impact" ... Ipeelee* at para 63.

108 *largely attributed to judges ...* ibid at para 60.

108 *comprising 32 per cent of federal ...* OCI, "Annual Report 2021–22"; *Gladue* at para 58.

112 *"Prison has been characterized ..."* See *R v Proulx*, [2000] 1 SCR 61 at para 69 (citing the Report of the Canadian Committee on Corrections, *Toward Unity: Criminal Justice and Corrections* (1969) for this proposition).

114 *been called a genocide ...* Pamela Palmater, "Overincarceration of Indigenous Peoples Nothing Short of Genocide", *The Lawyer's Daily* (30 January 2020).

114 *"it results in bodily ..."* Prisoners' Legal Services, "The Role of Prison in Genocide and Crimes against Humanity against Indigenous People in Canada" (29 September 2021) at 2.

6. "The Usual Suspects"

117 *their physical appearance and clothing ...* Desmond Cole, "The Skin I'm In: I've Been Interrogated by Police More Than 50 Times – All Because I'm Black", *Toronto Life* (21 April 2015) [Cole, "Skin I'm In"].

117 *The Skin We're In ...* Desmond Cole, *The Skin We're In: A Year of Black Resistance and Power* (Doubleday Canada, 2020).

117 *at least fifty times ...* Cole, "Skin I'm In".

118 *a $2.7 billion class action ...* Peter Small, "Police Union Sues Star over Race-Crime Series", *Toronto Star* (18 January 2003); "Top Class Action Cases in Canada", online (blog): *Klein Lawyers LLP* <https://www.callkleinlawyers.com /full-disclosure/top-class-action-cases-in-canada/>.

118 *lawsuit was eventually abandoned ...* CBC, "Here's What You Need to Know about Carding", online: <https://www.cbc.ca/firsthand/features/heres-what-you -need-to-know-about-carding>.

118 *In Vancouver in 2018 ...* BC Civil Liberties Association, "Civil Liberties and First Nations Groups File Amendment to Complaint on VPD Street Checks; Concern with Over Representation of Indigenous Women in New Numbers Released" *Press Release* (12 July 2018).

118 *"The VPD does not ..."* Mychaylo Prystupa, "Blacks, Indigenous Over Represented in Vancouver Police Stops: 10 Years of Data", *CTV News* (14 June 2018).

118 *"An unwillingness to discuss ..."* Ontario Human Rights Commission, *Paying the Price: The Human Cost of Racial Profiling – Inquiry Report* (21 October 2003).

119 *The Commission's inquiry found ...* ibid at 12.

119 *Jamiel Moore-Williams ...* Liam Britten, "Vancouver Police Officers Criminally Charged over Violent Takedown That Victim Says Was Racially Motivated", *CBC News* (8 December 2020).

120 *remained on active duty ...* ibid.

120 *In February 2023, Constable ...* CBC News, "Vancouver Police Officer Guilty of Assault with Weapon in Arrest of Black Man Stopped for Jaywalking" (13 February 2023).

120 *370 per cent more likely ...* Akwasi Owusu-Bempah, *Race-Based Criminal Justice Data in Canada: Suggestions for Moving Forward* (Public Safety Canada, March 2011) at 6 [Owusu-Bempah, "Race-Based Criminal Justice Data"].

120 *"Indigenous people and Black ..."* Jennifer Yoon & Jaela Bernstein, "Black, Indigenous People 4 to 5 Times More Likely than Whites to Be Stopped by Montreal Police", *CBC News* (7 October 2019).

121 *three times more likely ...* Scot Wortley & Akwasi Owusu-Bempah, "The Usual Suspects: Police Stop and Search Practices in Canada" (2011) 21:4 Policing and Society 395.

121 *Policing Black Lives ...* Robyn Maynard, *Policing Black Lives: State Violence in Canada from Slavery to the Present* (Fernwood Publishing, 2017) at 87 [Maynard, "Policing Black Lives"].

121 *"more that a group..."* David M Tanovich, "E-Racing Racial Profiling" (2004) 41:4 Alberta Law Review 905.

121 *"disproportionate over-surveillance ..."* Maynard, "Policing Black Lives" at 87.

122 *"Black people are not ..."* ibid.

122 *Another major set of factors ...* For a more detailed discussion of the "higher offending thesis" and "bias thesis," see Scot Wortley & Maria Jung, *Racial Disparity in Arrests and Charges: An Analysis of Arrest and Charge Data from the Toronto Police Service* (Ontario Human Rights Commission, 2020) at 4.

122 *Both Ontario ... Collection of Identifying Information in Certain Circumstances – Prohibition and Duties*, O Reg 58/16, s 5.

123 *"While celebrated by some ..."* Akwasi Owusu-Bempah, "Ontario's 'Ban' on Carding Isn't Really a Ban at All", *CBC News* (18 January 2017); see also Jacques Gallant & May Warren, "Police Carding Should Be Banned in Ontario, Independent Review Says", *Toronto Star* (31 December 2018).

123 *"significant racial differences with ..."* Canadian Association of Black Lawyers, *Race and Criminal Injustice: An Examination of Public Perceptions of and Experiences with the Ontario Criminal Justice System* (Ryerson University Faculty of Law, 2021).

123 *"overtly bans stopping someone ..."* Simon Little, "The VPD Has Updated Its 'Carding' Policy. Here's What It Means for You", *Global News* (21 January 2020).

124 *white people don't ...* Mychaylo Prystupa, "Blacks, Indigenous Over Represented in Vancouver Police Stops: 10 Years of Data", *CTV News* (14 June 2018) at 01:11, online (video): <https://bc.ctvnews.ca/blacks-indigenous-over-represented-in-vancouver-police-stops-10-years-of-data-1.3973823>; see also Wortley & Owusu-Bempah.

125 *One in five Black people ...* Cotter, "Perceptions".

125 *"the ability of police ..."* ibid.

125 *An Environics Research survey ...* Canadian Association of Black Lawyers.

126 *7 per cent of Black and Indigenous ...* Cotter, "Perceptions".

126 *In an Ontario study ...* Wortley reviewed 784 incidents in 2000–6 that were before Ontario's Special Investigations Unit. See Scott Wortley, *Police Use of Force*

in Ontario: An Examination of Data from the Special Investigations Unit – Final Report (Ipperwash Inquiry, 2006) at 40–2.

126 *Troublingly, there is no ...* For a discussion of race-based criminal justice data in Canada, see Owusu-Bempah, "Race-Based Criminal Justice Data".

126 *four times more likely ...* Maynard, "Policing Black Lives" at 107.

127 *2.3 times more often ...* Pagliaro.

127 *twenty times more likely ...* Wendy Gillis & Jim Rankin, "Nearly 20 Times as Likely to Be Shot Dead. Six Times More Likely to Be Taken Down by a Police Dog. Inside a Landmark Report on the 'Disproportionate' Use of Force on Black Torontonians", *Toronto Star* (17 August 2020); see Ontario Human Rights Commission, *A Disparate Impact: Second Interim Report on the Inquiry into Racial Profiling and Racial Discrimination of Black Persons by the Toronto Police Service* (10 August 2020).

127 *"Our own analysis of ..."* "Read the Landmark Toronto Police Report on Race and Officer Use of Force", *Toronto Star* (15 June 2022).

128 *two-hundred-year history of slavery ...* See, e.g., Matthew McRae, "The Story of Slavery in Canadian History", online: *Canadian Museum for Human Rights* <https://humanrights.ca/story/the-story-of-slavery-in-canadian-history>.

128 *including Lester Donaldson ...* Maynard, "Policing Black Lives" at 105.

128 *"In 2014, the police ..." ibid.*

129 *3.7 times more likely ...* Wortley & Jung at 108.

129 *more likely to be denied bail ...* Maynard, "Policing Black Lives" at 107–8.

129 *disproportionately imprisoned and have been ...* See Akwasi Owusu-Bempah et al, "Race and Incarceration: The Representation and Characteristics of Black People in Provincial Correctional Facilities in Ontario, Canada" (2021) Race and Justice.

129 *From 2005 to 2015 ...* Howard Sapers, *Annual Report of the Office of the Correctional Investigator 2014–2015* (26 June 2015).

130 *8.1 per cent of federally incarcerated people ...* Public Safety Canada, *2020 Corrections and Conditional Release Statistical Overview* (2022) at 60.

130 *42 per cent of people convicted ...* Department of Justice Canada Research and Statistics Division, *The Impact of Mandatory Minimum Penalties on Indigenous, Black and Other Visible Minorities* (Department of Justice Canada, 2017).

130 *"incarceration is heavily concentrated ..."* Owusu-Bempah et al.

130 *"Black men were five times ..." ibid.*

131 *"My investigation of race ..."* Office of the Correctional Investigator, "Correctional Investigator's 2020–21 Annual Report Finds Incarcerated Black and Indigenous Persons Are More Likely to Be Involved in Use of Force Incidents" (10 February 2022).

132 *40 per cent of the city's murder ...* Scot Wortley, "A Province at the Crossroads: Statistics on Youth Violence in Ontario" in Roy McMurtry & Alvin Curling, eds, *The Review of the Roots of Youth Violence*, vol 4 (Queen's Printer for Ontario, 2008) at 56.

133 *"It is a little known ..."* Michael H Tulloch, *Report of the Independent Police Oversight Review* (Queen's Printer for Ontario, 2017) at 26.

133 *Justice Mahmud Jamal ...* Supreme Court of Canada, "The Honourable Mahmud Jamal" (10 January 2023), online: <https://www.scc-csc.ca/judges-juges/bio-eng.

aspx?id=mahmud-jamal>; Peter Zimonjic, "Justice Mahmud Jamal Is First Person of Colour Nominated to the Supreme Court of Canada", *CBC News* (17 June 2021).

133 *Justice Michelle O'Bonsawin* ... Supreme Court of Canada, "The Honourable Michelle O'Bonsawin" (11 January 2023), online: <https://www.scc-csc.ca /judges-juges/bio-eng.aspx?id=michelle-obonsawin>; Nick Boisvert, "Michelle O'Bonsawin Becomes 1st Indigenous Person Nominated to Supreme Court of Canada", *CBC News* (19 August 2022).

134 *"Too little and too late"* ... Johnson, "Peace and Good Order" at 146.

7. "An Alien System of Law"

135 *"beat the American detachment ..."* Mohawk Council of Kahnawà:ke "Tsi Niti-ohtón:ne Oká:ra, History of Kahnawà:ke" (24 April 2017).

136 *"Within less than a hundred years ..."* ibid.

137 *the Mohawk Resistance at Ka'nehsatà:ke* ... Melinda Meng, "Bloody Blockades: The Legacy of the Oka Crisis" (2020) 41:3 Harvard International Review 38 at 38–9.

139 *while some on-reserve Indigenous* ... See Public Safety Canada, "First Nations and Inuit Policing Program" (21 March 2022).

139 *over half of First Nations* ... The Council of Canadian Academies, *Towards Peace, Harmony, and Well-Being: Policing in Indigenous Communities – The Expert Panel on Policing in Indigenous Communities* (2019) at xv.

139 *68,718 police officers* ... Patricia Conor et al, "Police Resources in Canada, 2019" (2020) 40:1 Juristat 1–29.

139 *a mere $149 million* ... Public Safety Canada, "FNPP Background and Program Stats" (13 September 2021) [PSC, "FNPP Background"].

140 *"physical and mental wellbeing"* ... Public Safety Canada, "Summary of the Evaluation of the First Nations and Inuit Policing Program" (22 April 2022) [PSC, "Summary"].

140 *"The First Nations Policing Policy ..."* Court of Appeal of Quebec, *Takuhikan c. Procureur général du Québec* (15 December 2022), online: <https:// courdappelduquebec.ca/en/judgments/details/takuhikan-c-procureur -general-du-quebec/> [English summary of *Takuhikan c. Procureur général du Québec*, 2022 QCCA 1699].

140 *"a 26% decrease ..."* PSC, "FNPP Background".

140 *Indigenous communities feel safer* ... PSC, "Summary".

141 *Under the 1992 Corrections* ... *Corrections and Conditional Release Act*, SC 1992, c 20, s 81.

141 *"self-identity, self-esteem ..."* Correctional Service Canada, "About the Different Lodges" (5 September 2019) [CSC, "Different Lodges"].

142 *Four are operated by* ... Public Safety Canada, *2020 Corrections and Conditional Release Statistical Overview* (2022) at 60; CSC, "Different Lodges".

143 *"Indigenous offenders released from ..."* Office of the Auditor General of Canada, *2016 Fall Reports of the Auditor General of Canada: Report 3 – Preparing Indigenous Offenders for Release – Correctional Service Canada* (Ottawa, 2016) at 3.63.

144 *"We feel that we ..."* AJIC, "Report".
144 *Prior to the arrival of ...* Val Napoleon & Hadley Friedland, "Indigenous Legal Traditions: Roots to Renaissance" in Markus D Dubber & Tatjana Hörnle, eds, *The Oxford Handbook of Criminal Law* (Oxford University Press, 2014).
144 *"a system which seeks ..."* Indian Residential School History & Dialogue Centre, "Timeline: John Cabot Arrives on the North Shore of North America (1497)".
144 *"Everything that has ..."* Johnson, "Peace and Good Order" at 11.
144 *"To say that law ..."* *ibid* at 14.
145 *"Indigenous-police relations are ..."* Tulloch at ch 1, para 23.
145 *"the great aim of ..."* House of Commons, "To an Order of the House of Commons, dated the 2nd May, 1887; – For copies of all title deeds, patents, correspondence, and all documents respecting the claim of the Six Nation Indians, as set forth in their Petition presented to this House on the 18th April, 1887", *Sessional Papers*, vol 16, No 20b (1887) at 37.
145 *"I want to get rid ..."* Brian Titley, *A Narrow Vision: Duncan Campbell Scott and the Administration of Indian Affairs in Canada* (UBC Press, 1986) at 50.
145 *"From an Indian perspective ..."* Chief Joe Mathias & Gary R Yabsley, "Conspiracy of Legislation: The Suppression of Indian Rights in Canada" (1991) 89 BC Studies 34 at 35.
146 *The legislation compelled ...* Indian Act, RSC 1886, c 43, s 138(2).
146 *criminalized Indigenous parents ...* Indian Act, RSC 1906, c 81, s 10 as amended by An Act to amend the Indian Act, SC 1919-20, c 50, s 1.
146 *prohibit Indigenous religious and legal ceremonies ...* The Indian Act, 1880, SC 1880, c 28, as amended by An Act to further amend "The Indian Act, 1880", SC 1884, c 27, s 3.
146 *provide funds for a lawyer ...* Indian Act, RSC 1906, c 81, s 149a, as amended by An Act to amend the Indian Act, SC 1926-27, c 32, s 6; Indian Act, RSC 1927, c 98, s 141, as amended by An Act to amend the Indian Act, SC 1930, c 25, s 16.
146 *"supreme law of Canada ..."* Constitution Act, 1982, s 52(1), being Schedule B to the Canada Act 1982 (UK), 1982, c 11.
146 *"To understand the nature ..."* "Sources of Criminal Law in Canada" in Department of Justice Canada Federal Prosecution Service, *The Federal Prosecution Service Deskbook* (Federal Prosecution Service, 2005) <https://www.ppsc-sppc.gc.ca/eng/pub/fpsd-sfpg/fps-sfp/fpd/ch01.html> [Federal Prosecution Deskbook, 2005].
147 *In Canada's Indigenous Constitution ...* John Borrows, *Canada's Indigenous Constitution* (University of Toronto Press, 2010) [Borrows, "Canada's Indigenous Constitution"].
147 *But, as Borrows points out ...* Borrows, "Canada's Indigenous Constitution" at 17. See also Johnson, "Peace and Good Order" at 125–6.
147 *"factually, legally and morally wrong" ...* Report of the Royal Commission on Aboriginal Peoples: Looking Forward and Looking Back, vol 1 (Canada Communication Group – Publishing, 1996) at 696.
147 *"formally repudiated by ..."* TRC Summary at 195 (see Calls to Action 47 and 49).
147 *the Vatican issued a statement ...* Holy See Press Office, "Joint Statement of the Dicasteries for Culture and Education and for Promoting Integral Human

Development on the 'Doctrine of Discovery', 30.03.2023" (30 March 2023), online: <https://press.vatican.va/content/salastampa/en/bollettino/pubblico /2023/03/30/230330b.html>.

148 *"When the settlers came ..."* Borrows, "Canada's Indigenous Constitution" at 18; *Calder et al v Attorney-General of British Columbia*, [1973] SCR 313 at 328.

149 *"without treaties, the so-called ..."* Borrows, "Canada's Indigenous Constitution" at 21.

149 *efforts to "Indigenize" the system ...* See, e.g., Katrina Eñano, "Law Society of British Columbia Now Mandates B.C. Lawyers to Take Indigenous Intercultural Course", *Canadian Lawyer* (1 March 2022); Canadian Judicial Council, "2021 Annual Conference on Indigenous People and the Law"; *Corrections and Conditional Release Act*, ss 80–84.1; *Criminal Code*, s 718.2(e); *Gladue* at para 68; *Ipeelee* at para 60.

149 *"The fundamental difference between ..."* Johnson, "Peace and Good Order" at 133.

150 *more stringent penalties do not deter ...* See, e.g., US National Institute of Justice, "National Institute of Justice Five Things about Deterrence" (5 June 2016), online: <https://nij.ojp.gov/topics/articles/five-things-about-deterrence>; Heather Mann et al, "What Deters Crime? Comparing the Effectiveness of Legal, Social, and Internal Sanctions across Countries" (2016) 7 Frontiers in Psychology 1–13; Daniel S Nagin, "Deterrence in the Twenty-First Century" in Michael Tonry, ed, *Crime and Justice in America: 1975–2025* (University of Chicago Press, 2013) 199–264.

151 *"is to lay before ..."* Boucher v The Queen, [1955] SCR 16 at 23.

151 *"duty is to protect the ..."* Law Society of British Columbia, *Code of Professional Conduct for British Columbia* (October 2021) at r 5.1-1, commentary 9.

152 *"pickpocketing more than ..."* Steven Wilf, *Law's Imagined Republic: Popular Politics and Criminal Justice in Revolutionary America* (Cambridge University Press, 2010) at 140.

152 *Torture was, for some ...* Charles H Randall, Jr, "Sir Edward Coke and the Privilege against Self-Incrimination" (1956) 8:4 South Carolina Law Quarterly 417 at 419.

152 *The last hangings in ...* EA Fattah, "Canada's Successful Experience with the Abolition of the Death Penalty" (1983) 25:4 Canadian Journal of Criminology 421.

152 *Other penalties included lashing ...* Correctional Service Canada, "Abolition of Corporal Punishment 1972" (5 March 2015).

152 *"were removed from the ..."* Hamish Maxwell-Stewart, "The Rise and Fall of Penal Transportation" in Paul Knepper & Anja Johansen, eds, *The Oxford Handbook of the History of Crime and Criminal Justice* (Oxford University Press, 2016) 635 at 636.

152 *Author Resmaa Menakem has ...* Resmaa Menakem, *My Grandmother's Hands: Racialized Trauma and the Pathway to Mending Our Hearts and Bodies* (Central Recovery Press, 2017) at 58ff.

153 *the presumption of innocence ...* See *Woolmington v DPP*, [1935] AC 462.

153 *"better ten guilty persons ..."* William Blackstone, *Commentaries on the Laws of England*, vol 4 (Clarendon Press, 1769) at 352.

153 *minor offences like shoplifting ... Criminal Code*, s 334(b)(i).
153 *pair of counterfeit sunglasses ... Copyright Act*, RSC 1985, c C-42, s 42(1)(b);
    Criminal Code, ss 408(b), 412(1)(a).
153 *and graffiti ... Criminal Code*, s 430.
153 *In 2019, without any ... Criminal Code*, s 787. See Jillian Rogin et al, "ACCLE
    and Bill C-75: Implications for Student Legal Clinics & Communities in Can-
    ada" (2020) 32 Journal of Law and Social Policy 91.

8. "Nobodies"

155 *"Why don't you leave ..."* Interview with "Skye," 12 April 2022 (to protect their
    privacy, a pseudonym has been used).
156 *Researchers cite myriad reasons ...* Alafair S Burke, "Domestic Violence as a
    Crime of Pattern and Intent: An Alternative Reconceptualization" (2007) 75:3
    George Washington Law Review 552 at 569–71; Cynthia K Sanders & Meg
    Schnabel, "Organizing for Economic Empowerment of Battered Women: Wom-
    en's Savings Accounts" (2006) 14:3 Journal of Community Practice 47 at 48;
    Maggie A Evans & Gene S Feder, "Help-Seeking amongst Women Survivors of
    Domestic Violence: A Qualitative Study of Pathways towards Formal and Infor-
    mal Support" (2014) 19 Health Expectations 62 at 66–8.
156 *related to "traumatic bonding" ...* Rebecca L Heron, Maarten Eisma & Kevin
    Browne, "Why Do Female Domestic Violence Victims Remain in or Leave Abu-
    sive Relationships? A Qualitative Study" (2022) 31:5 Journal of Aggression, Mal-
    treatment & Trauma at 9–10; Matthew H Logan, "Stockholm Syndrome: Held
    Hostage by the One You Love" (2018) 5:2 Violence & Gender 67 at 67; Donald
    G Dutton & Susan Painter, "Emotional Attachments in Abusive Relationships: A
    Test of Traumatic Bonding Theory" (1993) 8:2 Violence & Victims 105 at 106.
156 *"that battered women are ..."* R v Lavallee, [1990] 1 SCR 852 per Wilson J.
156 *"outside the common understanding ..."* R v Malott, [1998] 1 SCR 123 at para 43
    per L'Heureux-Dubé J.
157 *known as "whacking" victims ...* Cristin Schmitz, "'Whack' Sex Assault Com-
    plainant at Preliminary Inquiry", 8:5 *The Lawyers Weekly* (27 May 1988) at 22.
158 *it remains a serious concern ...* Elaine Craig, *Putting Trials on Trial: Sexual As-
    sault and the Failure of the Legal Profession* (McGill-Queen's University Press,
    2018) at 41–60 [Craig, "Putting Trials on Trial"].
158 *"unwillingness to cooperate" ...* See Benjamin Perrin, *Victim Law: The Law of
    Victims of Crime in Canada* (Thomson Reuters, 2017) at 80, 249, 261 [Perrin,
    "Victim Law"].
158 *One in five Canadians ...* Adam Cotter, *Criminal Victimization in Canada, 2019*
    (Statistics Canada, 2021) [Cotter, "Criminal Victimization"]. Unless otherwise
    noted, the statistics in this section are from this report.
159 *Indigenous people are seven ...* Amelia Armstrong & Brianna Jaffray, "Homicide
    in Canada, 2020" (Statistics Canada, 2021).
159 *"The missing and murdered women ..."* Wally T Oppal, *Foresaken: The Report of
    the Missing Women Commission of Inquiry – Executive Summary* (British Co-
    lumbia, 2012) at 24.

159 *were treated as "nobodies" ... ibid* at 25.
160 *"This figure is consistent ..."* Cotter, "Criminal Victimization".
160 *one of the highest rates ...* Julie Sauvé & Kwing Hung, "An International Perspective on Criminal Victimisation" (Statistics Canada, 2009).
162 *women are twice as likely ...* Cotter, "Criminal Victimization".
163 *since childhood with ADHD ...* Anita Thapar & Miriam Cooper, "Attention Deficit Hyperactivity Disorder" (2016) 387:10024 Lancet 1240 at 1240.
163 *significant association between childhood ...* Nicole M Brown et al, "Associations between Adverse Childhood Experiences and ADHD Diagnosis and Severity" (2017) 17:4 Academic Pediatrics 349.
166 *standard is so high ...* R v Lifchus, [1997] 3 SCR 320 at para 39.
166 *simply be deemed "unfounded" ...* See Robyn Doolittle, "Unfounded: Why Police Dismiss 1 in 5 Sexual Assault Claims as Baseless", *Globe and Mail* (3 February 2017).
166 *35 per cent of charges are ...* Statistics Canada, "Adult Criminal Courts, Number of Cases and Charges by Type of Decision", Table 35-10-0027-01.
166 *test in R. v. Jordan ...* R v Jordan, [2016] 1 SCR 631.
167 *upwards of 90 per cent ...* Simon N Verdun-Jones & Adamira A Tijerino, *Victim Participation in the Plea Negotiation Process in Canada* (2002) at vi.
167 *"The process largely takes ..." ibid* at iii.
167 *"would bring the administration ..." R v Anthony-Cook*, [2016] 2 SCR 204 at para 32.
167 *"our justice system would ..." ibid* at para 40.
167 *considered in determining the accused's ... Canadian Victims Bill of Rights*, SC 2015, c 13, s 2 at s 15; see also *Criminal Code*, s 722.
168 *"years after the Victims ..." R v Aklok*, 2020 NUCJ 37 (CanLII) at para 57.
168 *Some judges are "troubled" ... ibid* at paras 92–4.
168 *"the physical or emotional ..." Criminal Code*, s 722(1).
168 *"Less than one percent ..."* Craig, "Putting Trials on Trial" at 3.
168 *"people who reported having ..."* Dyna Ibrahim, "Public Perceptions of the Police in Canada's Provinces, 2019" (Statistics Canada, 2020).
170 *received the worst grades ...* Benjamin Perrin & Richard Audas, *Report Card on the Criminal Justice System #2* (Macdonald-Laurier Institute for Public Policy, 2018).
171 *overwhelming proportion (87 per cent) ...* Cotter, "Criminal Victimization".

9. "Do No Harm or Injustice"

172 *The police had Melissa's ...* Interview with "Melissa," 4 April 2022 (to protect her privacy, a pseudonym has been used).
173 *"Victims of crime and ..." Canadian Victims Bill of Rights*, s 2.
173 *there's no actual enforcement ... ibid*, ss 28–9.
178 *"In other words, individuals ..."* Jo-Anne M Wemmers, *Victimology: A Canadian Perspective* (University of Toronto Press, 2017) at 101 [Wemmers, "Victimology"]. All excerpts reproduced with permission.
179 *or "second injury" emerged ...* Martin Symonds, "The 'Second Injury' to Victims of Violent Acts" (1980) 70:1 American Journal of Psychoanalysis 34.
179 *Wemmers notes that victims ...* Wemmers, "Victimology" at 115.

179 *"The trial process can ..." ibid* at 116.

179 *In her book Putting ...* Craig, "Putting Trials on Trial".

180 *One woman who underwent ... ibid* at 4.

180 *"in some cases women ..." ibid.*

180 *request "testimonial aids" ... Canadian Victims Bill of Rights,* s 13.

180 *measures like excluding the ...* See Perrin, "Victim Law" at 106–28.

181 *"interfere with the proper ..."* See *ibid* at 113.

182 *"The secondary victimization endured ..."* Wemmers, "Victimology" at 207.

184 *it was imposed ...* See Alan W Mewett, "The Criminal Law, 1867–1967" (1967) 45 Canadian Bar Review 726; "Sources of Criminal Law in Canada" in Federal Prosecution Deskbook, 2005 at ch 1; Desmond Brown, *The Genesis of the Canadian Criminal Code of 1892* (University of Toronto Press, 1989).

184 *"the victim is a witness ..."* Melanie Randall, "Restorative Justice and Gendered Violence? From Vaguely Hostile Skeptic to Cautious Convert: Why Feminists Should Critically Engage with Restorative Approaches to Law" (2013) 36:2 Dalhousie Law Journal 461 at 494 [emphasis added] [Randall, 2013].

184 *from 1887 to 2019 ...* Search on Westlaw using the phrase "crime against the state" on 27 April 2022 found 117 reported decisions. See, e.g., *Dwight and Macklam (Re)*, [1887] OJ No 126, 15 OR 148 at para 16; *Regina v Jeffers*, 1963 CanLII 737 (NS SC), [1964] 2 CCC 346; *R v Wedawin*, 2009 NWTSC 49 at para 34; *R v Irwin*, 2019 ABPC 290 at para 40.

184 *"A crime is not a ..."* Federal Prosecution Deskbook, 2005.

185 *"Thus, crime ceased to ..."* Wemmers, "Victimology" at 8.

185 *"Little by little, the ..." ibid.*

186 *"experienced by victims as alienating ..." R v BP*, 2015 NSPC 34 at para 22.

187 *"[t]raditional legal theories are ..."* Wemmers, "Victimology" at 207.

188 *"In retributive theory, victims ..." ibid* at 208.

10. "Perfectly Designed"

190 a *"significant contributing cause" ... R v Nette*, [2001] 3 SCR 488, 2001 SCC 78 at para 71 per Arbour J; *R v H.(L.I.)*, [2003] MJ No 232, 2003 MBCA 97.

193 *"Every system is perfectly ..."* Earl Conway & Paul Batalden, "Like Magic? ('Every system is perfectly designed ...')" (21 August 2015), online (blog): *Institute for Healthcare Improvement Blog* <http://www.ihi.org/communities/blogs/origin-of-every-system-is-perfectly-designed-quote>.

194 *"an actual process of ..." R v Briscoe*, 2010 SCC 13, [2010] 1 SCR 411 at para 24.

194 *"knowledge of a danger ..." Sansregret v The Queen*, [1985] 1 SCR 570 at para 22.

11. A New Vision

202 *"Substance abuse, there's another ..."* Interview with "Matthew," 5 April 2022 (to protect his privacy, a pseudonym has been used).

204 *"Transformative justice includes victims ..."* Ruth Morris, *Stories of Transformative Justice* (Canadian Scholars Press, 2000) at 3.

204 *"Transformative justice sees crime ..." ibid* at 21.

205 *other versions of transformative justice ...* See, e.g., Mariame Kaba, *We Do This 'Til We Free Us: Abolitionist Organizing and Transforming Justice* (Haymarket Books, 2021); Ejeris Dixon & Leah Lakshmi Piepzna-Samarasinha, *Beyond Survival: Strategies and Stories from the Transformative Justice Movement* (AK Press, 2020).

12. Healthy Kids and Communities

210 *"is a foundation for ..."* Harvard University Center on the Developing Child, "The Science of Early Childhood Development", online: <https://harvardcenter. wpenginepowered.com/wp-content/uploads/2007/03/InBrief-The -Science-of-Early-Childhood-Development2.pdf> [emphasis added].

210 *Some jurisdictions, like Washington ...* US, SHB 1965, *An Act Relating to Public and Private Partnership in Addressing Adverse Childhood Experiences*, 62nd Leg, 1st Spec Sess, Wash, 2011 (enacted); US Centers for Disease Control and Prevention, National Center for Injury Prevention and Control, Division of Violence Prevention, *Learning from Washington's Adverse Childhood Experiences (ACE) Story* (undated).

210 *"to reduce child abuse ..."* WAVE Trust, "The 70/30 Campaign", online: <https://www.wavetrust.org/7030>.

211 *"earlier the intervention the ..."* George Hosking & Ita Walsh, *The WAVE Report 2005: Violence and What to Do about It* (WAVE Trust, 2005) at 40.

211 *the Nurse-Family Partnership ...* Nurse-Family Partnership, "About Us", online: <https://www.nursefamilypartnership.org>.

211 *"are less likely to ..."* Hosking & Walsh at 45; see also David L Olds, "The Nurse-Family Partnership: An Evidence-Based Preventative Intervention" (2006) 27:1 Infant Mental Health Journal 5.

212 *The Rand Corporation estimated ...* Children's Health Policy Centre, "How Does Nurse-Family Partnership Work in Canada?", online: <https://childhealthpolicy. ca/nurse-family-partnership/>.

212 *British Columbia with 739 participating ...* Children's Health Policy Centre, "BC Health Connections Project", online: <https://childhealthpolicy.ca /bc-healthy-connections-project/>; Nicole LA Catherine, "The British Columbia Healthy Connections Project: Findings on Socioeconomic Disadvantage in Early Pregnancy" (2019) 19:1161 BMC Public Health 1; Donna Jepsen & Nicole Catherine, "The British Columbia Healthy Connections Project (BCHCP): A Scientific Evaluation of Nurse-Family Partnership in Canada" (Lecture delivered at the Healthy Mothers and Healthy Babies Conference, 1–2 March 2018) at 34, online: <https://interprofessional.ubc.ca/files/2018/03/ D3ii_Jepsen.pdf>.

212 *The Roots of Empathy (ROE) ...* Roots of Empathy, "About", online: <https:// rootsofempathy.org/about/>.

213 *"Students use maths skills ..."* Roots of Empathy, "What Is Roots of Empathy?" (4 July 2019), online (video): *YouTube* <https://www.youtube.com/watch?v= WSqP9Vef664>.

213 *"Babies are 100 per cent accepting ..."* *ibid.*

213 *Evaluations of the ROE ...* Hosking & Walsh at 42; Kimberly A Schonert-Reichl et al, "Promoting Children's Prosocial Behaviors in School: Impact of the 'Roots of Empathy' Program on the Social and Emotional Competence of School-Aged Children" (2012) 4 School Mental Health 1; Kimberly A Schonert-Reichl & Fiona Scott, "Effectiveness of 'The Roots of Empathy' Program in Promoting Children's Emotional and Social Competence: A Summary of Research Outcome Findings" in Mary Gordon, *The Roots of Empathy: Changing the World Child by Child* (Thomas Allen Publishers, 2009) 239. See also Roots of Empathy, "Research Summaries of Published Studies Conducted on the Roots of Empathy Program", online: <https://rootsofempathy.org/wp-content/uploads/2022/01/Research-Summaries-of-Published-Studies-on-Roots-of-Empathy-2021.pdf>; Roots of Empathy, "Summary of Roots of Empathy Research 2001–2018" (4 March 2019), online: <https://rootsofempathy.org/wp-content/uploads/2022/04/Roots-of-Empathy-Full-Research-Summary-2021.pdf>.

214 *Table 2 – Preventing Adverse Childhood Experiences ...* Centers for Disease Control and Prevention, *Preventing Adverse Childhood Experiences (ACEs): Leveraging the Best Available Evidence* (CDC, 2019) at 9.

215 *"The changes that are ..."* Robert Maunder & Jonathan Hunter, "How Childhood Trauma Can Lead to Chronic Illness", *The Walrus* (30 May 2017).

215 *"Long-term unemployment and ..."* Mikko Aaltonen, Janne Kivivuori & Pekka Martikainen, "Social Determinants of Crime in a Welfare State: Do They Still Matter?" (2011) 54:2 Acta Sociologica 161 at 161.

216 *Providing meaningful education ...* See Correctional Service Canada, Evaluation Division, Policy Sector, *Evaluation of CSC's Education Programs and Services* (CSC, February 2015); Patrick Oakford et al, *Investing in Futures: Economic and Fiscal Benefits of Postsecondary Education in Prison* (Vera Institute of Justice, January 2019); Kelly M Babchishin, Leslie-Anne Keown & Kimberly P Mularczyk, *Economic Outcomes of Canadian Federal Offenders* (Public Safety Canada, 2021); Lori L Hall, "Correctional Education and Recidivism: Toward a Tool for Reduction" (2015) 66:2 Journal of Correctional Education 4 at 25; Torbjørn Skardhamar & Kjetil Telle, "Post-Release Employment and Recidivism in Norway" (2012) 28:4 Journal of Quantitative Criminology 629; Christopher Uggen, "Work as a Turning Point in the Life Course of Criminals: A Duration Model of Age, Employment, and Recidivism" (2000) 65:4 American Sociological Review 529.

216 *nearly one million job ...* Nojoud Al Mallees, "The Labour Shortage Isn't Over – And Employers Are Having to Lower Their Hiring Expectations", *CBC News* (6 April 2022).

216 *mechanics, welding, electrical engineering ...* Colin R Singer, "Canada Labour Shortage: These Are the Top 15 Most In-Demand Jobs for 2022" (1 February 2022), online: <https://www.immigration.ca/canada-labour-shortage-these-are-the-top-15-most-in-demand-jobs-for-2022>; TC Global, "What Are the Skills Shortages in Canada?" (25 May 2022), online: <https://helpcentre.tcglobal.com/hc/en-us/articles/360036923651-What-are-the-skills-Shortages-in-Canada->.

216 *64 per cent of businesses are ...* Brooklyn Neustaeter, "These Canadian Industries Are Currently Facing the Biggest Labour Shortages", *CTV News* (5 October 2021).

216 *cost the economy $25 billion ...* Al Mallees.

217 *"is a recovery-oriented ..."* Hanie Edalati et al, "Examining the Relationships between Cumulative Childhood Adversity and the Risk of Criminal Justice Involvement and Victimization among Homeless Adults with Mental Illnesses after Receiving Housing First Intervention" (2020) 65:6 Canadian Journal of Psychiatry 409 at 411.

217 *"is strongly successful in ..."* *ibid* citing Julia R Woodhall-Melnik & James R Dunn, "A Systematic Review of Outcomes Associated with Participation in Housing First Programs" (2016) 31:3 Housing Studies 287.

217 *some Housing First projects in Canada ...* Government of Canada, "Housing First", online: <https://www.infrastructure.gc.ca/homelessness-sans-abri /resources-ressources/housing-first-logement-abord-eng.html>.

217 *18 per cent over a two-year ...* Edalati et al at 413.

218 *will also need specialized ...* *ibid* at 415.

218 *"a significant increase in ..."* Susanne Alm, "Isolating the Effect of Eviction on Criminal Convictions: Results from a Swedish Study" (2018) 61:3 Acta Sociologica 263 at 263.

218 *"People are products of ..."* Ryan Meili, "Upstream Justice: A Look at the Social Causes of Crime", *Huffington Post* (15 January 2016).

218 *the social determinants of health ...* Government of Canada, "Social Determinants of Health and Health Inequalities", online: <https://www.canada.ca /en/public-health/services/health-promotion/population-health/what -determines-health.html>.

219 *Nationally, 46 per cent of Indigenous ...* Paula Arriagada, *The Achievements, Experiences and Labour Market Outcomes of First Nations, Métis and Inuit Women with Bachelor's Degrees or Higher* (Statistics Canada, 20 October 2021) at 1.

219 *chronic underfunding of Indigenous education ...* See Dustin William Louie & Dianne Gereluk, "The Insufficiency of High School Completion Rates to Redress Educational Inequities among Indigenous Students" (2021) 28:1 Philosophical Inquiry in Education 43. See also Andrew Stobo Sniderman & Douglas Sanderson, *Valley of the Birdtail: An Indian Reserve, a White Town, and the Road to Reconciliation* (HarperCollins, 2022).

219 *most Black youth (94 per cent) ...* Statistics Canada, *Canada's Black Population: Education, Labour and Resilience* (Statistics Canada, 25 February 2020) at 7.

219 *"even after controlling for ..."* *ibid.*

219 *"significantly less likely to ..."* *ibid* at 8; see Philip Oreopoulos, "Why Do Skilled Immigrants Struggle in the Labor Market? A Field Experiment with Thirteen Thousand Resumes" (2011) 3:4 American Economic Journal: Economic Policy 148; Paul Eid, "Les inégalités 'ethnoraciales' dans l'accès à l'emploi à Montréal: Le poids de la discrimination" (2012) 53:2 Recherches sociographiques 415.

220 *"Black communities have been ..."* Maynard at 230.

220 *"What would it look ..."* *ibid* at 231.

13. Decriminalizing People

221 *"Shame on you!" shouted ...* Zoë Dodd, "This is a small clip of me disrupting the House of Commons today. It was my first time there. Those who voted no are murderers, cowards and should be ashamed. Especially @Carolyn_Bennett."

(1 June 2022 at 17:32), online: *Twitter* <https://twitter.com/ZoeDodd /status/1532158067537809408?s=20&t=t0Kz46_7eKY1IoasdpBNeg>.

221 *MPs voted on Bill C-216 ...* Bill C-216, *An Act to Amend the Controlled Drugs and Substances Act and to enact the Expungement of Certain Drug-related Convictions Act and the National Strategy on Substance Use Act*, 1st Sess, 44th Parl, 2021 (first reading 15 December 2021).

221 *The vote was 71 ...* House of Commons, *Votes*, 44-1, No 114 (1 June 2022), online: <https://www.ourcommons.ca/Members/en/votes/44/1/114>.

222 *73 per cent of ...* 1,785 overdose deaths in BC compared to 6,500 total overdose deaths in Canada in 2020: Canada, Public Health Agency of Canada, Special Advisory Committee on the Epidemic of Opioid Overdoses, *Opioid- and Stimulant-Related Harms in Canada* (Public Health Agency of Canada, 2022).

222 *The youngest opioid-related ...* Amy Smart, "Suspected Overdose Death of 12-Year-Old Pushes Government to 'Do Better': Minister", *CBC News* (8 May 2021).

222 *the Canadian Drug Policy Coalition ...* Canadian Drug Policy Coalition, "Letter to Ministers Bennett and Duclos Re: Proposed Cumulative Threshold of 4.5 Grams in B.C." (13 April 2022).

224 *"health, safety, and well-being ..."* Centers for Disease Control and Prevention, "The Public Health Approach to Violence Prevention" (18 January 2022).

226 *research has found that ...* See Perrin, "Overdose" at 163ff.

226 *"People can instead focus ..."* ibid at 165.

226 *Pilot safer supply programs ...* Health Canada, "Early Findings from Safer Supply Pilot Projects" (17 March 2022), online: <https://www.canada.ca/en/health-canada/services/opioids/responding-canada-opioid-crisis/safer-supply/early -findings-safer-supply-pilot-projects.html>; National Safer Supply Community of Practice, "Resources", online: <https://www.nss-aps.ca/resources-overview>.

227 *The Vancouver Declaration on ...* ibid at 236–8.

229 *vast gap between how ...* See JHSO, "Broken Record".

230 *"invest significantly in addressing ..."* Amanda Butler & Doug LePard, *A Rapid Investigation into Repeat Offending and Random Stranger Violence in British Columbia* (September 2022) at 8.

234 *"concerted efforts towards seeing ..."* Maynard at 232.

14. Transforming Trauma

236 *Poilièvre – then a Catholic priest ...* Jason Warick, "Sask. Priest Calls on Catholic Church to Release Records of Abusive Priests, Enablers", *CBC News* (27 December 2019).

236 *release records of abusive priests ...* ibid; Jason Warick, "Priest Slams 'Pitiful' Lack of Catholic Fundraising for Residential School Survivors", *CBC News* (10 July 2021); Seyit Aydogan, "Former Canadian Priest Slams Catholic Church for Treatment of Indigenous Children at Residential Schools", *Anadolu Agency* (11 July 2021).

237 *"Well, I have no idea ..."* Andrea Hill, "Str8 Up Looking to Restructure amid Financial Difficulties", *Saskatoon StarPhoenix* (14 November 2018). Only this quote from Poilièvre is from this source. The rest are from my interview with him, unless otherwise noted.

238 *report commissioned by Public Safety* ... Jana Grekul & Patti LaBoucane-Benson, "An Investigation into the Formation and Recruitment Processes of Aboriginal Gangs in Western Canada" (Public Safety Canada, 2006) at 35.

239 *"new and better stories ..."* Johnson, "Firewater" at xi.

241 *In 2008, André was* ... Governor General of Canada, "Father André Poilièvre: Order of Canada" (2009), online: <https://www.gg.ca/en/honours /recipients/146-9031>.

241 *Justice Canada featured STR8 UP* ... Department of Justice Canada, "Transform-ing the Criminal Justice System: Indigenous Over-representation – Devon" (27 November 2017), online (video): *YouTube* <https://www.youtube.com /watch?v=7d6qrv3nKds>.

241 *Independent evaluations of STR8 UP* ... Laura Ortin et al, *Process Evaluation of the Saskatoon STR8UP Program: Evaluation Report* (University of Saskatchewan, 2012) at 9–10.

242 *STR8 UP has published* ... *STR8UP and Gangs: The Untold Stories* (Hear My Heart Books, 2013); Kristine Scarrow, ed, *STR8UP: Stories of Courage* (Hear My Heart Books, 2017).

243 *mould on reserve land* ... Marina von Stackelberg, "Homes on Remote First Na-tions Are Mouldy before They're Even Built, Experts Say", *CBC News* (28 March 2019).

245 *"No human being is ever ..."* Gabor Maté, *In the Realm of Hungry Ghosts: Close Encounters with Addiction* (Penguin, 2009).

246 *Realizes trauma has a* ... Adapted from SAMHSA Guidance at 9. See also Max-ine Harris & Roger D Fallot, *Using Trauma Theory to Design System Services* (Jossey-Bass, 2001). The SAMHSA Guidance is followed by a wide range of organizations: see, e.g., BC Mental Health & Substance Use Services, "Trau-ma-Informed Practice"; Public Health Ontario, *Trauma-Informed Practices for Children and Families during the COVID-19 Pandemic* (Public Health Ontario, 2020) at 2; Australia, State of New South Wales, Agency for Clinical Innovation, *Trauma-Informed Care in Mental Health Services across NSW: A Framework for Change*, ACI 4035 [03/22] (State of New South Wales, 2022) at 1; The National Association for People Abused in Childhood (UK), "Trauma-Informed Prac-tice"; Bristol, North Somerset & South Gloucestershire, *Principles for Trauma Informed Practice* (2021).

247 *"take into account an ..."* TIP Guide at 12.

247 *"in ways that recognize ..."* ibid.

247 *"safety and empowerment for ..."* ibid.

247 *"create an environment where ..."* ibid.

247 *"more directly address the ..."* ibid at 13.

248 *"pay scant attention to ..."* Naomi Murphy, "Sensorimotor Psychotherapy" in Jason Davies & Claire Nagi, eds, *Individual Psychological Therapies in Forensic Settings: Research and Practice* (Routledge, 2017) [Murphy, "Sensorimotor Psychotherapy"].

248 *sensorimotor psychotherapy* ... See Pat Ogden & Janina Fisher, *Sensorimotor Psy-chotherapy: Interventions for Trauma and Attachment* (WW Norton, 2015).

248 *"offers a helpful framework ..."* Murphy, "Sensorimotor Psychotherapy".

248 *Internal Family Systems (IFS) therapy ...* Ethan Ryan Jones et al, "Integrating In-
  ternal Family Systems and Solutions Focused Brief Therapy to Treat Survivors of
  Sexual Trauma" (2022) 44 Contemporary Family Therapy 167–75; Nancy Won-
  der, "Making the Unconscious Conscious in IFS Consultation of Sexual Abuse,
  Sexual Offending, and Sexual Compulsivity Cases" in Emma E Redfern, ed, *Internal Family Systems Therapy: Supervision and Consultation* (Routledge, 2022);
  Erin M Di Fulvio, "Alternative Paradigms in Correctional Treatment: Internal
  Family Systems and the Risk–Need–Responsivity Model", Pacifica Graduate
  Institute ProQuest Dissertations Publishing (3 February 2019), online: *ProQuest*
  <https://www.proquest.com/openview/4390ddb9a3b2187625c0f2b60c615d5e
  /1?pq-origsite=gscholar&cbl=18750&diss=y>.
249 *"Trauma-informed care emphasizes ..."* Maunder & Hunter, "Damaged" at 145.
249 *"Highlight successful adaptation rather ..."* ibid at 147.
251 *Table 3 – Overview of Basic ...* Wemmers, "Victimology" at 115.
251 *In Victim Law: The Law ...* Perrin, "Victim Law".

15. Real Safety

253 *A woman is walking across ...* These calls have been slightly reworded to be
  comprehensible to lay people without losing the meaning: Eugene Police Crime
  Analysis Unit, *CAHOOTS Program Analysis* (2021).
253 *(CAHOOTS) who was dispatched ...* See "What Is CAHOOTS?" (29 October
  2020), online: *White Bird Clinic* <https://whitebirdclinic.org/what-is-cahoots>
  ["What Is CAHOOTS?"]; "Case Study: CAHOOTS" in Jackson Beck, Melissa
  Reuland & Leah Pope, *Behavioural Health Crisis Alternatives: Shifting from
  Police to Community Responses* (Vera Institute, November 2020); Ben Adam
  Climer & Brenton Gicker, "CAHOOTS: A Model for Prehospital Mental Health
  Crisis Intervention" (29 January 2021) 38:1 Psychiatric Times.
254 *"When a police officer goes ..."* Chris Stewart, "CAHOOTS: Crisis Assistance
  Helping Out On The Streets" (19 July 2020), online (video): *YouTube* <https://
  www.youtube.com/watch?v=nflxiuytb8w>.
254 *"There are lots of ..."* ibid.
254 *In 2019, CAHOOTS responded ...* "What Is CAHOOTS?".
254 *on-scene 311 times ...* ibid. Note: there's some discrepancy with CAHOOTS
  saying 150 times police backup was called, with the Eugene police saying it was
  311 times. Either way, it is very low. I have used the latter figure.
255 *5–8 per cent of police calls ...* Eugene Police Crime Analysis Unit, 2021.
255 *almost doubled between 2014 ...* "CAHOOTS", online: *Eugene Police Department*
  <https://www.eugene-or.gov/4508/CAHOOTS>.
255 *people who are disoriented ...* ibid; "CAHOOTS", online: *White Bird Clinic*
  <https://whitebirdclinic.org/cahoots/>.
255 *"trauma-informed de-escalation ...* "What Is CAHOOTS?".
256 *"A team will respond ..."* ibid.
256 *community-based "sobering service" ...* Rob Waters, "Enlisting Mental Health
  Workers, Not Cops, in Mobile Crisis Response" (2021) 40:6 Health Affairs 864;

"Buckley's Sobering Services", online: *Willamette Family Inc* <https://wfts.org/sobering.htm>.

256 *police are US$90 million ...* "What Is CAHOOTS?".
256 *crisis worker is paid ...* Waters, 2021; US, City of Eugene, *Salary Schedule July 1, 2021 through June 20, 2022*, FY22 (2022).
256 *created "988" ...* Waters, 2021.
257 *pilot project in Denver, Colorado ...* Grace Hauck, "Denver Successfully Sent Mental Health Professionals, Not Police, to Hundreds of Calls", *USA Today* (6 February 2021).
257 *"STARS calls were focused ...* ibid.
257 *Toronto Community Crisis Service ...* City of Toronto, "Toronto Community Crisis Service", online: <https://www.toronto.ca/community-people/public-safety-alerts/community-safety-programs/toronto-community-crisis-service/>.
258 *"If policing were the ..."* Irvin Waller, *Science and Secrets of Ending Violent Crime* (Rowman & Littlefield, 2019) at xvii, xxiv.
258 *"England and Wales, for ..."* ibid at 38. See also *ibid* at 40.
259 *68 per cent of registered nurses ...* Abigail Cukier & Lauren Vogel, "Escalating Violence against Health Workers Prompts Calls for Action" (2021) 193:49 Canadian Medical Association Journal E1896.
265 *An EPO could immediately ...* See, e.g., *Family Law Act*, SBC 2011, c 25, ss 182–91; *Domestic Violence Intervention Act*, SNS 2001, c. 29; *Family Violence Protection Act*, SNL 2005, c F-3.1, s 6; *Family Violence Prevention Act*, RSY 2002, c 84, s 4(3). See *Victim Law* for extensive discussion of relevant federal, provincial, and territorial legislation and related jurisprudence.

16. Peacemaking and Accountability

268 *Dave looked in the ...* "Dave" and "Pierre" are pseudonyms to protect their privacy. Their story was recounted by Kimberly Mann, with permission.
268 *"anger is an acid ..."* This quote is often attributed to Mark Twain, but this may be suspect.
268 *"a non-adversarial, non-retributive ..."* Department of Justice Canada, "Reconciliation through Restorative Justice" (21 July 2021), online: <https://www.justice.gc.ca/eng/news-nouv/photo/video3.html>.
269 *an evaluation commissioned by Public Safety Canada ...* Tanya Rugge, James Bonta & Suzanne Wallace-Capretta, *Evaluation of the Collaborative Justice Project: A Restorative Justice Program for Serious Crime* (Public Safety and Emergency Preparedness Canada, 2005) at 2.
271 *Table 4 – Aspects of Restorative ...* Howard Zehr & Harry Mika, "Fundamental Concepts of Restorative Justice" (1998) 1 Contemporary Justice Review 47 at 54–5.
271 *"One was the neglect ..."* Howard Zehr et al, "Working Luncheon – Restorative Justice" (Panel discussion delivered at the United States Sentencing Commission Symposium on Alternatives to Incarceration, 14 July 2008) at 54.

272 *three overarching principles ...* Zehr & Mika at 50–1; Zehr et al at 55.
272 *"fundamentally a violation of people ..."* Zehr & Mika at 51.
273 *"[U]nlike the criminal justice ..."* Randall, 2013 at 494.
273 *"violations create obligations ..."* Zehr & Mika at 51.
273 *"make things right as ..."* ibid.
273 *"Offenders are provided opportunities ..."* ibid.
273 *"the welfare of its ..."* ibid at 52.
273 *"seeks to heal and ..."* ibid.
273 *"the more you involve ..."* Zehr et al at 55.
274 *75 per cent to 98 per cent of cases ...* Lode Walgrave, "Investigating the Potentials of Restorative Justice Practice" (2011) 36:1 Washington University Journal of Law & Policy 91 at 107. See Ivo Aertsen et al, *Rebuilding Community Connections – Mediation and Restorative Justice in Europe* (Council of Europe Publishing, July 2004).
274 *"meet with someone who ..."* Canadian Resource Centre for Victims of Crime, *Restorative Justice in Canada: What Victims Should Know* (March 2011), online (pdf): <https://crcvc.ca/docs/restjust.pdf>.
275 *"may also be helpful ..."* ibid.
275 *"restorative justice programs are ..."* Jeff Latimer, Craig Dowden & Danielle Muise, *The Effectiveness of Restorative Justice Practices: A Meta-Analysis* (Department of Justice Canada, Research and Statistics Division, 2001); Jeff Latimer, Craig Dowden & Danielle Muise, "The Effectiveness of Restorative Justice Practices: A Meta-Analysis" (2005) 85:2 Prison Journal 127. For a good review of the evidence supporting the effectiveness of restorative justice, as well as the methodological challenges these studies face, see Carrie Menkel-Meadow, "Restorative Justice: What Is It and Does It Work?" (2007) 3 Annual Review of Law & Social Science 161 at 172–9.
275 *A rich tradition of ...* Katherine Beaty Chiste, "Faith-Based Organizations and the Pursuit of Restorative Justice" (2006) 32:1 Manitoba Law Journal 27.
276 *the significant majority of ...* Department of Justice Canada, *State of the Criminal Justice System 2019 Report* (Department of Justice Canada, 2019) at 14–15.
276 *"[w]here offenders are ..."* Harry Mika et al, "Listening to Victims – A Critique of Restorative Justice Policy and Practice in the United States" (2004) 68:1 Federal Probation 32 at 33.
277 *"You know, I've been ..."* As recounted by Kimberly Mann. "Derek" is a pseudonym to protect his privacy.
279 *"Only when an offender's ..."* R v Moses, 1992 CarswellYukon 2, [1992] YJ No 50 (YT Terr Ct).
279 *"You know, at first ..."* R v Bullen, 2001 YKTC 504, [2001] YJ No 96 (YT Terr Ct) at para 13.

17. Rehabilitation and Healing

287 *"The basic question that ..."* NowThis News, "How Norway's Prisons Are Different from America's" (6 August 2020), online (video): *YouTube* <https://www.youtube.com/watch?v=zNpehw-Yjvs> [NowThis News, "Norway's Prisons"]. See also Jan R Strømnes, "Nordic Correctional Policies, Values, Methods and

Practice – What Are They – And Can and Should They Be Transferred to the US?",
online (pdf): <https://waynenorthey.com/wp-content/uploads/2019/02/Halden-
prison-ACA-Winter-Conference-New-Orleans-januar-2019-pdf-version.pdf>.

287 *called the "most innovative" … ibid.*

287 *"We make sure an …"* Emma Jane Kirby, "How Norway Turns Criminals into
Good Neighbours", *BBC News* (7 July 2019).

287 *recidivism in Norway has fallen …* In contrast, there's a lot of debate and contested definitions of recidivism in Canada, with a wide range of recidivism
rates measured at between 9 and 90 per cent, according to the Department of
Justice (with the highest rates being 80 per cent for Indigenous adults and 90 per
cent for Indigenous youth having recontact with police in Saskatchewan). See
Department of Justice Canada, *Recidivism in the Criminal Justice System, 2020*
(Department of Justice Canada, 2020).

288 *"serve their sentence under …"* Norwegian Correctional Service, "About the Norwegian Correctional Service", online: <https://www.kriminalomsorgen.no/?%20
cat=265199> [NCS, "About the NCS"].

289 *Residents take skill-based …* Norwegian Correctional Service, *Halden Prison:
Punishment That Works – Change That Lasts!* (Halden fengsel, 2019) at 48–53,
online: *Issuu* <https://issuu.com/omdocs/docs/magasin_halden_prison_issu>
[NCS, "Halden Prison"].

289 *a 40 per cent increase in …* Manudeep Bhuller, Gordon B Dahl & Katrine V
Løken, "Policies to Reintegrate Former Inmates into the Labor Force" in Melissa
S Kearny & Amy Ganz, eds, *Expanding Economic Opportunities for More Ameri-
cans: Bipartisan Policies to Increase Work, Wages, and Skills* (The Aspen Institute
– Economic Strategy Group, February 2019) 128 at 133.

289 *restraint equipment, physical handling …* CSC, "Use of Force".

289 *"contact officer" who is …* NCS, "Halden Prison" at 37.

290 *"Guards and prisoners are …"* Kirby, 2019.

290 *"law and policy, use …"* Paula Mallea, *Beyond Incarceration: Safety and True
Criminal Justice* (Dundurn Press, 2017) at 146; Correctional Service Canada,
"Hiring Process – Correctional Officer – Training and Appointment" (23 April
2019); Justice Institute of British Columbia, "Correctional Officer", online:
<https://www.jibc.ca/career/correctional-officer>.

290 *"Creating good relationships with …"* NCS, "Halden Prison" at 34.

290 *a rigorous two-year training program …* See NCS, "About the NCS"; NowThis
News, "Norway's Prisons".

291 *are expected to be respectful …* Mallea at 146–7.

291 *"There was an inmate …"* NCS, "Halden Prison" at 34.

291 *Halden is designed to …* Jessica Benko, "The Radical Humaneness of Norway's
Halden Prison", *The New York Times Magazine* (26 March 2015).

292 *programs dealing with relationships …* NCS, "Halden Prison" at 42.

292 *generally small capacity …* Mallea, 2017 at 145–6.

292 *include low-security facilities …* NCS, "About the NCS".

293 *"Just as the size …"* Waller at xxv.

299 *less restrictive safety measures …* See Maya Schenwar & Victoria Law, *Prison by
Any Other Name* (The New Press, 2020).

18. Indigenous Justice

300 *"To Indigenous peoples across ..."* Johnson, "Peace and Good Order" at 146.

301 *"unwilling to accept responsibility ..." ibid* at 135.

301 *"[s]imply providing additional ..."* "Chapter 7 – Aboriginal Justice Systems" in AJIC, "Report".

302 *A "plurinational state" is ...* John Borrows, "Foreword" in Sarah Morales & Joshua Nichols, *Reconciliation beyond the Box: The UN Declaration and Plurinational Federalism in Canada* (Centre for International Governance Innovation, 2018) ix at ix.

302 *inherent right to self-government ...* See *United Nations Declaration on the Rights of Indigenous Peoples,* GA Res 61/295, UNGAOR, 61st Sess, Supp No 49, Vol III, UN Doc A/61/49 (2007) 15. See, e.g., arts 3 (self-determination), 4 (autonomy/self-government), 5 (political/legal institutions), 6 (nationality), 7 (freedom/peace/security), 22(2) (protection from violence), 24(2) (physical and mental health), 33 (determine identity/membership), 34 (juridical systems and customs), and 35 (determine responsibilities of individuals); TRC Summary at 199 (Call to Action 45), 207 (Call to Action 51).

303 *the American tribal court system ...* See "Chapter 7 – Aboriginal Justice Systems" in AJIC, "Report".

303 *"In the United States, while ..."* John Borrows, "Policy Paper: Implementing Indigenous Self-Determination through Legislation in Canada" (Assembly of First Nations, 20 April 2017).

303 *"are strong evidence that ..."* AJIC, "Report".

303 *"address conduct [that] threatens ..." United States v Cooley,* 141 S. Ct. 1638 citing *Montana v United States,* 450 US 544, 566 (1981).

303 *greater coordination and collaboration ...* Savannah Maher, "Supreme Court Rules Tribal Police Can Detain Non-Natives, but Problems Remain", *NPR* (9 June 2021).

304 *In January 2023, minister ...* Olivia Stefanovich, "Ottawa Laying Groundwork for Indigenous Justice Systems, Says Lametti", *CBC News* (13 January 2023), online: <https://www.cbc.ca/news/politics/lametti-caron-indigenous-justice-strategy-1.6712300> [Stefanovich, 2023].

304 *a mere 0.04 per cent of ...* Based on the estimate of $25.5 billion per year that my research assistant calculated for the settler criminal justice system. Calculations on file with author.

304 *just one high-risk offender ...* See chapter 19 for figures.

304 *"It's re-assuming jurisdiction ..."* Stefanovich, 2023.

306 *"When working with Indigenous ..."* Borrows, "Canada's Indigenous Constitution" at 24.

307 *"maintain peace, order ..." Kahnawà:ke Justice* Act, K.R.L. c., J-1 (enacted by MCR #1/2015-2016 on 15 Ohiarí:ha/June 2015; amended by MCR # 3/2015-2016, on 14 Ohiarihkó:wa/July 2015), s 1.

307 *"entry point for the Kahnawà:ke ..." ibid,* s 6.2.

307 *address all "situations of conflict" ... ibid,* s 6.3.

307 *"the court of original ..." ibid,* s 8.1.

307 *"to integrate traditional Kanien'kehá:ka ..." ibid,* s 4.

307 *enforced by the Kahnawà:ke Peacekeepers ... ibid*, s 3.3. See *Kahnawá:ke Peacekeepers Law*, KRL c P-1, s 1.4–1.5.
308 *"In the Mi'kmaq legal ..."* The Council of Canadian Academies, *Towards Peace, Harmony, and Well-Being: Policing in Indigenous Communities – The Expert Panel on Policing in Indigenous Communities* (2019) at 15.
309 *"wait, observe, and collect ..."* Hadley Louise Friedland, *The Wetiko Legal Principles: Cree and Anishinabek Responses to Violence and Victimization* (University of Toronto Press, 2018) at 109–10.
309 *"despite the ongoing presence ..." ibid* at 110.
309 *For Métis people, while ...* Lawrence J Barkwell, Anne Carrière Acco & Amanda Rozyk, *The Origins of Métis Customary Law with a Discussion of Métis Legal Traditions* (Louis Riel Institute, 2007).
309 *"the men would replace ..." ibid* at 11.
309 *"The disruption to community ..." ibid.*
309 *"values, knowledge, behaviour, perceptions ..."* Qajaq Robinson, *Nunavut Legal Information Manual for Violence Support Services* (YMCA, 2014).
310 *"to be safer and more ..."* "The BC First Nations Justice Strategy", online: *BC First Nations Justice Council* <https://bcfnjc.com/landing-page/justice-strategy/>. See BC First Nations Justice Council et al, *BC First Nations Justice Strategy* (February 2020).
311 *In 2013, the BC First ...* "About", online: *First Nations Health Authority* <https://www.fnha.ca/about>; "First Nations Health Governance Structure in BC" and "First Nations Health Governance Journey in BC", online (pdf): *First Nations Health Authority* <https://www.fnha.ca/Documents/First-Nations-Health-Governance-Structure-in-BC-Placemat.pdf>.
312 *"relearn, revitalize, and ..."* First Nations Health Authority (BC), "What Is Land-Based Treatment and Healing?", online: <https://www.fnha.ca/Documents/FNHA-What-is-Land-Based-Treatment-and-Healing.pdf>.
312 *culture and language camps ... ibid.*
312 *"Then we tried land-based ..."* Harold Johnson, "Land-Based Healing", *Inroads* 48 (2021), online: <https://inroadsjournal.ca/land-based-healing/>.

19. "New and Better Stories"

319 *"new and better stories ..."* Johnson, "Firewater" at xi.
323 *well exceeding $25.5 billion ...* Calculations on file with author.
323 *estimated at $1.7 million ...* Paul Gendreau, Claire Goggin & Francis T Cullen, *The Effects of Prison Sentences on Recidivism* (Public Works and Government Services Canada, 1999). Note that $1 million in 1997 dollars is equivalent to $1.7 million in 2022 dollars: "Inflation Calculator", online: *Bank of Canada* <https://www.bankofcanada.ca/rates/related/inflation-calculator/>.
323 *substance use is $794.92 ...* Inflation-adjusted based on Holly Ellingwood, *A Better Estimation of Police Costs by Offence Types* (Public Safety Canada, 2016), which provides a figure of $637.08 in 2013 dollars. This is $794.92 in 2022 dollars based on the Bank of Canada's "Inflation Calculator", online: *Bank of Canada* <https://www.bankofcanada.ca/rates/related/inflation-calculator/>.

323 *estimated that every dollar ...* National Institute on Drug Abuse, *Principles of Drug Addiction Treatment: A Research-Based Guide*, 3rd ed (January 2018) at 14.

324 *"One example of cost-benefit ..."* Thomas Gabor, *Costs of Crime and Criminal Justice Responses* (Ottawa: Public Safety Canada, 2016) at 10. See Damon Jones et al, *The Economic Return on PCCD's Investment in Research-Based Programs: A Cost-Benefit Assessment of Delinquency Preventing in Pennsylvania* (Pennsylvania State University, March 2008).

324 *"Governments in Canada spend ..."* TRC Summary at 182.

326 *Almost two-thirds of ...* Louis Cornelissen, "Religiosity in Canada and Its Evolution from 1985 to 2019" (Statistics Canada, 28 October 2021).

326 *the John Howard Society blog ...* Benjamin Perrin, "A Christian View on Criminal Justice" *The John Howard Society of Canada* (4 December 2018), online: <https://johnhoward.ca/blog/christian-view-criminal-justice/>; see also Benjamin Perrin, "What Would Jesus Think of Our Criminal Justice System and Why Should You Care?" *Church for Vancouver* (22 November 2018), online: <https://churchforvancouver.ca/what-would-jesus-think-of-our-criminal-justice-system-and-why-should-you-care/>.

326 *"Blessed are the merciful ..."* Matthew 5:7 (NIV).

326 *"forgive us our trespasses ..."* Matthew 6:12 (KJV).

326 *"Settle matters quickly with ..."* Matthew 5:25 (NIV).

327 *"Let any one of ..."* John 8:7 (NIV).

327 *"I was in prison ..."* Matthew 25:36 (NIV).

327 *we have all fallen short ...* See Romans 3:23, John 3:16, Romans 5:8; Ephesians 2:8–9.

327 *"We serve a God ..."* Dominique DuBois Gilliard, *Rethinking Incarceration: Advocating for Justice That Restores* (IVP, 2018) at 199.

Index

First Nations Policing Program
(FNPP), 139–40
flashbacks, 51, 89. *See also* post-
traumatic stress disorder
Fleisher, Kevin, 308
Floyd, George, 128–9
forced labor, 152
forgiveness, 308
foster care, 78, 98, 243
freeze, 12
Friedland, Hadley, 308–9
Frøvik, Maria, 290, 291

Gabor, Thomas, 67–8
gangs, 92. *See also* STR8 UP
genocide, 76–7, 85, 114
God, 3, 52–3, 327. *See also*
Christianity
"Good Samaritan" overdose laws, 261
Gordon, Mary, 210–13
Greg, 1–4, 315–17, 330

Haag, Julius, 73, 116–17, 122, 124–5,
127, 132, 133–4, 161, 234, 260,
262–3
Halden Prison, 286–92, 294, 297
harm by criminal justice system,
178–83, 189–97, 264
Harper, Stephen, 103, 197
healing: overview, 319–22;
Angeline, 84; and balance, 21;
and Cree legal tradition, 308;
Danny, 243–4; Dave, 269; Greg,
2–3, 316–18; Jessica, 15; Kaila,
42–3; as key aspect of new
transformative justice, 206 (*see also*
rehabilitation); land-based healing,
311–13; Mandy, 242–3; Savannah,
170; Skye, 164. *See also* Indigenous
justice; new transformative justice
vision; restorative justice programs
healing lodges, 142–3
healthy kids and communities:
overview, 220; ACEs reduction

laws (*see* healthy kids and
communities); dealing with
ACEs, 208–9; investing in early
childhood development, 210–13;
investing in social determinants of
justice, 210, 215–20; as key aspect
of new transformative justice,
205; prevention of childhood
trauma, 210–15, *214*; teaching
socialization, 209
Henry II (king of England), 185
heroin, 32–3, 46
historical trauma, 10
Høidal, Are, 287, 290
holistic services, 250–2, 276–7, 311
homelessness: overview, 191–2; and
crime, 218; and criminal justice
system, 61–2; families, 91–2;
Housing First, 217–18; and prison,
41, 72, 297; and STARS support,
257
homicides, 55, 68, 190
Horstman, Fritzi, 32, 249, 280, 289, 325
Hosking, George, 210–11
housing, 41, 99–100, 217–18
Housing First, 217–18
hunger, 97
Hunter, Jonathan, 16, 215, 249
hyperarousal, 12

identity, 239–40
Iftene, Adelina, 62–3, 234–5, 260,
263, 293, 297
Indian Act, 27, 135–6, 144–5
indictment definitions, vi
Indigenous justice: overview,
151–2; and aftercare, 313; BC First
Nations Justice Strategy (2020),
310; Canada's lethargic start, 304;
as completely sovereign, 301–2;
Cree legal tradition, 308; and
different legal systems, 306; as
diverse, 306; FNHA, 311; FNPP,
139–40; forgiveness, 308; Inuit

Indigenous justice (*continued*)
principles, 309–10; Johnson
on, 300–1; Kahnawà:ke Justice
System, 307–8; land-based healing,
311–13; in law schools, 310; Métis
law, 309; Mi'kmaq legal tradition,
308; as new creation, 305, 308;
vs. other crisis, 305; policing
own communities, 136–41, 303;
vs. settler colonialism laws, 152;
transition to, 301; and trauma-
informed approach, 308–9; in
United States, 303
Indigenous Knowledge, 109, 244, 312
Indigenous Knowledge Keepers, 110
Indigenous peoples: overview, 192;
and ACE risk, 16; and alcohol,
27–8; and *Anthony-Cook* decision,
168; assimilation, 136, 145; and
child welfare, 78; children and
gangs, 92, 99; children taken
away, 76–7, 98, 174; conversing
with, 5; correctional services,
141–4; decriminalization of,
234; dismissed by criminal
justice system, 90, 92–3; and
doctrine of discovery, 147–8;
and education, 219; FSIN, 236–7;
guilt and innocence, 13, 103; as
homicide victims, 159; *Indian Act*,
27, 135–6, 144–5; "Indigenous
courts," 109–10; intergenerational
trauma, 324 (*see also* residential
schools; Sixties Scoop); as judges,
133; Kanien:keha'ka People,
135–8; killed by police, 94; mental
health and police, 55; naming
ceremonies, 15; and overdose risks,
31; and police (overview), 89–90,
145; and police strip searches, 127;
process in criminal justice system,
13, 91, 102–3; racial profiling,
118, 120, 126; and recidivism, 40,

377n287; self-government, 144,
148–9; sentencing circles, 110–11;
and settler colonialism laws,
144–51; and specialized criminal
courts, 109–10; system trauma
overview, 195–6; targeted, 90–1;
traditional ceremonies, 95; and
transgenerational trauma, 246;
trusting criminal justice system,
84–5; victim/offender overlap, 18;
as victims, 218–19; violence against,
80–4, 87–8, 90; vision quests, 2–4,
315–18, 330. *See also* racialized
people; STR8 UP; *specific people*
Indigenous peoples in prison:
and ongoing colonialism,
73; overrepresentation of,
100–1, *101*, 107–8, 114–15, 149;
overrepresentation of youth, 95–6;
prison as exacerbating criminality,
112–14; and sense of loss, 70; and
use of force, 67–8, 93
Indigenous Women's Healing Centre,
141–2
injectable opioid agonist treatment
(iOAT), 225–6
instincts, 316–17
intergenerational trauma, 10, 17, 102,
214–15, 324
Internal Family Systems (IFS), 248–9
interviews for book, 5–6
Inuit Qaujimajatuqangit, 309–10
investing in social determinants of
justice, 215–20, 223, 224, 229–30,
231–2
isolation in prison, 6–7, 67, 69, 100,
105–6

Jackson Lake Healing Camp, 313
Jake, 174–8
Jessica, 10–11, 13–14, 166–7
Jesus, 2, 326–7. *See also* Christianity
Jimmy, 32–3

drug possession thresholds,
222; harassing victims, 175–6;
Indigenous peacemakers, 136–8,
303–4; and Indigenous peoples
(overview), 89–91, 145; Indigenous
policing, 136–41, 303; Jessica's
kind officer, 15; and LGBTQ+,
79; and mental health issues,
37–8, 50, 53–6, 57–60; and non-
responsiveness, 60; numbers and
crime statistics, 258; and overdoses,
261; overlooking violence against
Indigenous peoples, 80–4; own
traumas, 59–60; racial profiling,
116–23, 126; reporting crime to,
14, 160–2, 166, 170; responding
only to criminal offences, 258–9;
shifting resources away from,
234, 267; and social workers,
259–60; targeting Indigenous
Peoples, 90–1; transitioning to
other work, 328; transparency,
126; as underprotecting Black
people, 131–3; use of force, 126–7;
victimizing victims, 132; violence
towards Black people, 119–20,
262; violence towards Indigenous
People, 87–9, 90; and white people,
124, 125. *See also* criminal justice
system
Policing Black Lives (Maynard), 121
post-traumatic growth, 20–1
post-traumatic stress disorder
(PTSD): assessment of, 353n51;
C-PTSD, 9; and police violence,
89, 175; from prison, 92; and
shelters, 45; and violent crime, 171
poverty: and criminal justice system,
72–3; criminalization of, 232;
and mental health issues, 73; and
prison, 41, 72–4, 113, 130
prison: abolition, 293–4; and ACE
risk, 19; alternatives to, 141–4; and
awaiting trials, 75; Black inmate

population increasing, 129–30;
Black people in maximum security,
129; changing the system, 292–8;
and community contact, 295;
corrections officers, 289–91, 296–7,
328–9; and criminality, 112–14;
death in, 68–9, 190; "drunk tanks,"
38; dynamic security, 289; fights
in, 44; Halden Prison, 286–92,
294, 297; and homelessness, 41, 72,
297; and Indigenous youth, 95–6;
juvenile jail, 104–5; leaving, 41; life
expectancy of prisoners, 71, 91; and
maladaptive coping, 64; and mental
health issues, 61–71, 92, 105; mixed
genders, 104–5; as new residential
schools, 103; in Norway, 286–92,
294, 297; and poverty, 41, 72–4,
113, 130; and rehabilitation (*see*
rehabilitation); segregation in, 6–7,
67, 69, 100, 105–6; self-harm in,
67, 69–70, 291; and skills training,
216–17; and substance use, 43–8;
suicide in, 68, 70; vs. support, 233;
as threat, 153, 298; and trauma,
63–5; vs. treatment, 35–6; and
unemployment, 73; use of force in,
65–9, 93, 106, 131, 289; violence
in, 62; and violence reduction,
293; and war on drugs, 130;
youth detention, 99–100. *See also*
criminal justice system; Indigenous
peoples in prison; recidivism
Prisoners' Legal Services (PLS), 114–15
probation, 99–100
protection order (PO), 266, 285
psychosis, 53
public health, 224–8, 230
punishment: vs. accountability,
278–80; commitment to, 151, 153;
death, 152; as deterrent, 150; and
Gladue decision, 112–13; harsh,
152–3; vs. inquiry, 37; vs. love, 209;
vs. rehabilitation, 286; vs.

governance, 262; community group support, 260–1; crisis intervention teams, 253–8, 259, 264; dynamic security in prison, 289; EPOs, 264–6; funding of community-based agencies, 262–3; as key aspect of new transformative justice, 205–6; police response, 258–60; POs, 266; sober services vs. drunk tanks, 261; and victims, 275; victims and non-police options, 264

Sapers, Howard, 223, 231–2, 295

Savannah, 169–70

Schwartz, Arielle, 20–1

Scott, Duncan Campbell, 145

Sealy-Harrington, Joshua, 34, 110, 127, 129

secondary victimization, 179–83, 189–96, 264

security. *See* safety/security

self-discovery, 42

self-esteem, 3

self-harm, 25–6, 67, 69–70, 191, 291

self-medicating, 17, 27–8, 32. *See also* coping strategies

self-protection, 13

sentencing circles, 110

service providers and trauma-informed approach, 247

settler exploitation, 136–7

sexual abuse/assault: ACE and further abuse, 19; and automatic response, 348n12; and charges stayed, 166–7; childhood, 11, 14, 19; and legal sanctions, 168; reporting, 14, 160; secondary victimization, 179–82; and strip searches, 67; and uprooting life, 169–70. *See also* Adverse Childhood Experiences

shame, 280

shelters, 45

Sidhu, Jarrod, 120

Simpson, Sandy, 30, 53, 54, 56, 63, 73, 74, 229, 230–1

single incident trauma, 9

Sixties Scoop, 76–7, 98, 174, 243

The Skin We're In (Cole), 117

Skinner, Chris, 253–4

Skye, 155–8, 162–4, 208–9, 219, 251–2, 270, 274, 293

slavery, 127–8

sober services, 256, 261

sobriety, 41, 42, 50–1, 179, 243, 318

Soltani, Jerry, 40–1, 86, 169–70, 207, 313

specialized criminal courts, 109

spirituality, 239–40

Stevenson, Louis, 144, 152

stigma, 329–30

Stories of Transformative Justice (Morris), 203

STR8 UP, 40, 43, 237–43, 299

STR8UP and Gangs: The Untold Stories, 242

STR8UP: Stories of Courage, 242

stranger attacks, 229–30

strip searches, 67, 127

Strømnes, Jan, 287

St'su̓lkwanem, 145–6

Stuart, Barry, 279

"stupid on crime," 325–6

substance use: abstinence conditions, 39; and ACE risk, 27; after prison, 106; and children, 32; as compulsive, 29; and conflict resolution committee, 283; cost of police stop, 323; criminalization of, 19, 28–31, 34–40, 190–1, 261; death in custody, 68; decriminalization of (*see* decriminalization of drugs); "drug courts," 39; and geographic restrictions, 228; misconceptions of, 29; and organized crime,

white people: and carding, 120; and
    crime, 80–4; and police reactions,
    124, 125, 126; in prison, 130;
    and prison sentences, 91; and
    surveillance, 121; and use of force
    by police, 127
white supremacy, 83. *See also* racism
Will, 49–51
The Wisdom of Trauma (film), 246
women: and adultery, 327; and
    Anthony-Cook decision, 168;
    carding, 118, 120; confidence in
    courts, 168–9; dual charging, 79–
    80; and education, 219; Missing
    and Murdered Indigenous Women

and Girls, 85–6, 88, 159; in prison,
    67–8, 71, 96, 102, 103–4, 130;
    reporting crime, 160, 161, 162;
    victimization statistics, 159
Wortley, Scot, 120–1, 126

Youth Criminal Justice Act, 96
youth detention, 99–100

Zacharie, Dwayne, 108, 111–12, 136,
    137–8, 140, 150, 307–8
Zehr, Howard, 271, *271*
Zinger, Ivan, 61–3, 66–7, 100–1,
    103–4, 131, 141, 142, 143–4,
    294–5, 302

About the Author

Benjamin Perrin is a professor at the University of British Columbia, Peter A. Allard School of Law, specializing in criminal law, constitutional law, and international law. He served in the Prime Minister's Office as in-house legal counsel and lead criminal justice and public safety adviser (including matters related to the Department of Justice, RCMP, Correctional Service of Canada, and Parole Board of Canada). He was also a law clerk at the Supreme Court of Canada. Professor Perrin is a national best-selling author. His books include *Overdose: Heartbreak and Hope in Canada's Opioid Crisis* (Penguin Random House, 2022) and *Victim Law: The Law of Victims of Crime in Canada* (Thomson Reuters, 2017). He has testified as an expert witness before legislative committees and regularly provides commentary in the media. He lives in Vancouver, BC. For more information, please visit www.benjaminperrin.ca.